Winds of Change

PETER LANG
New York • Washington, D.C./Baltimore • Boston
Bern • Frankfurt am Main • Berlin • Vienna • Paris

Winds of Change

The Transforming Voices of Caribbean Women Writers and Scholars

Edited by
Adele S. Newson
and Linda Strong-Leek

PETER LANG
New York • Washington, D.C./Baltimore • Boston
Bern • Frankfurt am Main • Berlin • Vienna • Paris

Library of Congress Cataloging-in-Publication Data

Winds of change: the transforming voices of Caribbean women
writers and scholars / edited by Adele S. Newson & Linda Strong-Leek.
p. cm.
Includes bibliographical references (p.   ) and index.
1. Caribbean literature—History and criticism.
I. Strong-Leek, Linda. II. Title.
PN849.C3N49   809'.897292—DC21   96–49833
ISBN 0-8204-3715-8

Die Deutsche Bibliothek-CIP-Einheitsaufnahme

Winds of change: the transforming voices of caribbean women
writers and scholars / Adele S. Newson & Linda Strong-Leek (eds.).
–New York; Washington, D.C./Baltimore; Boston; Bern;
Frankfurt am Main; Berlin; Vienna; Paris: Lang.
ISBN 0-8204-3715-8

Cover illustration by David L. Horst.

The paper in this book meets the guidelines for permanence and durability
of the Committee on Production Guidelines for Book Longevity
of the Council of Library Resources.

Printed in the United States of America.

Contents

Preface

This book is a result of the gathering of Caribbean women writers and scholars who participated in the 1996 International Conference of Caribbean Women Writers and Scholars held April 24–27 at Florida International University. Over three hundred academics, students, scholars, and literature mavens assembled to discuss the theme "Winds of Change: The Transforming Voices of Women." The conference sought to bring to the fore the contributions Caribbean women have made to the literature, culture, and politics of the region.

The excitement of familiarity marked the occasion, which was largely attended by women. Both Caribbean and African American women have had interruptions in cultural insularity by virtue of the Middle Passage, slavery, the plantation system, and domestic servitude. Both created and lay claim to artful language development and verbal dexterity. Both share the spiritual energy of generations of courageous and entrepreneurial foremothers who tirelessly cultivated, nurtured and harvested, bartered and sold in order to provide the best for their families. These experiences are revealed in the works of Caribbean women writers.

Yet a significant point of divergence between Caribbean and African American women is in the concept of place as cultural or imaginative construction, as well as in the evocation of place. That is, what does it mean to inhabit an island where, after colonization, the seats of government are run by people of one's own racial group? And when does social class become the greater divide, as in the Caribbean, while race and color mount social divisions and distinctions in North America?

The concept of place also embraces separation or exile from a cherished and particular place. Both African American and Caribbean women have endured and written about the experience of living in exile. While in the case of the latter, exile may be rendered as physical and geographical, the spiritual exile of the African American woman in her own community or county has been no less real. Exile, both physical and psychological, is very much a feature of the communal landscape of many Caribbean writers. On the question of Caribbean women writing in exile, Barbadian-connected Elaine Savory explains that:

"wherever you live in the world, if you live in a space which is connected to the Caribbean and you recognize Caribbean cultural sovereignty, you write within Caribbean space. . . .Our divisions, if set out oppositionally, or to privilege one identity over another, only weaken our communal capacity to share and to go home to work alone in a fully creative way."

While African American writers, as Surinamese Astrid H. Roemer points out, do not have to live in exile as do many Caribbean writers, a literary tradition binds both groups: language subversion and invention, oral traditions, and the trickster-mask traditions, to name a few elements.

The antithesis of exile might be called sanctuary, and here too, Caribbean and African American women have shared the common goal of creating safety zones—physical, emotional, spiritual, and economic—for their communities and their loved ones. Within the literature of the African Diaspora, the neighborhood, the village, and the parish, as well as the home, the church, and the family, are all sanctuaries from which characters emerge to do battle with the world and to which they return for solace and comfort. Conferences such as the one from which the essays in this volume were generated are, as Astrid H. Roemer says, "substitutes for the neighborhood."

Astrid H. Roemer compares the efforts of African Caribbean writers to those of African American writers in her essay contained in this volume. Echoing June Jordan's assertion of language as being political, Roemer advances the idea that "there is no novel, no story, no poem without interests" and expresses the belief that language, as a power medium, must be deconstructed before women of color use it. According to Roemer: "It is a necessity that the neighborhood 'understands' the language and that the outside world just 'overstands' the text because it is not made 'in their size' and the text is not dealing with their interests." In taking on the editing of such a collection as this, we acknowledge that the fear of appropriation is a valid one. Concerns about appropriation and perhaps even cultural chauvinism are issues against which all women of color struggle. It is with the utmost sincerity that we appeal to our Caribbean sisters for goodwill and good reading of the project. With the exception of Sybil Seaforth's fictional narrative, the language of many of the essays has been converted to Standard American English for editorial purposes. This volume includes sixteen essays presented at the Conference, a fictional work, and a section on Guyanese writer Beryl A. Gilroy, who received from the Association of Caribbean Women Writers and Scholars a special award honoring her lifelong work in literature and education. Additionally, we reference papers not included in this volume but presented at the conference to help the reader gain a sense of participation in the dialogue that was the 1996 International Conference of Caribbean Women Writers and Scholars.

We wish to offer our sincere appreciation to Malvina Engelberg, University of Miami, and Cynthia Davis, Barry University, for their insightful readings of the manuscript and for their contributions to the 1996 International Conference of Caribbean Women Writers and Scholars. We would also like to thank the Department of English, Donald G. Watson, and the College of Arts and Sciences at Florida International University for their generous support of the Conference and of this project.

Introduction

The literatures of the Caribbean represent the multilingual, multiracial, multi-plicitous societies which are hallmarks of the region. The voices of the women of the Caribbean now fill the halls of academe with new, yet hauntingly familiar murmurs conversing on the political, social, economic, and spiritual possibilities which affect and are affected by these women of color. They include the biting satire of the novels of Beryl Gilroy, the Guyanese woman who would become the first Black head teacher in London, and the voices of new writers such as Patricia Powell whose work *A Small Gathering of Bones* brings one into the astonishingly painful lives of a gay Caribbean society pre-1978. These writers create a mélange of spaces and ways of being in the world for the Caribbean character, as well as of interpretations open to the reader.

Gilroy and Powell are representative of the Caribbean woman writer whose range extends outside of the immediate mental landscape of the writer. Gilroy's efforts in her three most recent novels reveal that the Amerindian, as well as the Asian and others, are very much features of her mental landscape. Powell's forthcoming novel *The Pagoda* focuses on the life of a Chinese immigrant to Jamaica. In her recently released novel *The Festival of San Joaquín,* Zee Edgell, the Belizean writer, adopts the persona of a mestizo woman to tell a story of domestic conflict. And of course Olive Senior, among other poets, has consistently conjured the myriad voices of the Caribbean to provide the portraits of her multiracial and culturally diverse society.

This collection is the result of the 1996 International Conference of Caribbean Women Writers and Scholars hosted by Florida International University, April 24–27, 1996. The writers and scholars featured speak to each other, revise each other, echo and complement each other. But above all there exists a sense of serious engagement in the entire enterprise. Its overriding theme "Winds of Change: the Transforming Voices of Women" addresses the diversity as well as the influence Caribbean women writers and scholars have had and continue to have in their various communities and abroad. The Conference was a call and response to their activities. The papers in this collection reflect concern with issues of insularity, of migration, of history, of development, and of critiques, among others. The authors of the essays do not situate themselves as "marginal" or on the margin, or even as literary objects; rather these writers provide the refreshing centrality that many readers and critics of their literature often fail to note. Centrality is also a function of audience and targeted readership. And as Merle Hodge points out in her essay, "for the moment, it is only a small fraction of 'our own people' who read our works." In this case she is referencing the constraints imposed on the use of nation language in the works of the Caribbean writers. But that Caribbean women writers revise and signify on each other is a point Régine Latortue advances in her essay on Marie Chauvet and Maryse Condé.

The founding conference of Caribbean women's writing was hosted by the Black Studies Department at Wellesley College on April 16, 1988. Spearheaded by Selwyn R. Cudjoe, it featured over fifty writers and scholars primarily from the English-speaking Caribbean who came together "to talk about their writings and to let the world know what they seek to achieve when they set out to write about their experiences."[1] The relevance of this conference as well as the subsequent conferences of Caribbean Women Writers and Scholars cannot be overstated. They serve as forums for the diffusion of female literature and orature of the Caribbean.

Helen Pyne-Timothy, the University of the West Indies, St. Augustine, Trinidad, hosted the second conference in 1991. Joceline Clemincia spearheaded the 1994 conference held in Willemstad, Curaçao. The fourth conference returned to Wellesley, and the fifth was hosted by Florida International University. With each conference, the programs expanded to accommodate as many cultural and linguistic representatives of the Caribbean as possible, and the number of participants grew substantially. At the Miami conference over three hundred participants from the Caribbean, Latin America, Canada, Europe, and all over the United States were in attendance. Of the phenomenon Cudjoe asserts:

> The rise of women's writing in the Caribbean cannot be viewed in isolation. It is part of a much larger expression of women's realities that is taking place in the postcolonial world and post-civil rights era in the United States. The enormous production of literature from the women of the Caribbean does not only contribute to our literary development but it begins to change the very contours of that literature as well.[2]

The conference from which the papers in this volume are garnered was appropriately titled "The Winds of Change: The Transforming Voices of Women," since its aim was to continue the discourse as well as highlight the very real contributions of women to the development of the North American and Latin American cultural and political landscapes. Its premise was that not only is the personal political but the very nature of art—its production process, its manifestations, and its creators—is fundamentally political. Caribbean writers have, as Astrid H. Roemer reminds us, "interests" which inform their craft and production. Indeed, the absence of the Cuban writers, owing to the politics of North America and Cuba, strongly attests to the political nature of art and its dissemination.

The Rise of Caribbean Women's Literature
The indigenous peoples of the Caribbean were swiftly conquered and marginalized as Europe expanded westward in the fifteenth century. Similarly, the Middle Passage and the plantation system contributed to the marginalization of the African population. Building on this African-Indigenous base, later migrations of Asian laborers, itinerant Europeans, and Ashkenazic and Sephardic Jews increased the diversity and nature of social classes in the Caribbean.

Shakespeare's character Caliban (*The Tempest*, 1611–1612) is representative of the outside world's conception of the inhabitants of the Caribbean colonies and their marginal status. In her article "Female Calibans," M. J. Fenwich observes that

> The paternalistic position assumed by Prospero toward Caliban projected the future relationship between the European nations and the colonies, and cultural hegemony can be measured by the extent to which the Prospero/Caliban paradigm has been and is accepted within the Caribbean.[3]

The Caribbean woman has been even further marginalized. While Fenwich uses Caliban to symbolize contemporary Caribbean women poets defying colonial orthodoxy, others challenge the entire model as not being even remotely inclusive or representational. In her essay "De Language Reflect Dem Ethos," Opal Palmer Adisa cites the creation of Shakespeare's Caliban (the model of the Caribbean man) as that crucial moment in which the Caribbean man is given voice. She goes on to say that "[i]t is out of this patriarchal structure, designed to make her an object, part of the landscape to be used and discarded as seen fit by the colonizer, that the Caribbean woman has emerged."

The link between history, diversity, marginalization, and Caribbean women is deftly explored in Mary Prince's *The History of Mary Prince, West Indian Slave* (1831). This work marks the first female resistance narrative issuing from the Americas, and it is a testimony of the struggle to possess self and personal space which the African Diaspora woman was denied from the beginning of her sojourn in the Americas. As Thomas Pringle explains in his preface to the narrative, "The idea of writing Mary Prince's history was first suggested by herself. She wished it to be done, she said, that good people in England might hear from a slave what a slave had felt and suffered."[4] Her will and her story intrude into the direct-account narrative of the atrocities of her existence in a way that, writes William L. Andrews, "must have surprised, if not shocked, many of her readers. Women, especially those of Prince's caste and class, were not expected to speak out so bluntly in public, especially about their supposed betters."[5] Prince's legacy is a direct discourse and positioning of the self as subject, activist, and literary persona. Other early texts include Gertrudis Gomez De Avellaneda's *Sab* (1841) and Mary Seacole's *Wonderful Adventures of Mrs. Seacole in Many Lands* (1857). Essential to these three early works of Caribbean women is the use of voice to insert the Caribbean female into the discourse of the day. If Prince and Avellaneda sought to advocate against slavery, then Seacole's work is as masterful in its exploration of female autonomy—ownership of self and economic independence.

The Politics of Language

It was not until the twentieth century that other voices rang out in acknowledgment of the female Caribbean self. Jean Rhys, Una Marson, Louise Bennett, and Phyllis Shand Allfrey, among others, dominated the literary landscape up to the 1960s. Though few in number, these writers continued the tradition begun by their foremothers with notable revisions and expansions of theme and personae. If these few writers tell us anything, they tell us that there is no monolithic Caribbean female character and that the landscape the Caribbean woman inhabits is as rich as it is diverse. Rhys's expression of the Creole woman; Marson's use of cultural traditions such as music and spiritual cadences; Bennett's celebration of African connections; and Allfrey's commitment to the rural community attest to the richness of the Caribbean mental and physical landscape.

Beginning in the late 1960s, a new generation of Caribbean women writers emerged. For a number of reasons, but chiefly owing to the imperialistic nature of the English "first world," Anglophone writers of the Caribbean dominated the new generation of Caribbean women writers, as they continue to dominate the present landscape. Paule Marshall, Jamaica Kincaid, Louise Bennett, Olive Senior, Lorna Goodison, Grace Nichols, Beryl Gilroy, Merle Collins, Merle Hodge, and Sybil Seaforth are among the best-known Caribbean women writers partly because they hail from the English-speaking Caribbean. With respect to the Francophone Caribbean, Edwidge Danticat's popularity is as much a function of her craft as it is of her Haitian American literary connections. Danticat's *Breath, Eyes, Memory* and *Krick, Krak* are written in English, making Haitian culture and literature accessible to a metropolitan audience, while older writers who have been publishing for much longer, and those who write in Creole, like Paulette Poujoul Oriol, are scarcely known. Even Maryse Condé, the most prolific female Francophone writer, though backed by the prestigious French cultural establishment and blessed with exceptional talent and an excellent translator, has not yet received the international attention her work deserves.

In terms of the Spanish-, Dutch-, and Portuguese-speaking countries, the situation is nearly as bad. While serious literature mavens know Astrid H. Roemer, Nancy Mórèjon, Myra Santos Febres, and Mirta Yañez, the reality is that these authors are popular in the United States, Canada, and the United Kingdom only to the extent that they are translated and marketed by their publishers. Like their Spanish- and Dutch-speaking sisters, the Afro-Brazilian women writers Lia Vieria, Miriam Aparecide Alves, and Leda Martins have begun to assert their unique racial and cultural identity, and to celebrate their Afrocentric heritage, albeit to a limited reading public.

One common thread which connects all of these women is the politics of publishing. The fact that publishers are located in the metropolis means that Caribbean writers incur considerable expense and inconvenience in order to bring their work to fruition. Another problem is that many wish to write in Creole or patois. Just as Maryse Condé and Simone Schwarz-Bart argue that the authenticity of one's literature is expressed through one's language, so too do these authors feel that their indigenous language is essential to articulate character, to celebrate invention, to validate culture, and even to support group consciousness. Unfortunately, given the economic realities of publishing and the insularity of the metropolitan consumer, the use of Creole and patois is often discouraged. As Paula Burnett observes in her introduction *to The Penguin Book of Caribbean Verse in English*:

> It is clear from the history of Greek and Latin that the languages of impe-
> rialism tend to outlast the empires. In a recent poem Derek Walcott com-
> ments on the British empire in the Caribbean: "It's good that everything's
> gone, except their language, which is everything."[6]

The 1996 International Conference of Caribbean Women Writers and Scholars
featured not only the writers listed above, but many others. In total, over thirty writers from every linguistic group of the Caribbean were invited to participate. From
the established writers such as Beryl A. Gilroy and Astrid H. Roemer to the newer
writers such as Patricia Powell and Lia Vieria, the participants of the conference gathered to share insight and discourse with their public on their crafts.

Issues in Caribbean Women's Literature
Anticolonial discourse is found in the writings of Jamaica Kincaid, whose works
Annie John and *A Small Place* speak to issues not only of identity within the colonial
patriarchy, but of identity within the world of those who acquiesce to the colonials,
and those who totally reject the ideas and ideals of the *other*. While Kincaid's works
seem inherently approachable from a postcolonial theoretical framework, Merle
Hodge finds in the deficient linguistic (Creole) spaces of Kincaid's rendering "a different kind of writing from that which concerns itself with exploring and affirming
the experience of a specific collective. Yet both kinds of writing rejoin the universal,
if the writer achieves truth." Both kinds of writing (introspective and collective),
Hodge concludes, are valid and necessary. Similarly, Elaine Savory asserts that divisions "only weaken our communal capacity to share and to go home to work alone
in a fully creative way." Savory distinguishes between exile (the condition of separation from the country of birth) and "ex/isle" (referring to the literal island as well as
the original cultural identity and connection). Lizabeth Paravisini-Gebert argues
that the range and depth of Caribbean experiences cannot be adequately accounted
for in postcolonial theorizing because of the very nature of the region's diversity, as
well as the difficulty of constructing a Caribbean identity informed by its many contradictions.

Thus, what began as a whisper years ago in the Caribbean is now a loud rever-
berant shout! A shout to be heard—a shout to be reckoned with—a shout, a scream
for acknowledgment. The voices of women like Guadeloupian Maryse Condé speak
to the literary imagination in the most unique and imaginative ways. Condé's
characters, one a "forgotten" part of the Salem witch trials, others caught in the slave
trade and the religious, social, and economic changes facing Africa after the colonials
arrive, question the accountability of all: black, white, mulatto, Muslim, Christian,
traditionalist, male and female, all play a major part in the inevitability of the even-
tual and total alteration of the African continent. In her essay "Francophone
Caribbean Women Writers and the Diasporic Quest for Identity: Marie Chauvet's

Amour and Maryse Condé's *Hérémakhonon*," Régine Latortue asserts that

> [t]he growing body of literature by women writers is redefining the canon
> of Caribbean literature, challenging accepted notions of self, gender, race,
> and history. Maryse Condé presents us with a superb, complex portrayal of
> the contemporary diasporic woman.

Tituba, Condé's "Black Witch of Salem," for example, questions Puritanic racism and
hypocrisy, much as Condé reflects on the current problem of racism in American society:

> Writing *Tituba* was an opportunity to express my feelings about present-
> day America. I wanted to imply that in terms of narrow-mindedness,
> hypocrisy, and racism, little has changed since the days of the Puritans.
> Every Black person living in America will tell you that racism still exists. A
> few success stories that are told over and over again for propaganda reasons
> must not hide the fact that for the majority of the blacks, life is still hell.[7]

However, it is not merely "American" morals or racism that Condé indicts, but more
importantly for Tituba, American sexism:

> Of course, racism is very important in *Tituba*. She was forgotten by history
> because she was Black. But it seems to be more important that she was for-
> gotten because she was a woman. It seems to me that I stress her condition
> as a woman more than I stress her condition as a Black. So the book is more
> about the discrimination against women than against people of color in
> general.[8]

In the present volume, Condé resurrects yet another woman, Suzanne Césaire, in an
effort to articulate Césaire's complex ideas on what is now Créolité—a call for writers to explore the self beyond the process of recuperating the past, while affirming
multiple origins. Condé dubs Césaire "the founding mother of all the postcolonial
critics who denounce simple pieties cloaked by the idiom of alterity."

Thus, although the female writers of the Caribbean may exist in different eth-
nological and ontological realms, they all exist in worlds which have, at one time or
another, attempted to censure, silence, or ignore the ideals and interests of women.
Caribbean-Diaspora—Anglo—Native—Indian—exile, living abroad, living at
home: all these labels attest to the challenges of being Caribbean women, writers, and
scholars.

This volume of essays includes a few of the myriad voices of the Caribbean,
women who, like Astrid H. Roemer, are faced with the difficult issues of identity and
voice, and who question their own use of the "masters-language." Roemer, born in
Suriname, living in The Netherlands, is acutely aware of the difficulty of writing and

speaking the various languages of the colonials, but she also acknowledges, like Chinua Achebe, that if one is to be heard, if one is to be read, one must often abandon the language of the native speaker:

> My first love was language (maybe the sound of "mamma") and of course there was a point of no return for me when I discovered the magic of written words. In the magnum opus *Segu*, by the distinguished Maryse Condé, there is that "point of no return" when one of the Bambara sons seems to be witched by the Koran—not because of its content but because of the magic of the written language. And that is where the tragedy started: a conflict between parole and script, between sound and silence, but more than that, Condé exposed the moment the Bambara son broke through his own tradition of language to let the "stranger" in. And by letting the stranger (white, male, European, Christian) in, Africa lost her heritage, her land, and even her peoples. We are all devoted to written texts; we are writers, novelists; our job is making books and selling the silence of the written speech.

Roemer's questions of heritage, of selfhood, of loss, of the "stranger," and the final acknowledgment that the stranger is indeed within all peoples of the African Diaspora, are deeply thoughtful, yet also lamentable. In order for one to write, to be successful, one must let the other, the "European" in; but that does not mean total acquiescence. Roemer's essay attests to the dignity of her Surinamese heritage and her ability to walk the fine line between acceptance of the language of the other and maintenance of one's spiritual being.

In "Ex/Isle: Separation, Memory, and Desire in Caribbean Women's Writing," Elaine Savory speaks of her position as a British woman writing about and criticizing the works of women in the Caribbean. Voice, identity, race, gender, and even language itself all find a place for commentary in this collection.

Opal Palmer Adisa's essay on language, like the work of noted African American scholar Geneva Smitherman, speaks to the creation of the language in Jamaica known as patois, while discussing the legitimacy of Jamaican patois as a language itself. Language is power, and the ability to disempower others by devaluing their indigenous language has been a consistent problem with people living in the various parts of the Diaspora. Adisa writes:

> Jamaicans, as a result of colonial conquest, were never thought to possess a language of their own. The widespread ideology is that the language the people speak is not really a language at all, but rather a dialect, commonly referred to as pidgin English or patois ... However, anyone who understands the hegemony of colonialism and neocolonialism knows the pejorative light in which the colonized people's tongue has been cast, particularly a people who were never considered in the first place to possess culture, or have a history, philosophy, or any original ideas.

The notion that the peoples of Africa never possessed language, culture, philosophy, or any system considered modern or worthy of reproduction by Europeans and non-Europeans features prominently in the myriad debates faced by Blacks throughout the Caribbean and indeed, across the Western world. For years Africanist scholars have sought to legitimize Black thought, Black philosophy, and the social and political structures present in Africa prior to colonization. While some progress is evident, all too often we find the opposite to be the case.

Yes, the people of Haiti speak a unique combination of French and indigenous African languages, but we call it Haitian Creole, and Jamaicans have their own unique language, but we call it patios. And those unfortunate enough to speak a Black English Vernacular are simply called unemployable. Language is power, and this collection of essays attests to the empowerment of people through the recognition of their language, their culture.

Bahamian Marion Bethel poses yet another intriguing question in her essay on capital punishment, "I'll Fly Away"—namely: What responsibility do we have to our young men? She analyzes the act of state-sanctioned "murder," and what it means to the average citizen. Speaking to the seeming popularity of the death penalty as a "quick fix" for societal ills, she observes:

> Our children will not forgive us for the quick fix of the gallows. They will despise our lack of creative possibilities; they will hate our legacy to them—a culture of death. What will they make of the gallows?—the event with no soul. What will they make of the State slaughterhouse? What will our youth feel about this display of State manhood? This threat to youthful creativity? Must we remain within the conqueror's paradigm and eliminate what we do not like and pretend not to understand? The gallows cannot ease our pain. The gallows—the naked and omnipotent power of the State, virile and unexamined brutality?

In societies gone mad, filled with acts of random violence, where the price one pays for the offense of stepping on someone's tennis shoes is a quick and violent death by a gunshot wound to the face, one may question Bethel's query. What is a civilized society to do? How must one react to uncontrollable hostility? Is it better, then, to begin to understand the source of the hostility, or merely eliminate those whose very being has become synonymous with the threat? This is but a sampling of the dialogue offered by the diverse group of scholars, writers, students, and teachers present at the 1996 International Conference of Caribbean Women Writers and Scholars. Here they addressed some of the most difficult issues of our times.

As we gathered in Miami, Florida, on April 24, 1996, for the Conference, anticipation filled the air. Hosting a group of writers from various cultures and countries throughout the Caribbean and indeed throughout the world, we focused our attention on the minute details of the last minute: transportation, lodging, swift propelling of panels, etc. We did not know exactly what to expect. What we would find over the next three days was a group, mainly of women, full of interest and inquiry, ready to participate in relevant conversations. We encountered sophisticated responses to difficult cultural and philosophical issues, and a myriad of languages, voices, and interpretations. This Conference attempted to include as many different faces and places in the Caribbean, and even South America, as possible. Women from Brazil, Haiti, Canada, Jamaica, Trinidad and Tobago, Europe, and a host of other regions gathered at Florida International University to discuss the issues most relevant to them as scholars, creative writers (poets, novelists, essayists), and interested participants. The results appear in the following essays.

Part One

Language, Orality, and Voice

Overview

Caribbean writers operate within a rich landscape of language. Their arsenal, derived from their people, is linguistically vast and includes indigenous influences as well as influences from Africa, Europe, and Asia. Creole or nation language is the main medium of spoken communication in most of these Caribbean countries. In her essay "Orality and Writing: A Revisitation," Merle Collins explains that when we speak of connections between orality and writing, "we are referring partly to ways in which the performance mode might be incorporated into the written work." The language one uses, the skill with which that language is employed and the authority which informs it, marks (though does not define) a person geographically, socially, and economically. The dialectic of language as political is an inescapable feature of the manifestation of language. Moreover, language is the element that informs the Caribbean women writers' literary tradition. Opal Palmer Adisa asserts:

> The discussion of language is not merely an academic or literary exercise; it is at the very root of Caribbean selfhood because without voice, without a language of our own, we will always be lagging behind as poor imitators.

The speech act validates lives and cultures, supports, as Geneva Smitherman has suggested "a group consciousness." This stamp of belonging defines a space for and a way of being in a society and world. Adisa says that when she thinks about the language of Jamaica she hears "the women's voices loudest and clearest." Merle Collins maintains that whenever she speaks, her "voice is informed by the stories of the women in [her] family." For her, it happens that "[t]he women . . . were the performers, the storytellers, the ones who argued, praised, insulted, threw around their poetry in laughter and sometimes in song." Merle Hodge celebrates "diamond-like clarity and precision of her English prose" as a product of Jamaica Kincaid's Creole foundation. Maryse Condé provides voice and thereby recognition to neglected writer Suzanne Césaire, while Sybil Seaforth explores the breakdown of communication in the lives of older Caribbean couples in an excerpt from her fictional work-in-progress *In Silence the Strands Unravel.* The contribution of women to nation language is celebrated in this section.

What do Caribbean women writers see as the distinctive traits and nuances of the language of the region? In this section, Opal Palmer Adisa, Velma Pollard, Merle Collins, Merle Hodge, Maryse Condé, Régine Latortue, and Sybil Seaforth address the defining issues of the language of the region in terms of literary products and philosophical achievement. In sum they suggest that language, culture, and autonomy exist in a symbiotic relationship—one which would define the individual character's way of being in the world. The construction of a Caribbean identity is a challenging enterprise. The vehicles for its production include language and the rendering of voice to clientele who are often rendered mute in external representation.

In her essay "De Language Reflect Dem Ethos: Some Issues with Nation Language," Opal Palmer Adisa argues that Caribbean speech is equivalent to nation language, that is, a language born of the "unrelenting fight to validate . . . lives through . . . speech . . . the right not to be slaves or servants to others also means the right to define, determine, and tell our own stories in our own words." She maintains that, until recently, Caribbean writers had used Caribbean nation languages sparingly (most often to depict uneducated or countrified characters), and that education has become the greatest enemy of the nation language. Rejecting nation language, she believes, is equivalent to the rejection of resistance. By so doing the writer is "unable to wrestle with him/herself and project his/her own values and worldview." She argues that language is indeed political and courage as well as full acceptance is needed "for the Caribbean writer to use her people's tongue, her own native tongue, in writing about the complexities and truth of their lives"—if the writer is to refrain from marginalizing her subjects and/or continuing colonial ideology. She challenges Caribbean women writers "to speak, and to speak in a language that their sisters can understand."

Velma Pollard, in her essay "Language and Identity: The Use of Different Codes in Jamaican Poetry," echoes Adisa's observation that protest is "at the forefront of the movement toward the full embrace of . . . nation languages." Pollard examines the different codes associated with the different levels of stratified Jamaican society as poets struggle to voice representational speech communities. She identifies three aspects of the Jamaican linguistic environment. The Jamaican dialect of English is "the language of the formal motions of the society and of education. . . ." Jamaican Creole is a Creole of English lexicon which everyone in the speech community understands, and Dread Talk is the code of Rastafari, a lexical adjustment invoked to satisfy the requirements of speakers sympathetic to the philosophy of Rastafari.

Pollard's analysis of Lorna Goodison's "Ocho Rios II" demonstrates "how language may be used as a mark of identity in a medium which must be at once terse and expressive." In "Ocho Rios II" language is used as an identification marker, and the poem's achievement rests with "the rendering of complex behaviors, complex voices, by the manipulation of lexicon and grammar." Pollard says that the opus represents a synthesis of all the codes operating in the Jamaican environment in an expression that escapes the feeling of contrivance. She notes that Goodison's poem is "less a sliding from one code to the other than an overlap of codes to represent the different identities of the sectors of the community represented by each speech code." Pollard's contribution speaks as well to the political nature of language while it celebrates nation language and difference.

Similarly, Merle Collins, in her essay "Orality and Writing: A Revisitation," argues that the mode employed by voices used in literature influences technique and affects the structure of the novel or the poem. Collins connects oral literature and written literature, adding another dimension to the issue of voice through her analysis of the performance mode in literary works. In her own case, the practice is developed intuitively, by recording an experience "fully savored but not necessarily fully analyzed." Hence she, like other Caribbean writers, works within a tradition and practice made possible by others. In some cases, she argues, the generation removed from the African or Indian influences, for example, may not have direct or cognitive understanding of the inheritances, yet the writers are nonetheless spiritually influenced by their inheritances. She thereby identifies the element of spirituality as informing the Caribbean women's literary tradition. For the purposes of analysis, Collins maintains that "to fully understand the poetic forms upon which our spirits have stumbled, we have to move outside of the British traditions which have generally been our classroom fare."

Merle Hodge, in her essay "Caribbean Writers and Caribbean Language: A Study of Jamaica Kincaid's *Annie John*," explores possibilities and challenges presented for the creative writer in choice of language registry. The Anglophone Caribbean offers a "spread of variations which can . . . be likened to a continuum, with Creole at one extreme and Standard English at the other," with a range of nuances between. Jamaica Kincaid, the subject of Hodge's essay, uses a register of English far removed from the Creole end of the continuum. Hodge asserts that because Kincaid's fictional works are novels of introspection whereby "the main speaking voice is the voice of the protagonist/narrator and the main dialogue is with her own, searching self," the use of Creole in dialogue would detract from the writer's theme. She concludes that Kincaid's works, while not concerned with affirming the experience of the collective, render the universal and achieve their own truth.

Literary truth reconstructed is the subject of Maryse Condé's contribution to this section. In her essay "Suzanne Césaire and the Construct of a Caribbean Identity," Condé resurrects the voice of Suzanne Césaire, wife of famed poet Aimé Césaire, as the first intellectual to invent literary cannibalism . . . a rewriting and magical appropriation of the literature of the *other*, a symbol of the noncolonized self. Condé traces Césaire's evolution of thought during the five-year period of 1941–1945 and concludes that Césaire was the first to validate multiple origins in the construction of the Francophone Caribbean identity, an idea which, at the time, mitigated the effects of Négritude. In the end, Condé celebrates Césaire as "the founding mother of all the postcolonial critics who denounce . . . 'the simple pieties that the idiom of alterity frequently cloaks.'"

In her essay "Francophone Caribbean Women Writers and the Diasporic Quest for Identity: Marie Chauvet's *Amour* and Maryse Condé's *Hérémakhonon*," Régine Latortue locates Condé's efforts in *Hérémakhonon* as a complex statement about race, gender, nationality, and identity in the diasporic subject—thereby linking Condé to Marie Chauvet, Nella Larsen, Richard Wright, and Ralph Ellison in a genealogical strand. Chauvet's *Amour* and Condé's *Hérémakhonon* "illuminate each other in the centralizing of the female protagonist's story and the woman's voice and perspective."

Sybil Seaforth reflects on the power of silence to affect long-standing relationships in her contribution to this section, "The Silent Game." She offers reflections on women who, after several decades of marriage, find that their husbands have the ability to "ease" out of the relationship. The "silent game," Seaforth gives the reader to understand, is an actional sociological phenomenon affecting the lives of middle-aged women of the Caribbean. As her women characters articulate, the problem rests with the fact that "Men seek achievement in their chosen field of endeavor; women seek theirs in marriage." This dichotomy results in a disdain for the commodity owned (the wife); the woman is subsequently rendered invisible as she becomes the victim of the unjust system of female subordination. The woman as wife (unequal and often silenced partner in the relationship) is an apt metaphor for the issues raised in this section, where the idea of the Caribbean as the site of great cultural germination is explored along with the realities and social functions of the Caribbean woman writer.

The writers featured in "Part One: Language, Orality, and Voice" speak to each other and revise each other, tracing and enhancing the trails of literary foremothers. At heart is language, the use of nation language, and the creation of language that would welcome old voices obscured by time and neglect.

1. *De Language Reflect Dem Ethos: Some Issues with Nation Language*

Opal Palmer Adisa

> *I come from people for whom language is an art form.*
> —PAULE MARSHALL

I cannot begin to speak about language without thinking of conversations I have had or have overheard. When I think about the language of Jamaica I hear the women's voices loudest and clearest. They speak with honesty and passion, and what follows is a sample of how they come to understand their lives:

"Alrite, sista, noboda mash him up wid you mouth."

"But you see me crosses. Me mindin me own business an dis piece a man come si down ah me table . . ."

"Lawd me chile. Is so some man stay. Dem no know which side dem bread butter. But mek him gwane. Him no worth it."

"You rite. Him look like piece of bruk down."

The moment a person opens her mouth, what comes out defines her character, places her geographically, and often is a telltale sign of her class affiliation. June Jordan, African American poet and essayist, states: "Language is political. And language, its reward, currency, punishment, and/or eradication—is political in its meaning and in its consequence."[1] This means that those with political and economic power can and do define the parameters of the language used as the social medium and decide what is acceptable, and what is inappropriate and therefore substandard.

Jamaicans, as a result of colonial conquest, were never thought to possess a language of their own. The widespread ideology is that the language the people speak is not really a language at all, but rather a dialect, commonly referred to as pidgin English or patois (Creole in academic circles). However, anyone who understands the hegemony of colonialism and neocolonialism knows the pejorative light in which the colonized people's tongue has been cast, particularly a people who were never considered in the first place to possess culture, or have a history, philosophy, or any original ideas. The assumption being that what such a people, in this instance Jamaicans, speak is merely a poor imitation of their oppressors' language. While it is evident that the language Jamaicans speak shares much of the vocabulary of English, these majority people of African descent have combined African syntax with English words to create a language of their own. As Frederic G. Cassidy, who has done extensive research on Jamaican speech, notes, "Jamaican folk speech . . . is decidedly different from any dialect of England—it has, indeed, been formed in a very different way."[2]

Mervyn Alleyne situates the Jamaican nation language in a historical context by pointing out that "any discussion of the history and evolution of African languages in Jamaica must start out from the recognition that African languages were spoken quite normally on the island."[3] He discredits the commonly held belief that in order to discourage communication between them, Africans were never clustered according to their ethnic group during slavery. Instead, he produces historical evidence to demonstrate that, in the case of Jamaica, the first dominant group of Africans were the Akan people, and that the Twi-Akan language was widely used. Some Twi-Akan words still exist today in the Jamaican vocabulary.

Alleyne further states that the retention by enslaved Africans of their native tongues was a form of resistance:

> Military revolt by Maroons was only one form of resistance to assimilation to the English norm: there was also resistance to cultural assimilation. This cultural resistance took many forms, including both resistance to the adoption of an English language norm and the preservation of language codes incomprehensible to outsiders.[4]

Like the Maroons, the masses of Jamaica resisted cultural annihilation. Black people in the Caribbean, throughout the Americas, and even on the African continent put up a fierce and unrelenting fight to validate their lives through their speech. However, not only are they censored by the colonial or neocolonial powers, but they are often condemned by some of their own who are members of the educated elite in positions of power. All too frequently, this group disassociates itself from the masses, and often dismisses the average Jamaican as inferior and unintelligent. Consequently, Geneva Smitherman's assertion that "an individual's language is intricately bound up with his or her sense of identity and group consciousness"[5] merits consideration. For the Caribbean man, woman, and child, the right not to be slaves or servants to others also means the right to define, determine, and tell their own stories in their own words.

Until very recently, the literature produced by Caribbean writers, including Jamaicans, has been ambivalent about the usage of Caribbean speech, which I refer to as the nation language with acknowledgment to Edward Kamau Brathwaite's seminal work *History of the Voice* (1984). Writers have used Caribbean nation languages sparingly, often to depict a so-called uneducated or countrified person; or they standardize the folk speech to resemble British English. This in part is because until the seventies, with the exception of Louise Bennett and a few others, Caribbean intellectuals all looked toward European models, and their writing audience was in Europe and North America, not in the Caribbean. Of equal importance was the sense of shame and inferiority that some Caribbean writers carried within themselves and felt in relation to Europeans. Many writers accepted colonial standards, and therefore devalued themselves in comparison to European esthetics.

What this means for the Caribbean writer whose sense of inferiority is connected to slavery or indentured service is that he must throw off all vestiges that would link him to the masses and the soil. To safeguard against being linked to ancestral history, some Caribbean writers sharpened their tongues so that every syllable sounded like it came from a European. By rejecting the language, the Caribbean writer/intellectual has in fact rejected his resistance, and has conceded to remain no more than a shadow, a colonized person unable to wrestle with him/herself and project his/her own values and worldview. As June Jordan concludes in her comparison of Black English (African American speech) and Standard American English, for African Americans to accept that what they speak is substandard is to "literally accept the terms of the oppressor, or perish: that is the irreducible, horrifying truth of the politics of language."[6]

The language of the Caribbean remains vibrant and alive in its everyday usage, and Caribbean writers, especially the dub poets, have recorded their people's speech and elevated it to the level of poetry. Paule Marshall, the Barbadian-American writer, astutely encapsulates the place of Caribbean language when she recalls her introduction to the Bajan language of her mother and her mother's friends:

> I was that little girl, sitting in the corner of the kitchen, in the company of poets. I was there, seen but not heard, while these marvelous poets carried on. And from way back I always wanted to see if I might not be able to have some of the same power they had with words—their wonderful oral art. . . .[7]

The language that Caribbean people speak is art, yet many writers have not rendered such art in print. Language is political and it requires courage and full acceptance for the Caribbean writer to use her people's tongue, her own native tongue, in writing about the complexities and truth of their lives. Those Caribbean writers who make a conscious effort to refrain from using the native languages of their regions suggest that the people are incapable of speaking for themselves or that the nation language is incapable of expressing the full breadth and range of emotions and ideas.

Progress and development are interpreted all too often to mean relinquishing one's cultural sensibilities in favor of those of the metropolis. Sadly, education has been one of the worst enemies of the Jamaican language, and that in part is a result of the British model of education which still dominates the island, even today after independence in 1962. Amon Saba Saakana pinpoints the double-edged aspect of education:

> Education, therefore, was understood to be a form of liberation (from the
> shackles of the plantation), but it cruelly prepared the mind for a psychic
> trauma that would colour and limit the politics and literature of Caribbean
> writers and scholars.[8]

The country's political and social outlooks have not changed drastically. The ties are
still entrenched, perhaps more firmly today due to loan agreements with North
America and Europe, so the aspiration toward metropolis standards remains firm.
This is compounded by the fact that the country is governed by an educated group,
most of whom were trained in North America and Europe, and many of whom so
far have been unable to disassociate progress and development from the acceptance
of the cultural norms of the metropolis. In discussing the implications of education
in the Caribbean, Saakana distinguishes two phases of the movement toward a
speech that approximates the English ideal norm. The first phase occurred during
slavery: "This movement could be explained almost entirely by the need for an instrument of communication between Africans and British."[9] The second phase,
which I believe is presently at its height, is what Saakana identifies as "the realization
by Blacks that command of English is a precondition for upward socioeconomic mobility."[10] This is in fact the dilemma that writers and intellectuals of the forties and
fifties struggled with: how to demonstrate to the world that they have been schooled
in the history, philosophy, and literature of Europe, yet write about their peoples and
cultures using a language that the ethnocentric governing group of Europe has
deemed substandard, illiterate, a poor imitation of their own. The Caribbean writer
is caught in a bind because the unspoken rule is that regional languages should be
avoided at all costs. Again, Saakana's observation is pertinent:

> Thus language is but a reflection of culture in motion, and if the literary
> critic is not aware of the significance of cultural dissimilarity, a value-judge-
> ment could be placed on a work, dismissing it, without contextual com-
> prehension of the culture from which it emerged.[11]

To a large extent this dilemma has not been resolved. The English-speaking
Caribbean does not have any publishing houses, and the audience for Caribbean
writers' works is comprised largely of Europeans and North Americans, many of
whom perceive the Caribbean as islands of paradise, places to vacation and relieve
oneself of the pressure of living and working in the metropolis. While an indigenous
Caribbean audience is growing, as are the local literary journals and newspapers,
owing to the high cost of and limited access to books, such an audience remains minimal. But there is a tremendous potential, since several schools now include books by
Caribbean writers in their curricula.

The peasant with little or no contact with urbanity or metropolitan values is very comfortable with her/his speech and ways of life. This is not to suggest that rural folks do not desire access to the society at large or want to feel as if their voices are being heard. Nevertheless, many resilient souls, even after confrontation with the educated urban elite, insist on the value of their speech. VèVè Clark's realization of the impact of this language duality on the individual provides insight:

> The toll on the individual's double consciousness at the level of language is deeply unsettling because out of place, signifying upon return to the regional landscape (if return does occur) an imagination out of mind. The past two decades of Creole revival and defense in the Anglophone, Francophone, and Dutch Caribbean have transformed the previously inferior status of amalgamated, New World languages into an increasingly valued form of written expression.[12]

This is certainly the case with the recent novels by writers from the Anglophone Caribbean. Most notable among these in terms of more authentic usage of the native language, not only in dialogue but also in narration, is *The Dragon Can't Dance* (1979) by the Trinidadian author, Earl Lovelace, and more recently *Clarise Cumberbatch Want to Go Home* (1987) by Guyanese writer Joan Cambridge.

Poets are of course at the forefront of the movement toward the full embrace of the nation languages, and many prose writers do attempt to approximate their nation language, although this is still often done only when the characters speak. The narrators are often still outsiders or from the educated elite, or they speak a different, more standardized language from the characters, except in the works mentioned above.

Any discussion of language must include a critique of culture. Language is at the root of any culture, and as Frantz Fanon states, "To speak means to be in a position to use a certain syntax, to grasp the morphology of this or that language, but it means above all to assume a culture, to support the weight of a civilization."[13] The question then seems to be whether or not Caribbean writers and intellectuals are willing to acknowledge and demonstrate that Caribbean cultures are different from, yet on par with Europe. For until Caribbean people are able to wrestle to the ground the conflict between local and foreign cultures, they will remain forever colonized. Fanon was emphatic on this point:

> Every colonized people—in other words, every people in whose soul an inferiority complex has been created by the death and burial of its local culture originality—finds itself face to face with the language of the civilizing nation; that is, with the culture of the mother country.[14]

Since Fanon pointed this out in 1952, the whole notion of "mother country" has changed as a result of independence. Mother is no longer England, France, or Spain. So how does a former colonized person overcome her/his colonial experience and assert his/her own cultural identity separate and apart from the "mother" culture? Recent novels from the Caribbean have indicated that this course of action is possible, but only for someone like the protagonist in Joan Cambridge's novel, whose actions are based on instinct and common sense rather than worldly knowledge and introspective analysis. So when Clarise finds herself smack up against the mother country—America—under the hegemony of neocolonialism, she rejects it, realizing that the cost to her personhood is too great. She does what many Caribbean persons covetous of the green card would call madness—she demands to be returned to Guyana:

> "You going call?"
> "Yes Clarise. I will call immigration for you."
>
> "Thanks, Andy. Tell them: My-name-is-Clarise-Cumberbatch-I-come-from Guyana-and-I-doesn't-have-greencard!"[15]

This novel ushers in a new era in Caribbean literature in which not only is the nation tongue validated at the level of character and narrator, but the nation, home, is given credence above the metropole as a place more suited for one's spirituality.

The relationship between language and literature as a reflection of the cultural ethos of a people is obvious. Language is the fabric from which the literature takes shape. Language informs not only about a specific culture, but also about the people's attitude and self-perception. Literature is the platform on which these perceptions and values parade, although this is more evident in oral performances. If the Caribbean is to have a renaissance then the ideology that Ngũgĩ wa Thiong'o advocates for Africa is relevant to the Caribbean as well:

> Equally important for our cultural renaissance is the teaching and study of African languages. We have already seen what any colonial system does: impose its tongue on the subject races, and then down-grade the vernacular tongues of the people. By so doing they make the acquisition of their tongue a status symbol; anyone who learns it begins to despise the peasant majority and their barbaric tongues. By acquiring the thought-processes and values of his adopted tongue, he becomes alienated from the values of his mother tongue, or from the language of the masses. Language after all is a carrier of values fashioned by a people over a period of time.[16]

Is the Caribbean prepared to study and teach its nation languages? Is independence of mind being achieved? The use of nation languages might limit the audience for Caribbean writers, but it seems to me that those who are truly interested in sharing in Caribbean peoples' lives will stretch themselves to discern our words.

Until readers show themselves willing to decipher the Caribbean language, they cannot fully know its people. Accepting Ngũgĩ wa Thiong'o's point that language is "a carrier of values fashioned by a people over a period of time," we can therefore acknowledge the importance of choice of language usage in literary texts. This being the case, we need to examine the Caribbean man's model for language, because herein lies the dilemma. Celebrated Caribbean male writers such as George Lamming and Derek Walcott have engaged in discourse with Shakespeare's Caliban, who would appear to be the model for the Caribbean man, his appearance in literature being the moment when the Caribbean man is given voice. But should Caliban's voice be an archetype for Caribbean discourse? Perhaps at this stage the question is rhetorical, and we should shift to focus on gender.

Caribbean women have always spoken poetry, but because of their domestication, they have not always been published. Until the 1960s it was primarily men who migrated to England and to metropolitan cities elsewhere. There they had access to publishing, and, free from the constraints imposed by Caribbean colonial societies, they could realize their own voices. But this did not mean that the Caribbean woman at home did not have a voice. So, if Caliban is the model for the Caribbean man, who is his counterpart, the model for the Caribbean woman? Caliban's counterpart is noticeably absent; the Caribbean woman is rendered not only dumb but invisible as well in this important play by Shakespeare. That Caribbean male writers and intellectuals have not so far argued for their mate is merely a reflection of the sexism inherent in the society, but of equal danger is their embracing of Caliban as a symbol of their emergence in literature and the beginning of their voice. The consequence of this canonization is the erasure of a vital part of their historical culture.

Perhaps, then, it is to the Caribbean woman's advantage that Shakespeare omitted her. Jamaican intellectual Sylvia Wynter, in her in-depth analysis of Shakespeare's *Tempest*, situates this play in its historical context while providing insight into the Caribbean woman's absence:

Nowhere in Shakespeare's play, and in its system of image-making, one which would be foundational to the emergence of the first form of a secular world system, our present Western world system, does Caliban's mate appear as an alternative sexual-erotic model of desire; as an alternative source of an alternative system of meanings. Rather there, on the New World island, as the only woman, Miranda and her mode of physiognomic being, defined by the philogenically "idealized" features of straight hair and thin lips, is canonized as the "rational" object of desire; as the potential genitrix of a superior mode of human "life," that of "good natures" as contrasted with the ontological absent potential genitrix—Caliban's mate—of another population of human, i.e., of a "vile race" capable of all ill.[17]

It is out of this patriarchal structure, designed to make her an object, part of the landscape to be used and discarded as seen fit by the colonizer, that the Caribbean woman has emerged.

Paule Marshall, in her short story "Brazil," takes this whole paradigm of Caliban as being representative of the Black in the New World, and she shows Caliban, the Black man, is not only marginalized as Wynter suggests, but also obfuscated. No one sees him beyond the mask that he dons for their entertainment. In this agonizing story an aged comic, Heitor Guimares, on the eve of retirement comes face to face with the fact that he is unknown as a man and person, even to his wife and his mistress of fifteen years. He has made his fame and fortune playing Caliban, and has perfected the role so well that no one remembers that before there was Caliban there was Heitor. Marshall skillfully dramatizes how Caliban the performer erases the Black man because he lacks language and depth. When Heitor (a.k.a. Caliban) returns to the restaurant where he used to work mopping up the floor before he became a success, hoping to find someone who remembers him as Heitor, he meets only Caliban, from whom he is trying to escape. And as he continues his futile search to find himself, he makes more painful discoveries which heighten his invisibility. In Miranda's mistress's house, Heitor (a.k.a. Caliban) realizes his place:

> For the first time Caliban was aware of how the room expressed the city, and of himself, reflected in one of the mirrors, in relation to it. He was like a house pet, a tiny dog, who lent the room an amusing touch but had no real place there.[18]

Heitor's final defeat comes after he confronts Miranda, his stage partner and white mistress for some fifteen years, and she admits to not knowing any Heitor Guimares. In fact, she denies Heitor's existence completely:

> "You? No, senhor, you are Caliban. O Grande Caliban!" And leaping from the bed, her great breasts swinging, she dropped to his familiar fighter's crouch, her fists cocked menacingly and her smile confirming what the others—his wife that morning, the boys on the Rua Gloria chanting behind him, the man in the restaurant that had been made into a shrine, and finally, the old man, Nacimento—had all insisted was true, and what he, and certainly Miranda, had really known all along: simply, that Caliban had become his only reality and anything else he might have been was lost.[19]

So not only does Caliban die, but Heitor, the spiritual representative of the Black man in the new world, dies as well, and is not allowed to emerge.

Until the rulers and elites of the Caribbean come to terms with the fact that any kind of development has to begin with the fundamental issue of naming oneself (call it self-determination and acceptance of one's linguistic birthright), the Caribbean will always remain a shadow of the metropolis to be used and manipulated at will. The discussion of language is not merely an academic or literary exercise; it is at the very root of Caribbean selfhood, because without voice, without a language of our own, we will always be lagging behind as poor imitators.

In view of Lamming's dismissal of Caliban in his essay "A Monster, a Child, a

Slave," I can't help but wonder: for whom does Caliban speak?

> For language itself, by Caliban's whole relation to it, will not allow his ex-
> pansion beyond a certain point. This kind of realization, this kind of ex-
> pansion, is possible only to those who reside in that state of being which is
> the very source and ultimate of language that bears them forward. . . . But
> Caliban is not a child of anything except Nature. To be a child of Nature, in
> this sense, is to be situated in Nature, to be identified with Nature, to be eter-
> nally without the seed of a dialectic which makes possible some emergence
> from Nature.[20]

So Caliban is trapped: he is not allowed to develop, to speak without being addressed. This was the relationship that the colonizer demanded from the slave who, if he transgressed that rule, would suffer dire consequences. The language that Prospero taught Caliban was useless, as it did not render him visible or human. As Chinua Achebe reminds us, "It has long been known that language, like any other human invention, can be abused, can be turned from its original purpose into something useless or even dead."[21] This is the sad fate of Caliban, no matter how brilliantly or equally his language mirrors his tutor's.

But the fate Shakespeare devises for Caliban has little to do with the average Jamaican person who, like his/her African American brother and sister, is quick with rejoinders, and is known for verbal dexterity. I have often overheard the dismissive sucking of teeth, followed by verbal vehemence at what is considered double-talk. The response might be: "But a wha him a chat seh. Dem chat so til dem chat stupidness. Rass. Him mouth mus stuck inna him batty." This, followed by the fanning out of one's hand, completes the dismissal. The ability to deflate and dismiss with a word illustrates language at its most creative level.

Woman, too, wields language and transforms it to echo her deepest pleasure or her most gnashing pain. As a daughter of the Caribbean community, and of the writing community, I have never conceived of language as being gender-specific or gender-biased, perhaps because like Paule Marshall I learned to manipulate language and wring it to suit my voice from imitating my mother and her friends. In the society in which I grew up women were praised equally as men for being able to transform ordinary language into poetry, and biased as my memory might be, the women seemed best at such manipulation. They were certainly more clever in their usages, with unusual turns and surprises in the blend and molding of the language.

The Jamaican poet who epitomizes this trait par excellence is Louise Bennett. Her poem "Dutty Tough (The Ground Is Hard)" takes its inspiration from an equally prolific Jamaican male poet, Bob Marley:

> Sun a-shine but tings noh bright,
> Doah pot a-bwile, bickle noh nuff,
> River flood but water scarce yaw,

Rain a-fall but dutty tuff!

Tings so bad, dat now-a-days wen
Yuh ask smaddy how dem do,
Dem fraid yuh teck I tell dem back
So dem noh answer yuh!

Noh care omuch we dah-work fa
Hard time still eena we shut,
We dah-fight, Hard-Time a-beat we,
Dem might raise we wages but—

One poun gwan awn pon we pay, an
We noh feel noh merriment,
For ten poun gwan on pon we food
Ann ten pound on we rent![22]

The next four stanzas of the poem recount the many manifestations of inflation, and the cost of different items. This poem is a commentary on the socioeconomic conditions that the average Jamaican has been facing since the 1970s, and in keeping with Bennett's life, the form is direct; the persona is unsolicitous, merely recounting his/her daily life. As in so much of Bennett's poetry the voice is not gender-specific, but takes on the collective wail of the Jamaican masses. Bennett, like a large number of the masses of Jamaican women, foremost among these the market women and higglers (street side traders), owns the language and uses it to effectively convey and relate stories.

In her poem "Discourse on the Logic of Language," Trinidadian writer Marlene Nourbese Philip effectively conveys the limitation that the imposition of colonial languages places on the Caribbean person:

English
is my mother tongue
A mother tongue is not
not a foreign lan lan lang
language
l/anguish
anguish
—a foreign anguish.

English is
my father tongue
A father tongue is
a foreign language,

                    therefore English is
                    a foreign language
                    not a mother tongue.

                    What is my mother
                    tongue
                    my mammy tongue
                    my mummy tongue
                    my momsy tongue
                    my modder tongue
                    my ma tongue?

                    I have no mother
                    tongue
                    no mother to tongue
                    no tongue to mother
                    to mother
                    tongue
                    me

                    I must therefore be tongue
                    dumb
                    dumb-tongued
                    dub-tongued
                    damn dumb
                    tongue.[23]

But of course Nourbese Philip is not "tongue dumb." To the contrary, her rendition of this poem is a testimony to how resourceful the Caribbean person is, even in trying to work through and recognize the foreignness of the language with which she/he must work. However, the mother imagery that Nourbese Philip evokes heightens the persona's neurosis and demonstrates how her self-esteem is lowered as a result of not being able to locate herself or her cultural identity in this foreign language she is forced to use. But use it she must, even if her tongue is "dumb-tongued."

For the only tongue that is dumb is a silent tongue. The Black, feminist, lesbian poet Audre Lorde, who knows and uses language effectively, reminds us, in her very eloquent essay "The Transformation of Silence into Language and Action," of the responsibility we have to voice our fears and not drown in silence:

I have come to believe over and over again that what is most important to me must be spoken, made verbal and shared, even at the risk of having it bruised or misunderstood. That the speaking profits me, beyond any other effect.[24]

The speaking not only profits the individual poet/writer, but paves a way for those others who have no access. In my essay "She Scrape She Knee: The Theme of My Work" I focus on why I wrote my short story collection, *Bake-Face and Other Guava Stories* (1986):

> It is a tribute to those women who never have access to microphones, who carry their madness sewed into their skirt's hems and tied to their hand-kerchiefs buried in their bosoms. Giving voice to this madness that besieges us, giving voice to the celebration of our lives, giving voice to our quiet fears and invisible tears, giving voice to our struggles, our victories, our determi-nation. . . .[25]

Caribbean women writers have a responsibility to speak, and to speak in a language that their sisters can understand. We must also write in a language that others can empathize with, for we speak for our people, who although they use language daily in their defense, may not have access to print.

Lorde asks: "What are the words you do not yet have? What do you need to say? What are the tyrannies you swallow day by day and attempt to make your own, until you will sicken and die of them, still in silence?"[26] Already too many have died with-out leaving us a legacy. When I think of the tremendous vacuum that is a part of my history because no one recorded the slave narratives of Jamaicans, I feel weak. I can surmise, but I will never really know the life they lived, the specific details, the atroc-ities they endured, the links they forged. I am left to invent, to dream these my peo-ple who were buried without a stone to mark their graves. I do not have their words, I do not have an essential part of me.

Like Lorde, I am "afraid, because the transformation of silence into language and action is an act of self-revelation, and that always seems fraught with danger."[27] What is the danger that Caribbean women writers face when they reveal their lives for all to examine? Like their sisters in the past, they are subject to censorship, to loud dis-claimers, to rejection and ostracism. But the other side to this is that they help their sisters and countrymen to hold their heads higher, to walk with more swagger, to speak with more assurance and clarity, and to embrace the commonality that they all share.

Caribbean societies are still fraught with the silence of colorism, classism, sex-ism. The partisan politics that over the last two decades divided many families, and many other ordinary people in Jamaican society—all of whom are bearing the brunt of neocolonialism and capitalistic exploitation—is a silence that needs to be blared on the loudspeakers. We must announce over the radio and on television the rape of women and young girls, the misogynist acts of violence committed against female bodies. The corruption and tyranny of politicians who exploit the masses while buy-ing Mercedeses and homes in Miami must be published in the newspaper, discussed at Half-Way-Three, at the circle at Parade, at the bus depot at Cross Roads. To make these transgressions public is to invite danger. But if the society is to develop, if

Caribbean people are to achieve total independence, then we must abandon silence. And writers have a responsibility to lead the way. Of course, since the 1970s women's groups have been publicizing many of the abuses—and the oral discourse, in the form of graffiti, popular songs, etc., has been ahead of writers in this area.

The debate will continue over the appropriate language to use, but the movement is already afoot. The mission of Caribbean women writers is to render in all its complexity the life of Caribbean people. As Lorde so aptly puts it, "We share a commitment to language and to the power of language, and to the reclaiming of that language which has been made to work against us."[28] Caribbean women writers are making the language work in their favor; they are decoding and deconstructing standard English so they can build a world more suited to their taste. Language, in the context of Caribbean literature, is a tool that women have always wielded, just as, traditionally, women were the ones who cracked stones to pave roads. So too they mold and knead words and make bread to feed the nation. So, in the mode of the common Jamaican woman, "Ah so me get it, and ah so me sell it. If you no gwane buy den walk by."

2. *Language and Identity: The Use of Different Codes in Jamaican Poetry*

VELMA POLLARD

The struggle to find a voice that is truly representative of the speech communities out of which they write has been a very real one for Caribbean creative writers ever since the primacy of the European languages they inherited came to be debated. Commenting more than a decade ago on writing in the Anglophone Caribbean, Gerald Moore, literary critic, noted some success in finding that voice, or a close approximation to it, in the drama and in the novels in the early fifties.[1]

Jean D'Costa, Jamaican linguist and fiction writer, extends the requirement to include the need for the voices to be understood by a foreign readership. Discussing her choices of language in the writing of her novels for children in the 1960s and 1970s, D'Costa comments that the West Indian writer who wishes to satisfy himself, his local audience and his foreign audience must evolve a "literary dialect" which not only must satisfy both audiences but must be an authentic representation of the "language culture" of his community.[2] Of her own style she writes, "Variation, code-switching and minimal shifting appear . . . to form a complete internalized reality."[3]

In the essay "Mother Tongue," I identify the prose of Olive Senior as an almost perfect match between life and its fictive reproduction which "might serve as a kind of laboratory for examining Jamaican speech" without losing its accessibility to the foreign reader.[4] Moore's complimentary comment with regard to drama and the novel is not echoed in his comment on poetry. According to Moore, "By contrast it seems to have taken rather longer for West Indian poetry to develop a full consciousness of the living language situation which surrounds it."[5] And later Pamela Mordecai finds only Brathwaite among the region's poets handling "the Creole continuum [that is, the range of language between the deepest Jamaican Creole and 'Standard' Jamaican English] with a versatility" comparable to that of Lorna Goodison, the author whose work is the subject of the present paper.[6]

This paper analyzes a single poem, "Ocho Rios II," by Goodison, not merely to indicate the distance the poetry has traveled since Moore's comment on the fifties, but to illustrate how language may be used as a mark of identity in a medium which must be at once terse and expressive. In Goodison's hands, different voices of the Jamaican community find their expression in discrete but overlapping codes which constitute what D'Costa describes as "language culture" and the "living language situations" identified by Moore. D'Costa's "code-switching and minimal shifting" is extended, in Goodison, to an intricate weave, facilitated by the fact that all the codes used in Jamaica are English-related. Goodison is able to manipulate the different grammars without losing intelligibility to the English-reading public. She accommodates, as will be illustrated later, as many as three codes within one sentence.

A brief description of the Jamaican linguistic environment is in order. The official language of Jamaica, as of all the territories of the Anglophone Caribbean, is Jamaican English (JE), a dialect of English. It is the language of the formal motions of the society and of education. The majority of Jamaicans, however, speak Jamaican Creole (JC), a Creole of English lexicon, which everyone in the speech community understands and which almost everyone can produce. Dread Talk (DT), the code of Rastafari, is a lexical adjustment available to both languages and may be invoked to satisfy the requirements of speakers sympathetic to the philosophy of Rastafari, a socioreligious movement which originated in Jamaica.

I have selected "Ocho Rios II" for this exercise because I think it represents a synthesis of all the codes operating in the Jamaican environment in an expression that escapes the feeling of contrivance that sometimes results from this kind of effort. The lines, to the ear of a Jamaican, are authentic. It is to this feature, I believe, that J.E. Chamberlain refers when he writes, "Goodison's language typically combines conversational naturalness with poetic artifice."[7]

Pamela Mordecai, commenting on Goodison's first collection of poetry, identifies the use of language as an outstanding feature of the work and makes special reference to the effective sliding from one to another code of Jamaican speech.[8] And Edward Baugh, commenting later on the development of Goodison's craft, notes the "continuous expending of linguistic possibility" and the refining of the skill of "sliding seamlessly between English and Creole."[9]

The present analysis sees Goodison's product as less a sliding from one code to the other than an overlap of codes to represent the different identities of the sectors of the community represented by each speech code. The fact that all the codes are English related allows Goodison a certain security in the knowledge that an audience that reads English can understand what she writes while the local audience will be satisfied that the representation of the different strands of the society is accurate.

Language is, in the poem to be discussed, an identification marker of the person whose opinion or whose reaction to a given circumstance the writer wishes to record. The poem begins with an individual who enters the stage soliloquizing: "Today I again I forward to the sea." The local reader immediately recognizes a Rastafarian. The first person pronoun "I" is an English form, but its repetition in the sentence suggests the "I an I" which functions as both singular and plural first person in Dread Talk. The choice of verb further identifies the Rasta man as the speaker. "Forward" to describe the act of walking is a particularly common verb in DT. It is rarely used with that meaning in either Jamaican Creole or Jamaican English. While the format identifies the speaker, the meaning is completely accessible to users of the other codes of the community.

The word "again" comments both on the habit of the Rasta man and the existence of an earlier poem, "Ocho Rios."[10] The first movement of the poem continues:

> . . . to the built-up beach where a faithful few
> lie rigid, submit to the smite of the sun.
> Today I bless you from the sore chambers of my temples. . . .

These lines are written in JE except for the item "smite," in which the verb/noun distinction of English is ignored in favor of DT usage, and the possibility of the English "I" in the last line being "I an I" or "the I" of Rasta convention. These items maintain the presence of the Rasta man although the words are from the repertoire of an English-speaking Jamaican.

In the next movement a larger Jamaican population joins the Rasta man on the scene. Voice and content are the sound and sentiment of the middle-class Jamaican. He/she speaks English (more or less) and understands the relationship between the tourist presence and the economy of the country, at a sophisticated level. He can banter about collaboration of Kaiser Bauxite Company and the Jamaican government. He puns on the term "exchange" using the language the society thinks of as his:

> bless you Mr. Hawaiian Print Cabana suit,
> I can smile at the exchange
> The package tour one-upmanship
> vs. the regular visitor.
> "Did-you-get-drawn-butter-with-your-lobster?"
> "Our-Naytive-floor-show-was-soupberb!"
>
> Bless even you burnt to the colour of Bauxite
> for the Kaiser is now our partner

The scene here includes the archetypal tourist in dress that has become classic tourist wear (the patterned shorts and shirt rarely worn by local men). The tourist might bargain with the local peddlar ("one-upmanship") if he belongs to a poorer class who must choose the package tour. He is less likely to do that if he is a "regular" who can afford to visit Jamaica perhaps every year and can accept the peddlar's price without discussion. The "exchange" is of course both dialogue and dollars, the latter being "foreign exchange."

A distinctly non-native code intervenes here in the exchange between tourists, overheard by the locals. The Jamaican ridicules, mildly, the tourist's newly acquired tan, comparing it, in an extended metaphor, with bauxite, for its redness, then continuing to bless the tourist: "for the Kaiser is now our partner." "Kaiser" is the name of a foreign bauxite company. The uneasy relationships between local and foreign people and businesses are indicated by the placing of the definite article in front of "Kaiser" and so making it both the bauxite company and the World War One archenemy.

The third movement involves sentiments shared by all of Jamaica. Language identifies three different representatives. A fine fabric is woven as the middle-class speaker continues to bless the tourist in JE, but switches in midsentence (in lines 1 and 2) to JC. Another way of looking at this is that in mid-sentence he passes the microphone, so to speak, to the JC speaker:

> bless you with a benediction of green rain
>> no feel no way
> its not that the land of sea and sun has failed,
>> is so rain stay.
> You see man need rain for food to grow
> so if is your tan, or my yam fi grow? is just so.
>
> P.S. thanks for coming anyway,

The rendering of complex behaviors, the sound of complex voices in a single statement by the manipulation of lexicon and grammar, is what I regard as Goodison's major contribution to the language of Caribbean literature.

In the real-life situation the JE speaker is able and even likely to code switch in this way. The artistic intention, however, is to involve the man whose stereotypical speech is JC. He is the peasant farmer for whom "green rain," which ruins the tourist's tan, is a blessing. It brings (green) lushness and the promise of productivity to the plants which earn him his living. He apologizes to the tourist for preferring rain to the desired sun and explains away what might seem to be a selfish preference. He is a good ambassador for Jamaica, which he exonerates from blame for lack of sun in a place advertised for sun and sea. His complete statement is: "no feel no way . . . is so rain stay"; it might translate to English as: "Don't be angry, that is how rain behaves," that is, unpredictably.

All the speakers identify with the sentiment expressed in the next line. But it is the voice of the Rasta man that articulates it. What might be the impersonal "man" of JE is equally a variant of the multifunctional pronoun of DT. "I-man," "the man," "man," "I an I" are all equally valid ways of identifying the Rasta person. The verb which follows, "need," is unmarked, as verbs are in JC and DT. But a mere marking of the verb ("needs") would make the sentence English. In fact, depending on whether you read "you see" with an anglicized pronunciation or a JC pronunciation, you favor one speaker or the other.

The Rasta man and the farmer are at one in their relationship to the land. Both claim it in a very real sense. For one, it is his means of livelihood; for the other, it is what Jah (Jehovah) has given him for an inheritance. Anything that enhances its worth and beauty is important to both: "so if is your tan, or my yam fi grow? is just so."

The voice, perhaps of the tourist board representative, speaks the afterthought of the stanza: "P.S. thanks for coming anyway." That voice mediates between the gentle ribbing of the tourist by farmer and Rasta man, and any possible negative reaction the tourist might have to it. In addition it serves as a link with the next movement, in which a radio or TV announcer quotes a tourist statement to the media:

> (we're here because we didn't believe a word of it Jamaica
>   is too beautiful
> the people so friendly . . . but watch that talk of equality
>   though)
> Dont watch that. Albertha baby in the green coconut hat,
>   bless you
> still, but dont watch that.

The statement ends with an unfortunate comment which is the cue for the Rasta man's admonishment of the tourist. The admonishment suggests that while tourists are welcome to enjoy sun and sea (or to experience rain), they should try not to comment on the politics of the Jamaican situation, which is what they meddle in when they attempt to define terms like "equality" in the local context.

The poem ends, as it started, with the voice of the Rasta man, who is usually the most vocal of the unsolicited speakers in the Jamaican society. His is the voice of the nation against the outsider. Nevertheless he bestows on the outsider, the tourist, the earner of foreign exchange, the benediction from young Jamaica:

> "Dont watch that. Albertha baby in the green coconut hat,
>   bless you
> still, but dont watch that."

The word "still" needs some elaboration here. Notice that it is located where it can be applied to either line or to both. In JE it means "yet" and suggests that a blessing is given to the tourist in spite of his attempt to interfere. In the code of the Rasta man it is a ubiquitous tag.

In these final lines once more the three codes are represented. "Dont watch that" is English if it is written. Spoken however, a slight phonological adjustment ("th" to "d") allows that utterance to be JC. And whether Albertha is a Jamaican mother or an American tourist (as Gordon Rohlehr, personal communication, suggests), the unmarked verb "bless" allows the rest of the line to be JC but near enough to English that it can be either, depending on the phonological representation.

Three distinct voices in three codes, each representing an individual from one social group, can be identified in the poem. The fourth code is foreign and alien to the environment. It is the voice of the tourist mentioned earlier, whose sunbathing is the trigger for the discourse. It is heard in the second movement of the poem. That voice and the content it introduces are entirely out of place on a Jamaican beach. Alien content in an alien language is dull and passes without comment. Tourists compare notes:

"Did-you-get-drawn-butter-with-your-lobster?"
"Our-Naytive-floor-show-was-soupberb!"

The native Jamaican has little idea what drawn butter might be; nor does he speak of himself and things that concern him as "native." When the voice comments on the local politics in the final movement, however, it awakens a response in the company.

The literary artist paints in words. Goodison—herself, in real life, a painter in watercolors—uses the available codes and the stereotypes associated with them to present a credible encounter on a Jamaican beach. Stereotyping is important here. Each code is associated with certain behaviors and certain recognizable physical and psychological types. R. B. LePage and Andree Tabouret-Keller say of language that through it "we can symbolize in a coded way all the other concepts which we use to define ourselves and our society."[11] "Ocho Rios II" exploits fully the possibilities of language in these terms.

3. *Orality and Writing: A Revisitation*

MERLE COLLINS

In his text *Orality and Literacy*, Walter Ong refers to primary and secondary orality.[1] The first is to orality in cultures not influenced by writing; the second orality in cultures which do have contact with the written word. As I think of the narrative forms, the forms of poetic expression which are usually referred to as orality in Caribbean writing, using Ong's construct I would refer to these as secondary orality. But the term leads me also to think of what might be another kind of secondary orality: the orality practiced by those Caribbean writers living for the most part outside of the region and writing from an attachment to and from the memory of cultures in which they may be frequently but not constantly immersed, cultures which are daily being transformed in linguistic and other terms; writing, too, out of the dynamism of linguistic and other changes overseas in Caribbean communities. The differences, to me, are not about being more or less Caribbean—or perhaps, migrant that I am, I am merely being hopeful. Language changes in different ways depending on individual location and on the influences of the surrounding culture. But the voice that continues to shape me and to represent home is Caribbean.

My experience of living in England and the United States has made me perhaps even more acutely aware not only of the sociopolitical dynamics of language but also of how much, to me, language represents home. At first, in England, there was the verbal engagement with words which were more book usage than everyday Grenadian usage. In the United States now, I listen to my pronunciation. Is this how the Americans pronounce it? Is this a British pronunciation? Is it a Caribbean pronunciation? In the "Anglophone" Caribbean, I am completely at home with language. If I'm visiting an Anglophone Caribbean country other than Grenada, I may not know particular terms, but my only feeling about language there is excitement or interest. I don't listen to myself in the same way. I don't wonder whose language I'm using. Perhaps this is not only because I'm at home there but also because the Caribbean has absorbed facets of both Britain and the United States and is constantly reshaping these creatively into something distinctly Caribbean. Perhaps, too, all of this thinking about language is because I work with words and am constantly aware of their dynamism.

I term this paper "A Revisitation" because it seems to me that in recent times I have been writing and speaking considerably about orality and writing. The fascination with identifying and defining different facets of what is referred to as orality in Caribbean writing is, I suppose, there partly because I am so often confronted in public forums with demands to explain this feature which is said to be so prevalent in my work. One response would be, well, these are the voices I hear. But in reality it is not only a question of recording voices; it is clear that the modes employed by these voices influence technique, affect the structure of the novel, or the poem.

Let us have some idea of what this orality is supposed to be. Gordon Rohlehr defines the oral tradition in the Caribbean as "a heritage of song, speech and performance visible in such folk forms as the litanic work songs, chants, battle songs, Queh Queh songs, sermons of both the grassroots and establishment churches, riddles, jokes and word-games."[2] About oral literature Ruth Finnegan explains:

> There is no mystery about the first and most basic characteristic of oral literature. . . . This is the significance of the actual performance. Oral literature is by definition dependent on a performer who formulates it in words on a specific occasion—there is no other way in which it can be realized as a literary product. In the case of *written* literature a literary work can be said to have an independent and tangible existence in even one copy, so that questions about, say, the format, number, and publicizing of other written copies can, though not irrelevant, be treated to some extent as secondary; there is, that is, a distinction between the actual creation of a written literary form and its further transmission.[3]

When we come to speak, then, of connections between orality and writing, we are referring partly to ways in which aspects of the performance mode might be incorporated into the written work; ways, that is, in which we might represent what Kenyan writer Ngũgĩ wa Thiong'o has referred to as orature.[4]

My own efforts to find ways of contextualizing this orality, and the similar kinds of efforts observed when other Caribbean writers are asked about this aspect of their practice, suggest to me that the practice is often something which is developed intuitively, a recording of experience fully savored but not necessarily fully analyzed. Many of us have, in a sense, started walking both where inclination led and where the example of other writers before us suggested it might be an acceptable place to go. So that Louise Bennett's work, for example, outlined a possible route for several Caribbean writers, directly or otherwise. Not because she was necessarily writing about themes or using approaches that all were interested in, but because, as her work became more widely known and recognized, throughout the Caribbean and internationally, people came more to accept the idea of the use of the dialect, now also Creole, in written literature. In some cases, as with a writer like Valerie Bloom, one might say that the Bennett influences on tone, structure, performance, are all clear; in others, as with Jean Binta Breeze and Linton Kwesi Johnson, one might say that the very fact that it is a performance mode and the language is familiar suggests an influence, even though mood, thematic focus, rendition, are distinct; with a writer such as Paul Keens-Douglas, one might say the performance mode, even if not necessarily always the thematic focus, suggests that a way was mapped out by many others before him.

Many of the long narrative poems by those who emphasize performance place considerable importance on the recounting of a story and, in performance, on the techniques of rendition which would make this recounting an absorbing, inspiring event for listeners. And so these poem-stories may be recounted again and again, for each new rendition is different because the poet's techniques, which disappear once the poet-actor is off the stage, are always new. If not in print, the work can't be read and learned by heart. It may of course then be listened to and learned; or it may appear on video and so can be experienced repeatedly, but there is a quality to the interchange of a live performance which is always new and worth capturing. Audience response is part of the performance, and each audience responds differently.

Questions about orality remind us that Caribbean poetry reflects the fact that its writers are shaped by the largely silent stories of a variety of traditions: in some cases, influences are African and European; in some cases Asian and European; in some cases, African, Asian, and European; in some cases Asian, African, and European; in some cases European and Asian, and so on. Generations removed from those African and/or Asian and/or European influences, even if grasping on a cognitive level little of the inheritances which are not European, may nonetheless, I venture, be spiritually influenced by them. And perhaps those little examined spiritual influences are what questions about orality urge me to explore.

Elements of many or perhaps all of what Gordon Rohlehr names as facets of the oral tradition find their way at various times and to various extents into the poetry and prose of many writers. In the work of a poet such as Lorna Goodison, chants and sermonic aspects would appear to be present. The way in which Goodison delivers her poems, the healing impact of hands, the calming force of a turn of the head which suggests all the time in the world to listen, are also important dimensions of the poems. Here we have what appear to be techniques of a religious tradition effectively employed in poetry. But even the phrase "effectively employed" suggests that although used in poetry, they are taken from elsewhere, namely religion. In fact, it may be that this form of poetry is influenced by traditions in some cases not followed anymore in a cognitive sense, traditions in which the secular was not evenly divided from the religious, where religious poetry was a part of the secular tradition; now, even when the words may not necessarily be speaking about institutionalized religion, they still call attention to a mode of existence which is as spiritual (and in traditions where we are attuned to institutionalized religion we may well read that, or hear that, as *religious*) as it is secular.

There is a tradition of religious poetry in the Caribbean which is demonstrated, for example, in the poetry of many reggae songs, with lyrics like Bob Marley's "Come we go chant down Babylon one more time." The tradition of religious poetry in the Caribbean might have its roots in a variety of cultural influences. In the particular case of Africa, Ruth Finnegan, for example, informs us: "There is a great variety of religious poetry in Africa. There are hymns, prayers, praises, possession songs, and oracular poetry, all with their varying conventions, content, and function in different cultures."[5]

In the Caribbean performance tradition, the song or chant may be part of the performance; speech, the use of the voice with its range of tones carefully utilized to express emotion, may be as important as the sight of the words on the page. But here we move to another dimension of experience, because as important as the voice may be to enjoyment of the poem, the poem may well be enjoyed and savored as printed artifact. There we have a different kind of savoring, the lingering over and repeating of a word, a phrase, a verse, which is not as possible when listening to a performance. And that reading, without access to the voice of the writer, also lends itself to the interpretation of the reader, to the reader's infusing the work with responses based on his/her own experiences.

Recently, when I listened to explanations by African writers about their own not so much return to as acknowledgment of the influence of oral traditions in their writing, I was particularly struck by a comment by Professor Kofi Anyidoho of the Institute of African Studies, University of Ghana, about oral poetry focusing on specific social situations. These, he said, were often about "communications among the living and between the living and the dead."[6] Listening to explanations of how he understood all of this in relation to his own writing, it seemed clear that this was partly about how the traditional is influencing the modern, and, in that case as well as in the particular Caribbean situation, how the modern is reshaping itself as it comes more and more not only to acknowledge but also to understand and value the traditional and recognize its potential for shaping new forms.

Now, for African writers, who are conscious of the presence of their traditions even if they were not taught them in school, the move back to exploration of the roots of their oral *poetic* traditions is perhaps easier than it is for the Caribbean writer. They know of a lot of the oral performance as "poetry"—that is, because of that perception of a traditional poetry, they did not have to wonder where a form such as the calypso fit into the concept of poetry. Knowing it, they could turn around and point to the monumental presence of old traditions. Speaking about his work, written in English and spoken in a voice resonant with influences from a tradition not British, Professor Kofi Awoonor noted:

> People who hear me can hear that this poetry is not what you are seeing on the page. I make it leap out of the page. I am helped by the fact that I am working out of a tradition. I am not the originator—absolute originator— or creator of all that I'll be telling you but I'm borrowing from thousands of years, from hundreds of ancestors, hundreds of kinsmen and women, and you can hear their voice through me also, because I'm only a spokesperson.[7]

In this explanation we have a perception of nationhood and of spirituality, of continuity. Now a Caribbean writer could have the same sense of say, speaking out of a tradition, conscious the while that hers/his is no longer the tradition of a discrete national group in Africa; that there are probably, for example, in the family spirit, the family ancestral stories, traditions coming, perhaps, from the Wolof and from the

Ashanti; that in addition to that there may be some Hindu traditions, that there are too the European traditions which Ghana's modern story also shares.

In my own work, I constantly feel that the exciting challenge is to find out which African traditions most closely influence my work, because there is this sense that where orality is concerned generally and with regard to my influences specifically there is a great deal to be learned. Some of the European influences I learned at school. For me, the largely unresearched element remains the African. But there is a great deal being learned. Increasingly, calypsos are being used as poetic texts in schools, a state of affairs which recognizes their existence as poetry, and which would not have been acceptable in my youth. Caribbean critic Gordon Rohlehr has done considerable work on this theme. In Ghana, Professor Kofi Anyidoho spoke to me of poetry as song, poetry as verbal insults from your mother; he spoke of a particular kind of poetry among the Akan, where the drummer as poet had the authority to call on the king to listen to advice. It was understood by all that his was a community voice and not an individual voice. Professor Agovi, also in Ghana, spoke of a tradition of poetry, observable in the kudum festival of the Nzima people.[8] In this tradition, information was collected during the year and then handed over to poet cantors, who put the poems in the form of songs which were taught to those who would perform in public. People went to hear these songs at the festival, to listen to the wisdom of the poet, to interpretations about events in the society. There certainly appears here to be a connection to the calypso, and in fact it was in order to show this connection, when I spoke to him of the social commentary impact of many calypsos, that Agovi detailed aspects of the Nzima festival.

Our Caribbean orality is a mixture of these and many other traditions, the background to which we have to study in order to value our oral poetic forms as simply poetry coming from traditions which are not British. To be able to trace and pinpoint these, for example, in the way that we may recognize a ballad form, or the tetrameter. So that when we confront a poem with a song stuck in the middle of it, we are not stumped, not simply marveling at the orality, as we generally do now, without being able to make informed comments about the form. In other words, in order to fully understand the poetic forms which our spirits acknowledge, we have to move outside of the British traditions which have generally been our classroom fare. Sometimes, too, forms which because of their unfamiliarity we have to think of as innovative seem to demand a different kind of production than the printed page. It seems to me that all of this is exciting: the Caribbean, a creation of many cultures, will have to develop the ways to best present our cultural product, and also do the research which would enable us to understand it.

Perhaps a great deal of the orality in Caribbean culture has been coming to the fore in discussions since the 1960s partly because of the politics of the period. It may also be that as more women write, and as more men not reticent about showing the influences of mothers, aunts, grandmothers put pen to paper, the influences of the socialization of mothers shape themselves on the page out of the forms and techniques of stories told.

Perhaps the coincidence of the two dimensions—identity politics, that is, involving both race and gender—gives a new dimension to the Caribbean voice. Which
is not, of course, to ignore other earlier voices like those of Samuel Selvon and Edward Kamau Brathwaite. Brathwaite's orality was, since the 1960s, both Caribbean
and African. He used forms of the praise chant and the dirge, Ghanaian forms which
Caribbean people have to research to identify closely as based on techniques of orality that go beyond, for example, the incantatory impact of various lines, or the use of
Creole language forms. As Kofi Anyidoho said, you learn poetry on one level, as song,
as verbal insults, as, in our case, calypso, and then you "go to school and there is a dis-
juncture and eventually you have to grow back from where you started from and that
realization begins to reshape your work."[9]

My own novel, *Angel* (1988), incorporates something of the idea of the bildungsroman, a form to which I was introduced in the education system, but also
tries to make use of orality, the dimensions of which I did not encounter in that education system, to reshape the bildungsroman. But at the point of writing *Angel*, I
was mainly employing narrative forms from the culture which shaped the story, recognizing that there had to be a divergence from certain accepted forms if the story
was to reflect all that I wanted it to reflect. Had to diverge, that is, from what I had
learned of the nineteenth-century British novel but at the same time employ techniques used there as well as in the African novel, the Caribbean novel, and in the
voices of Caribbean oral storytelling. So that what emerges is truly a mixture of formal and informal education, attempting to privilege the voices of oral narrative, yet
perhaps contradicting that privileging by the very method of presentation, and perhaps even more so by the voice of analysis today. So the admixture continues.

In *Angel* an attempt is made to have language encapsulate the power of speech
in proverbial headlines, as it might do before or after a conversation, which proceeds
with a certain amount of circularity, back to the point of the original proverb. Then
there are the ubiquitous religious signs and symbols, photographs, holy pictures,
signs of the cross, sayings, which are part of the traditional culture—Gordon
Rohlehr's "sermons of both the grassroots and establishment churches"—and more.

Religion, perhaps partly reflecting the role of the churches in post-emancipation
education, has been an important shaping dimension of Caribbean culture, of
Caribbean secular consciousness, of Caribbean orality. A person doesn't have to be
particularly religious to say, "God self see I ain't lie. You see that kerchief that fall out
of he pocket? That is the selfsame kerchief I talking about. Bon Dieu! Look how God
prove the thing for me!" Or, "I going see you tomorrow, if God spare life—" or sometimes just "if God spare," "life" being understood. It is an attitude to existence which
acknowledges the potential of a force greater than ourselves. That may well owe its
development both to a Caribbean experience post-Africa, post-Europe, post-Asia, or
it may be buried deep in the ancient cultures of Africa, Asia, and Europe.

And this circularity leads me temporarily again away from religion to consider
how, recently, when I had the opportunity to listen to Anansesem (people telling
Ananse stories) in a Ghanaian village, I was struck by several different things. Speak-

ing to Professor Agovi, I listened to his perception of how a Ghanaian audience would probably be more attuned than a Caribbean one to the particular significance of each animal in some of the animal stories, the character traits of each. Thinking of the Compere Tigre stories I had known in my childhood, I reflected that I was probably more concerned with the general moral of the story than with Compere Tigre himself. After all, what he brought to the Caribbean jungle was his experience more than his physical presence, so perhaps I knew him differently. Listening to the Anansesem, I was also struck by how different performances elicited responses based to a great extent on the skill of the storyteller, and also by the part that song played in these stories. Sometimes song acted as a transition; at times it was introduced to demonstrate a particular character's feeling; at times the omniscient narrative voice appeared to be itself moved to song. I was excited listening to all of this simply because it mirrored techniques that I found myself employing in both poetry and fiction, partly because of a socialization in which storytelling was used in this way. In Ghana, those whom I met were conscious that this was a tradition which they were revisiting because they recognized its value in the shaping of traditions considered modern. It is a rejection of neither modernization nor tradition; nor is it a grasping of one to the detriment of the other, but an assessment that the future belongs to both, and that whether acknowledged or not, the older one informs the newer to a greater or lesser extent. And whatever Caribbean political or other thought may direct, religion, for example, remains embedded in the language.

In my second novel, *The Colour of Forgetting*, I quite often use the formulation "And time come and pass . . ." in order to advance the story. It is a formulation which I grew up hearing. Someone would be telling a story then a shift would come with something like "Well . . ."—a pause, a movement sideways on the chair, a hand passed across the face, which all indicated some temporal shift in the story, and then the voice—"time come and pass, and after a space of about five years or so, now, all of a sudden, she start up with this thing again. So the mother say, eh, eh! Well something funny . . ." Here I ask you to forget about the rest of that story, which won't be forthcoming, and go back to "Well, time come and pass, and after a space of about five years or so, now . . ." This seems remarkably similar to Old Testament formulations like "And when the days of weeping for him were past, Joseph spoke to the household of Pharaoh, saying . . ." (Genesis 50:4, the Death of Israel). Or consider "In course of time the wife of Judah, Shua's daughter, died . . ." (Genesis 38:12). Perhaps those early narratives that shaped my imagination were a mixture of various influences, among them biblical forms and techniques from Ghanaian Anansesem, adapted and transformed in the Caribbean.

In Grenada, recently, I listened to explanations of his practice from a man who believes in the Orishas.[10] This is what I grew up knowing as Shango, and what he refers to now as African traditional religion. He repeated for me what he said was the *Our Father* in African. Dr. Maureen Warner-Lewis, who researches African religions in Trinidad and Tobago, explained to me that what the man was actually doing was translating the spirit of the prayer, the religious or spiritual idea which he felt informed it. Much of African religion in the Caribbean represented what Warner-Lewis referred to as an "inter-African syncretic process," the creolization that is the Caribbean, that is there in our poetry, in our fiction.[11] One wonders how many such translations we have in our movement, in our gestures, in the mimed perceptions of existence, translations of the spirit of cultures which shaped our ancestors and which now reshape themselves in the meeting with others.

What are some of our stories? And what are some of these meetings? When I write, my voice as represented on paper, as conceptualized, as it is when it fills the space wherever I speak, is informed by the stories of the women in my family. The men's stories are there, too, but perhaps because my father was always a quieter, more listening presence, those stories had to be teased out of his imagination, and many of them I am only just beginning to understand. The women around me were the performers, the storytellers, the ones who argued, praised, insulted, threw around their poetry in laughter and sometimes in song. My father too, sometimes, gave his story in song, often religious, although in practice he appeared less given to institutionalized religion than my mother. His strong singing voice—and, sometimes, my mother's stories—would give him the confidence to tell one of his own or to encourage questions about himself which would help to shape his story.

As I think of their stories, of the stories still to be shaped around their lives and ours, of the old techniques to be used and of the new techniques that our perceptions of orality and writing could create, I remember some of Agovi's words. "The folk tale," he said, "encompasses the moral universe of our people. It defines the relationship between man and his environment and nature, and the cosmos, even more so than all other forms of oral literature."[12] It also, he says, challenges one's creativity, trying to get you to cope with a distorted environment, an environment you don't understand. And listening to that, I thought of Simone Schwarz-Bart and *The Bridge of Beyond*. I thought, too, of Caribbean creolization and the many tales of different kinds finding every variety of voice in this mixed experience. The search for my own, I think largely African, antecedents in this story is only the beginning, only one small part of a wider project; the search for an understanding of the varied roots of the Caribbean experience of orality is the wider project.

Consider, as a final word, the following poem from an—if you will—African American Jamaican student who usually lives in Miami and who, in 1996, completed a creative writing program at the University of Maryland. In the poem, the writer, Shara McCallum, speaks, apparently, of Venezuelan origins which found their way to Jamaica. And then to Miami? Talk about creolization and orality and the Caribbean and beyond:

Descubriendo una Fotografia de Mi Madre

If I had left Venezuela with you, been on the boat moving
from your world of Papá, Mamá, abuelos, tíos y primos,

I could watch granny cooking en la cocina,
taste frijoles negros y arepas hot on my tongue.

If I had worn your clothes, dressed like this niña bonita
you left behind, I would be able to conjure up the collar

moored to your neck, feel its lace scratching my skin.
If I had the memory you lost to the Atlantic

(the blur of a white house in the background, las caobas
lining the front walk, the music box dancer still spinning

in your hand), if I could do more than imagine you
as this child, I would understand how tierra, pais

y casa became untranslatable words. From Spanish
to Patwa, something unnameable must have gone wrong.[13]

And can you imagine! This writer assures me that at the time of writing she hadn't even read Ana Lydia Vega. It's a testimony to where what is referred to as Caribbean orality can lead us in our writing. And we don't even have to understand what it is for it to invade our writing. All we have to do is relax, respond and enjoy when it calls because its essence appears to be the Caribbean experience of literature in all its forms. Relax and respond, too, when the critics tell us who it was that visited. Perhaps, as happened in my case, also get curious about finding out more about the nature and origins of this particular dynamic resident/visitor.

4. *Caribbean Writers and Caribbean Language: A Study of Jamaica Kincaid's* Annie John

MERLE HODGE

C aribbean writers operate in a language situation which is both problematic and full of possibility, and the relationship between the Caribbean writer and the language of the people who are the focus of Caribbean literature is an area of study yet to be fully explored by literary critics. In most Caribbean countries the main medium of spoken communication is a Creole language which is the product of contact between European and West African languages. However, in every case the official language, the language of education and the written word, is a European language. The pattern is, by and large, that the Creole spoken in a particular place shares the lexicon of the official language, while in its sound system and its grammatical structure it owes more to Africa than to Europe. The essential features of this underlying grammatical structure are the same across all the Caribbean Creoles.

The Anglophone Caribbean presents not a cut-and-dried bilingual situation of two languages confined to separate compartments, but a spread of variations which can more accurately be likened to a continuum, with Creole at one extreme and Standard English at the other, and a range of nuances between. In speaking situations West Indians produce different admixtures of Creole and the standard which may reflect differences in education, social class, or age, or may give other important information about speakers and the context of communication, such as self-concept, mood, attitude, relationship. Writers may therefore effectively use these nuances of language for the purposes of characterization and the development of theme and plot. The language situation is in itself a resource not available to creative writers in societies where language variety is less complex.

Using this resource, however, is not without its challenges. The language forged out of a people's experience may be the medium which most accurately describes that experience and most faithfully records the worldview of that people. Yet unlike the artist of the oral tradition (storyteller, calypsonian, dub poet) for whom the Creole is the natural medium, the writer of novels and short stories has entered a tradition shaped by the culture of the official language. The Creole is something of an intruder into that tradition.

Moreover, Caribbean writers are themselves the product of an education process which may have alienated them from their first language so that they are not as proficient in it as in the standard language. Or, education may have produced at worst contempt, at best a certain discomfort with the Creole which does not allow one to take it seriously or to see it as having artistic potential. Some Caribbean writers in exile are simply not able to accurately reproduce a Creole language, and in our literary history there can be found some truly disastrous attempts at creating Creole-speaking characters from imperfect memory. (Such disasters are not, however, the exclusive preserve of writers in physical exile.)

Then there is the problem of audience. Who are the targeted readership of the Caribbean writer? And who are the real readership? We cling fondly to the ideological position that our primary audience is our own people. But for the moment it is only a small fraction of "our own people" who read our works. And our people are only a small fraction of the Anglophone world, so that when the revolution comes and Caribbean people turn to consuming Caribbean literature, they will probably still constitute an audience too small to sustain the writer. Our audience, therefore, is the larger English-speaking world, which is to say that we write largely, overwhelmingly, for foreigners. This imposes certain kinds of constraints on the use of our native language, which in turn compromises our relationship with our wished-for primary audience.

Caribbean writers of prose fiction have approached the question of language in a number of different ways, and some writers use more than one approach. The most traditional and most enduring language strategy is to render the speech of Caribbean people realistically in dialogue but to use the standard for the narrative voice. Beginning with the work of Samuel Selvon, there is also a whole tradition of Caribbean fiction in which Creole is used as the medium of both dialogue and narration. There are also Caribbean writers who do not attempt realism but who might simply translate the dialogue of Creole speakers into the standard language, or use an avoidance strategy such as affecting some form of stylization in order to indicate that the language being spoken is different from the standard.

There can be no imposed orthodoxy of language use for the Caribbean writer. The language situation offers writers not only a rich range of expression, but also a variety of options regarding how one responds to this language situation. One of these options is not to engage with the language situation at all. This is the option exercised by Jamaica Kincaid, who has lived outside of the Caribbean and out of earshot of Caribbean language for all of her adult life, having left Antigua at the age of seventeen.

Kincaid's writings contain occasional references to language and language issues which allow us some insight into the level of her awareness of the Caribbean language situation as well as her attitude to it. In a number of places Kincaid refers to the French-lexicon Creole which her mother (who is from Dominica) spoke to her.[1] This Creole remains part of Kincaid's language repertoire, although today she might have only passive competence in it. Kincaid's essay on Antiguan society, *A Small Place*, contains a few reflections on language, most of which are asides, physically enclosed in parentheses, but quite passionate in their tone. In two places she seems to bring into focus the highly developed Caribbean art of open-air verbal confrontation:

Since we were ruled by the English, we also had their laws. There was a law against using abusive language. Can you imagine such a law among people for whom making a spectacle of yourself through speech is everything? When West Indians went to England, the police there had to get a glossary of bad West Indian words so they could understand whether they were hearing abusive language or not.[2]

and

Here is this: On a Saturday, at market, two people who, as far as they know, have never met before, collide by accident; this accidental collision leads to an enormous quarrel—a drama, really—in which the two people stand at opposite ends of a street and shout insults at each other at the top of their lungs. (56)

Elsewhere in the essay she speaks of colonialism as having robbed "millions of people" of culture and tradition, and her comment does not seem to indicate a recognition that Caribbean people have a language of their own:

and worst and most painful of all, no tongue. (For isn't it odd that the only language I have in which to speak of this crime is the language of the criminal who committed the crime? . . .) (31)

In another aside she comments on the English language competence of young Antiguans, again based on the premise that Standard English is their first and only language:

In Antigua today, most young people seem almost illiterate. On the airwaves, where they work as news personalities, they speak English as if it were their sixth language. . . . What surprised me most about them was . . . how unable they were to answer in a straight-forward way, and in their own native tongue of English. (43–44)

Toward the end of *Annie John*, the adolescent describes her overwhelming feelings of unhappiness and a desire to turn her back on the environment of her growing up: ". . . the world into which I was born had become an unbearable burden" (128).

There is enough in published interviews given by Jamaica Kincaid to establish the closely autobiographical nature of her writing and in particular the intensity of these feelings of alienation from her milieu. In *Annie John* she seems to indicate that part of her act of withdrawal was a deliberately cultivated change in her language: ". . . I acquired a strange accent—at least, no one had ever heard anyone talk that way before—and some other tricks" (129).

In *Lucy*, which takes up where *Annie John* leaves off, the language of the newly arrived West Indian girl working *au pair* in a New York household draws the mistrust of the housemaid who deduces from her speech mannerisms a wider renunciation: "One day the maid who said she did not like me because of the way I talked told me that she was sure I could not dance. She said that I spoke like a nun . . ." (11). The girl has cast off the pronunciation and intonation patterns ("accent") of Antiguan speech and concocted a special dialect that began to set her apart from her speech community even before she physically took her leave of this community.

Yet in the essay *A Small Place* Kincaid's last word on language in her native land is an expression of fondness. In a lyrical passage near the end she reflects on the beauty of Antigua (although her ultimate point is the impression of unrealness), and she sees as part of this beauty the language of Antiguans:

> . . . and the way people there speak English (they break it up) and the way they might be angry with each other and the sound they make when they laugh, all of this is so beautiful, all of this is not real like any other real thing that there is . . . (79)

Perhaps the major achievement of Jamaica Kincaid is the beauty of the language that she herself has created, the diamond-like clarity and precision of her English prose. In appropriating the work of this outstanding writer into Caribbean literary history, we might seek to trace her verbal ability to the stimulating language environment of her childhood, when she functioned in three languages: the French-lexicon Creole of Dominica from her mother, the English-lexicon Creole of Antigua spoken all around her, and the Standard English acquired through formal education and hours of immersion in books. It is quite conceivable that close analysis of Kincaid's language might yield deep affinities and influences attributable to her Creole foundation, but on the surface there is very little that seems to connect her written English to a Caribbean vernacular.

Kincaid's language in *Annie John*, which is set in Antigua, is only minimally sprinkled with Creolisms. In the narration there are certain adverbial set phrases not found in Standard English. For example, "it was her duty to accompany her father up to ground on Saturdays" (68). Or, "the unhappiness of wanting to go to cinema on a Sunday" (85). Standard English would require that the singular countable nouns *ground* and *cinema* be preceded by an article or some other determiner. (Creole has extended the English "irregular" pattern of *to bed, to school, to church* to a larger group of countable nouns. In this pattern the noun refers to a concept, an abstraction rather than a single item, and therefore cannot in this context strictly be categorized as "countable.") The narrator calls bananas by the name they carry over a large part of the Caribbean, "figs" (68, 101), and once uses "dunce" as an adjective, which is Creole usage: "Ruth sat in the last row, the row reserved for all the dunce girls" (73). The protagonist in one place addresses her mother as "Mamie" (101), and she and her school friends chant in Creole as they dance: "Tee la la la, come go. Tee la la la, come go" (81).

For dialogue, Kincaid does not attempt to reconstruct Creole speech. All discourse is translated into Standard English, with a very few notable exceptions. The rare occurrences of Creole speech are poignant in their isolation and unexpectedness. These flashes of dialogue in Creole seem to come as part and parcel of certain intimate and unprocessed memories, preserved in such detail that the actual language used is indelibly recorded, resisting translation. During a prolonged illness, the young girl wakes up one night in her father's lap and sees her mother changing the bedsheets. Her father explains: "You wet, Little Miss, you wet" (112). What makes the incident memorable to the child is her experience of sexual arousal associated with this physical contact with her father, although the child is unable to account for her own train of thought at the time: "I do not know why that lodged in my mind, but it did" (113).

Recall of another, related incident also pulls up an intact recording of Creole speech. The speaker is one of a pair of fishermen who seem to have been a source of fascination for the young girl and who turn up again in *Lucy*. One of them particularly engages the girl's attention. In both novels, but more explicitly in *Lucy*, the protagonist remembers this man in details and images suggestive of her awakening sexuality. During the same period of illness this man delivers fish to the home and looks in on her:

> As I was thinking of how much he reminded me of my father, the words "You are just like Mr. John" came out of my mouth.
> He laughed and said, "Now, mind, I don't tell him you say that." (121)

Another piece of Creole emerges during the same recollection of Mr. Earl. It has been preserved as part of a family legend about her great-great-grandfather who was also a fisherman, and whose dying words were: "Dem damn fish" (122). This last utterance is indisputably intended to be Creole because the writer has used the phonetic spelling for "dem." The other two leave room for ambiguity in their interpretation. "You wet, Little Miss, you wet" could be read as English, with "you" as the subject of the sentence and "wet" a verb in the past simple tense. Heard as Creole, however, "wet" is here an adjective, or more precisely a Creole adjectival verb, indicating not an action but a state. "You wet" is formed on the Creole sentence pattern which involves a subject followed by an adjective functioning as the predicate.

The other Creole sentence, "Now, mind, I don't tell him you say that" (121) is punctuated in a curious way. The word "mind" is followed by a comma which makes no sense, and suggests an editorial "correction" by someone reading the sentence as English. The comma separates "mind" from the rest of the sentence, making this word a mere interjection attached to a declarative sentence in the present habitual tense/aspect: "I don't tell him you say that." In the Creole interpretation the sentence is not declarative—it does not give information. "Mind" is a verb in the imperative mood, it gives, or pretends to give, a warning. Then, the meaning of the unmarked verb "say" is perfective, not habitual. The man is playfully threatening to tell her father what she has said, not informing her that he habitually does not tell him something that she habitually says. "Mind" is the main verb, not a spliced-in, nonessential element. The comma, which assumes that the sentence is English, enforces a quite different intonation pattern and a different meaning from the Creole structure. The ambiguous identity of these two sentences has its advantages. They can be recognized as Creole by those who know Creole, and they can equally well pass for English on the page, escaping the notice of the English-speaking reader. That is to say, to the majority of readers they are unobtrusive.

There is overall very little direct speech in *Annie John*, and only one exchange between speakers prolonged enough to be called a conversation (65–66). Direct speech is largely restricted to utterances of one sentence, one phrase or even one word, punctuating at wide intervals the flow of the narrative. Instead, the writer favors reported speech:

> When I got home, my mother asked me for the fish I was to have picked up from Mr. Earl, one of our fishermen, on the way home from school. But in my excitement I had completely forgotten. Trying to think quickly, I said that when I got to the market Mr. Earl told me that they hadn't gone to sea that day because the sea was too rough. "Oh?" said my mother. (12)

One might be tempted to see in the low incidence of direct speech an avoidance strategy, a way around the language of Kincaid's prototypes who would have been mostly Creole speakers, except for the fact that *Lucy*, set in an English-speaking environment, shows the same scarcity of dialogue.

This is simply a feature of Kincaid's narrative style in which the main speaking voice is the voice of the protagonist/narrator, and the main dialogue is with her own, searching self. Kincaid's fictional works are novels of introspection, only one central character is drawn in depth. The other characters are experienced by the narrator, and therefore by the reader, only insofar as their behavior has an impact upon her development. This applies, I think, even to the portrayal of the mother with whom the child is so intensely involved. Our perception of the mother remains quite limited. We gain only a partial view of her. The subject is the girl's journey, her inner life, and there is no attempt at complete and detailed characterization in the case of the other actors in her life story. Not much attention is therefore paid to their individual speaking styles. The predominance of reported speech signifies that the content of her characters' speaking is more important than anything their speech might reveal about them individually. There is no obvious differentiation of characters' language.

The fact is that neither the personal speech patterns of individual characters nor the distinguishing features of Antiguan speech are relevant to the writer's purpose. Certainly the decision (if conscious decision there was) not to attempt realism in creating dialogue for her Creole-speaking characters is a judicious one. An artist cannot successfully use a medium that s/he does not completely control. It is very likely that Kincaid's competence in her native language has succumbed to amnesia induced not only by the passage of time, but possibly also by the deliberate distancing of her adolescent years.

Kincaid's medium is English, a register of English far removed from the Creole end of the continuum. Out of this medium she has produced a distillation so rarefied that to juxtapose with it any vernacular at all would be unwise. Vernaculars are by definition spontaneous, unself-conscious, uncut. The speech of Kincaid's characters even shies away from the more informal, conversational varieties of Standard English, and in *Annie John* all dialogue displays to some extent the fine-tuned precision and educatedness of the narrator's language. There are, for example, sentences such as this one spoken by mother to child: "Until this moment, in my whole life I knew without a doubt that, without any exception, I loved you best" (103).

The novels of Jamaica Kincaid actually sit on a cusp between fiction and essay. They are a genre unto themselves in which both narrator and fictional characters may be said to speak in the reflective style of the essayist. Dialogue in Creole would have set up such a contrast of codes as to create a focus which is not part of the writer's theme. Code-shifting invites attention to issues such as class and cultural difference, issues which are not central to the novel. Creole speech in the context of Kincaid's fiction would simply seem idiosyncratic, distracting, except for Creole speech that is not too obviously another language, such as the snatches of dialogue discussed earlier (*Annie John*, 112, 121).

There is sufficient reference, in *Annie John*, to details of the physical environment and the indigenous culture to ground the novel in a specific place. This is very important, for completely disembodied fiction does not work. But the specificity of Antiguan experience is not in itself a major preoccupation of the writer. *Annie John* is not primarily about collective experience. It is about individual experience, which in the telling expands into universal experience, often approaching the mythological in its dimensions.

Kincaid's is a different kind of writing from that which concerns itself with exploring and affirming the experience of a specific collectivity, a task which has informed a large part of Caribbean writing to date. Yet both kinds of writing rejoin the universal, if the writer achieves truth. Both kinds of writing are valid, and necessary.

5. *Francophone Caribbean Women Writers and the Diasporic Quest for Identity: Marie Chauvet's* Amour *and Maryse Condé's* Hérémakhonon

RÉGINE ALTAGRÂCE LATORTUE

Maryse Condé's *Hérémakhonon*[1] is located as commentary, revision, and extension in a complex web of the problematics of the diasporic novel. Its contribution to the diasporic tradition is best understood in a series of genealogical strands that trace from Marie Chauvet's *Amour*,[2] Nella Larsen's *Quicksand*,[3] Richard Wright's *Native Son*,[4] and Ralph Ellison's *Invisible Man*.[5] These genealogical strands locate Condé's *Hérémakhonon* as a complex statement about race, gender, nationality, and identity in the diasporic subject.

Certainly one of the clearest strands is Marie Chauvet's *Amour*. As Vèvè Clark points out in her article "Developing Diaspora Literacy and Marasa Consciousness": "To borrow Henry Louis Gates's term, Chauvet is Signifyin(g) on Claire Clamont, the central figure in *Amour*, and on Chauvet's detached narrative technique."[6]

With *Hérémakhonon*, Maryse Condé brilliantly posits the diasporic female heroine of the contemporary era. In many ways, Chauvet's last novel before she died as an exile in New York in 1973 following the publication of the politically charged *Amour, Colère et Folie* in 1968, and Condé's first novel, published eight years later in 1976, illuminate each other in the centralizing of the female protagonist's story and the woman's voice and perspective. Chauvet restricts her story to the national and the local, whereas Condé casts hers in an international and modernist context. Chauvet's model might seem rather narrowly defined, too restrictive for the modern diasporic woman, while Condé casts the political net of her intrigue more broadly, encompassing the personal, sexual, and political.

Initially, the heroines of *Amour* and *Hérémakhonon* appear to share a similar trajectory. Claire, Chauvet's protagonist, and Veronica, Condé's central character, have grown up in Francophone Caribbean islands, Haiti and Guadeloupe respectively, and have both been traumatized and alienated by their family, the patriarchal nature of their society, and the class and color conflicts of the Francophone Antilles. Symbolic of that alienation, both have been made to suffer in unflattering comparisons with their two sisters who embody the values of family, patriarchy, and nation. Says Claire bitterly, speaking of her sisters: "*Car ces deux mulatresses blanches sont mes soeurs. Je suis la surprise que le sang-mêlé a réservée à nos parents; surprise désagréable sans nul douse, car ils m'ont fait assez souffrir"* [For these two white-mulattas are my sisters. I am the surprise that mixed blood saved for our parents; a disagreeable surprise undoubtedly, for they caused me a lot of misery] (12). And Veronica explains: "I still have a complex from my awkward days of childhood . . . Years of being downgraded in comparison with my two sisters" (24). Both heroines tell their story in the first person narrative, and both emerge from their childhood neurotically scarred.

Chauvet's novel is set in a small village in Haiti, where Claire, the thirty-nine-year-old spinster sister, manages the household of her younger sister's French husband. Traumatized by a childhood which made the dark color of her skin a negative attribute, the ironically named Claire has remained insecure and has never believed she could be loved. Although quite aware and conscious of the injustices of class, color, and gender in her society, Claire remains politically passive for most of the novel, cherishing her privileged status as a member of the provincial aristocracy. As in most of Chauvet's novels, Claire undergoes a process of self-examination followed by self-actualization. Sexually frustrated and tormented by an unwanted virginity, Claire neurotically tries, through a series of unsuccessful attempts, to manipulate her sisters and brother-in-law into situations she imagines would fulfill her desperate need to now live vicariously through others. She even briefly considers suicide. But she is saved from that fate by a climactic act of criminality: she strikes down Calédu, the appropriately named representative of the terrorist regime, who has been sadistically torturing women and generally oppressing members of all classes. For Chauvet, and Haitian women writers in general, as Condé has remarked in *La Parole des femmes*, women's personal and political oppression coexist.[7] Through the (forcedly) political victory gained in killing Calédu, Claire finally achieves a state of self-respect and self-appreciation, at the same time as she eliminates the common oppressor of the community. As I have argued elsewhere: "By turning the dagger against Calédu, [Claire] turns it against its proper target, against the forces which have denied her and women like her, freedom, erotic dignity, and full womanhood."[8]

Unlike Chauvet's, Condé's novel embraces the four corners of the African Diaspora, therefore breaking the neat homology between family, patriarchy, and nation that defines Claire's world in *Amour*. Condé's work is in fact set in Africa, where Veronica reflects upon her past life as she strives to understand her present and tries to carve out a future for herself. Unlike the sexually repressed Claire, Veronica rebelled against the sexual status quo of her society, first taking an inappropriate lover (inappropriate according to the dictates of her black bourgeois parents, for her lover is a mulatto of the haute bourgeoisie), which led to her precipitated departure for Paris and higher education, where she will take a second inappropriate lover, a white French man. The story begins and ends at the airport. Having secured a job as a French *coopérante* (technical assistant), Veronica travels to Africa to "find herself" and is welcomed to the land by Saliou, the supervisor of the high school where she will be an instructor in philosophy. Veronica soon ends up in the arms of Saliou's brother-in-law, Ibrahima Sory, her mythical "nigger with ancestors," Minister of the

Interior of the corrupt authoritarian regime of a newly independent African nation. Ibrahima invites her to stay at Hérémakhonon (which means "Welcome House" or literally "Happiness Awaits" in Mande), a superb mansion in the select residential quarter of town, clearly an ironic omen for Veronica in search of happiness and self-fulfillment. In spite of her sympathy for Saliou and a number of her students, activists who are prepared to fight and die for a more equitable society, Veronica, absorbed in her own alienation, remains totally indifferent to the political climate of this African country in the throes of neocolonialism. She never bothers to learn any of the five local languages spoken there, and prefers to hang out with other French expatriates. It is only when Saliou, and a student named Birame III, who had led a demonstration against the government, are killed that she begins to be aware of the political situation, and, horrified at her own hypocrisy in her stance as politically neutral, flees back to Paris, ostensibly wiser.

For Veronica remains a stranger even in "the land of her ancestors." Carrying around a baggage of a mythical Africa à la Harlem Renaissance or Négritude, she willfully ignores the tragic realities of an oppressive political system that is growing increasingly authoritarian. As Françoise Lyonnet points out in *Autobiographical Voices*, even with her lover Ibrahima Sory, Veronica cannot communicate.[9] She is quite aware that theirs is an affair of the flesh, bragging that "There's a secret unhealthy voluptuousness in being treated like an object" (89) and telling herself "*En somme ce qu'il me faut pour voir la vie presque en rose, c'est a good fuck* [What I need to see life through rose colored glasses is a good fuck]" (222/125). Nevertheless, when she attempts to explain to Ibrahima why she came to Africa, and he responds: "*En somme, vous avez un problème d'identité?*" [In other words, you have an identity problem?] (100/52), Veronica realizes fully the extent of the cultural gap that cannot possibly be bridged as long as she maintains the posture of a jaded apolitical foreigner—the plight of the "neurotics from the Diaspora" (52), to use Condé's own phrase.

Like Claire throughout most of *Amour*, Veronica is acutely conscious of her status as an upper-middle-class, educated Black woman of the Diaspora, and she adopts an attitude of contempt and condescension toward the African militants fighting for change, "the attitude of the super-assimilated" as Léon Gontran Damas calls it in his poem "So Souvent." The only episode which seems to momentarily shake her serene impassibility is her recollection of seeing (and distancing herself from) an African street sweeper in Paris. The episode echoes Aimé Césaire's scene of recognition and self-confrontation with "*le vieux Nègre*" (the old Negro) in the metro in Paris in *Return to My Native Land*.

The novel *Quicksand*, published by the Harlem Renaissance writer Nella Larsen in 1928, also suggests itself in this equation. Although Larsen's heroine, Helga Crane, does not reach the African corner of the Diaspora, she travels from her small hometown in the South of the United States to Harlem at the height of the Renaissance and then to Copenhagen, where she briefly enjoys notoriety as the exotic phenomenon of the season. Of mixed heritage by way of an African American mother and a white European father, Helga Crane goes in quest of herself but fails to find her niche in any of these locales. Uncomfortable with her blackness and unsatisfied with what the white world offers her, she returns to the States, dejected, to bury herself in an unfulfilling and frustrating life as the wife of a small-town preacher, physically weakened by rapid and successive pregnancies. Like the tragic mulatta of the literature of the era, Helga embraces oblivion at the end of the novel. Larsen was the first to capture this image of the cultured young black woman, trapped between two worlds and alienated from both, unable to find her own space. Maryse Condé incorporates and reuses the themes of race, nationality, and gender that inform this precursor text. Her heroine is entrapped by three or even four worlds within the Diaspora.

Chauvet's and Condé's role within a diasporic literary tradition is akin to the relationship between Richard Wright and Ralph Ellison around the middle of the century. Ellison criticized Wright's portrayal of Bigger Thomas in *Native Son* as too localized and narrow in its construction of black manhood whereas the protagonist of Ellison's own *Invisible Man* exhibited a broader and finally more ambivalent consciousness which opened up possibilities of identity outside of the already existing social order. Further, the theme of Claire finding purpose and a true sense of self through criminality echoes Bigger Thomas's experience in Wright's naturalist novel. It is Bigger Thomas's fully conscious acceptance of himself as the criminal that society perceives him to be which horrifies and finally alienates his lawyer Max, the last human contact still accessible to Bigger. Bigger Thomas understands that criminality somehow inspired the full exercise of his potential as a human being, and when he utters: "What I killed for, I am!" at the end of the novel, Max is forced to recognize the existentialist stranger Bigger has become. Likewise, after the murder of Calédu, Claire is rid of her neurotic obsessions and has finally reached a state of self-acceptance and validation. As one literary critic noted, Wright's intention was to show that, denied normal social outlets, the individual turns naturally to antisocial behavior. That interpretation applies to both Bigger Thomas, denied on account of his race, and Claire Clamont, denied on account of her gender.

As concerns Ellison and Condé, the Invisible Man, after his surrealistic journey from "visibility to invisibility," confides to the reader at the end of the novel that, empowered by the full consciousness of his invisibility, he is coming out of his hole (presumably to act), but the reader remains perhaps unconvinced. Likewise, Veronica, after her sentimental-education-type journey of three months in Africa, speaks of "Spring in Paris" as she awaits her plane at the end of the novel—an allusion to rebirth and growth that the reader perhaps feels is unlikely. It is doubtful that this "neurotic from the diaspora" will "find" herself and ever return to Guadeloupe or Africa. Indeed, perhaps she will not act on her newfound awareness. As in Ellison's *Invisible Man*, the change in characterization that we observe is primarily for the reader's sake rather than the protagonist's sake. Even Ellison's hero is confined within a broadly enriched national scenario. In *Hérémakhonon*, Condé creates a heroine with diasporic possibilities and augments Ellison's quest for identity. The uncertainty of trajectory of the hero of *Invisible Man* or the heroine of *Hérémakhonon* leaves an open space for readers to question themselves about the nature and creation of the diasporic protagonist. Condé, like Ellison, sharply increases the options of being but does not resolve the complexities that those options provide.

More importantly, Condé confronts the myth of the return to "Mother Africa" and the alien and exile theme of Negrismo, the Harlem Renaissance, and Négritude, which had an impact on the Pan-African literature of the sixties as well. African descendants from the Caribbean and North America "returned" to Africa only to discover that in many African languages, the words "white" and "foreigner" were one and the same. Many never quite recovered from the fact that, far from being regarded as "lost, prodigal" brothers and sisters, they were considered at best as a type of very distant cousin. However, like Veronica and Claire, they often chose to remain oblivious of the tragic reality of power and politics in African nations, reluctant to accept the full range of human failings in these African contemporaries.

Haitian woman critic Yanick Lahens notes in a recent interview on Haitian women writers in *Callaloo* that "the first truly individual and personal words in fiction were articulated by women writers." During Indigenism and Négritude, she says, "the male writers wrote protest literature [and] situated themselves within the problematics of social realism. . . . It is the women writers who sought to pave the way for a new form of literary expression."[10] The growing body of literature by women writers is redefining the canon of Caribbean literature, challenging accepted notions of the self, gender, race, and history. Maryse Condé presents us with a superb, complex portrayal of the contemporary diasporic woman. As we celebrate her work here at this conference, even though, sadly, due to illness, she was not able to join us, I think it is particularly *à propos* to conclude with a quotation from VèVè Clark's "Developing Diaspora Literacy: Allusion in Maryse Condé's *Hérémakhonon*":

If one reconsiders Alaine Locke's call in 1925 for communication with Africa, one recalls how he predicted the seminal role the "new Negro" would play in fusing the Diaspora. Through Veronica, Maryse Condé has accomplished that feat in literature some fifty years after Locke's pronouncement. None of the male writers of the Indigenist, Harlem Renaissance or Négritude movements achieved such an integration, for Africa remained mythical and remote for most of them. The "new Negro," it would seem, is an Antillean woman.[11]

6. *Unheard Voice: Suzanne Césaire and the Construct of a Caribbean Identity*

MARYSE CONDÉ

There is a geographical expression—"the Caribbean"—associated with a certain space. There are many people who describe themselves as Caribbean persons and many foreigners who attest that they went to a place called the Caribbean. However, the truth is that the Caribbean, even as a geographical expression, is difficult to define. Some analysts include Florida, the Yucatan, and portions of Colombia and Venezuela in the Caribbean. Others exclude the mainland and concentrate on the islands. Even if you are in favor of the second interpretation, there is no racial unity in any definition of the Caribbean, since throughout the islands there are whites, Blacks, yellows, and every shade in between.

Gordon Lewis observes that the only period when a single racial type has occupied the Caribbean was in pre-Columbian times.[1] Following European contact and ever since, the Caribbean has been home to the entire range of biological types. There is the same diversity as far as languages and religions are concerned. People speak in a multitude of tongues and worship a multitude of gods. For example, some people are Christians and Hindus while others are Rastifarians, Santeros, and believers of Vodun. Perhaps no other region of the world is so diverse and varied. The construction of a Caribbean identity, therefore, is caught up in many contradictions. The Caribbean, although sharing common historical founding experiences, erupted into a collection of social orders with distinctive features. One may then ask a formidable array of questions.

When does Caribbean history start? Does it begin with the Middle Passage and the plantation system, eradicating everything that existed before, or does it begin before Columbus? The indigenous peoples, i.e., the Amerindians, were swiftly marginalized and subsequently wiped out. Does this mean that their cultures, even as memory, did not serve as a significant factor in the creation of the ensuing societies? Had the Caribbean islands been "discovered" by Europe and could they be rightly regarded as a New World? Owing to the flux of migration and displacement, are they not an extension of the preexisting worlds—Europe, Africa, and India? Is it legitimate to speak of the African Diaspora as far as the people of African descent of the Caribbean are concerned? Some years ago at a conference in Milan, Italy, Anthony Phelps, a Haitian writer, created an uproar when he declared: "I am a black man from the Americas. I am not an African American; I am not an Afro-American; I am not a black man with a prefix; I am an American."

Nowadays the Créolité movement from Martinique makes almost identical claims. The well-known sociologist Franklin Knight sums up these differences:

> The contemporary Caribbean, less a melting pot than a mélange, remains a strangely fascinating fusion of race, ethnicity, class, and culture, and the inescapable legacies of slavery and the plantation system have enormously complicated the social stratification of the region.[2]

Derek Walcott, the Nobel laureate poet, echoed this view metaphorically in his "Fragments of an Epic Memory" speech at Stockholm:

> That is the basis of the Antillean experience, this shipwreck of fragments, these echoes, this shard of a huge tribal vocabulary, these partially remembered customs. They survived the Middle Passage and the *Fatel Razack*, the ship that carried the first indentured Indians from the port of Madras to the canefields, that carried the chained Cromwellian convict and the Sephardic Jew, the Chinese grocer and the Lebanese merchant selling clothes samples on his bicycle.[3]

One of the first intellectuals who tried to piece together the broken fragments of the Antillean identity and restore the shattered Caribbean history is certainly Suzanne Césaire, the wife of the Martinican poet Aimé Césaire. Suzanne Césaire is the first intellectual who invented what we now call literary cannibalism (i.e., a rewriting and magical appropriation of the literature of the *other*). The list of Caribbean writers who rewrote the canonical texts of the European tradition is long. I shall cite only Jean Rhys from Dominica, who rewrote *Jane Eyre;* Derek Walcott, who rewrote *The Odyssey;* Vincent Placoly from Martinique, who rewrote *A Planter's Diary;* and I, who rewrote *Wuthering Heights* in my last novel, *Les Migrations du Coeur.*

Suzanne Césaire is at the same time a myth and an enigma. We know very little about her. Her shining face adorns the opening page of the reprint collection of the magazine *Tropiques* that she founded with her husband and a faithful group of followers. André Breton, the Surrealist poet, praised her beauty, and in the preface to *Return to My Native Land* by Aimé Césaire he writes: "*Suzanne Césaire, belle comme la flamme du punch.*"[4] [Suzanne Césaire, as lovely as the fire of a rum punch.] Michel Leiris, the French anthropologist who spent several years in Martinique, complained of her aggressiveness in putting forward Communist-oriented ideas and did not believe that it went well with her duties as the mother of five children. More recently, in his critical work *Aimé Césaire: un homme à la recherche d'une patrie*, Zairean George N'Gal dismissed her with the stroke of a pen and declared that all her ideas were taken from her illustrious husband.[5]

However, in the magazine *Tropiques,* which lasted from 1941 to 1945, we find a dozen articles that she wrote on subjects as varied as the German historian Leo

Frobenius, the French philosopher Alain, Black American poetry, André Breton, and Martinican folklore. Forgotten for many years by the critics, Suzanne Césaire emerges now as a Caribbean icon. In the preface to the translation of his novel *L'Isolé Soleil* (*Lone Sun*), the Guadeloupian writer Daniel Maximin confides:

> *Lone Sun* had to do with a major mythical figure of mine as well, with Suzanne Césaire. I discovered Suzanne Césaire in *Tropiques*, particularly in the last essay of the last issue that I had learned by heart. *Lone Sun* is the dialogue I have wanted to have with her, with all the women of four races and dozens of blood lines, to borrow Suzanne's unusual phrase.[6]

As Maximin points out, Suzanne Césaire has the last word as the magazine ends with one of her articles, "*Le grand camouflage*" ("The Great Smokescreen"). After that, she became forever silent. This last article signals a striking departure from the previous ones she wrote. For the first and last time, Suzanne Césaire ceases to be the contrived essayist, the convinced exponent of Négritude and Surrealism, to become the lyrical writer, conscious of the magical beauty of the Caribbean landscape, although in previous issues of *Tropiques* she had dismissed as exotic all references to Nature.

Here I trace the evolution of her thought during those five crucial years when the umbilical cord linking Martinique to France was severed by the war and the American blockade. For the Second World War is regarded in Guadeloupe and Martinique as a golden age when a measure of cultural independence was achieved. Hundreds of historians have written about this "blesse'" time, and it is the favorite setting of all of Raphael Confiant's novels. Suzanne Césaire, in her first writing, seemed to be extremely infatuated with the poetry of André Breton and could find no fault with him. "Breton," she writes in one of the first issues of *Tropiques*,

> *habite un merveilleux pays ou à ses dèsirs se plient les nuages et les étoiles, les vents et les marées, les arbres et les bêtes, les hommes et l'univers.* [Breton inhabits a marvelous country where the clouds and the stars, the winds and the tides, the trees and the animals, mankind and the universe submit to his desires.][7]

And she concludes: "*André Breton, le plus riche et le plus pur.*" [André Breton, the richest and purest of them all.][8] Here I cannot resist the pleasure of telling once more the story of how Breton and the Césaires met. In April 1941 Breton was fleeing occupied France and in the company of the well-known anthropologist Claude Lévi-Strauss was seeking refuge in the United States of America. Their ship was forced to dock in Fort-de-France, Martinique. Breton, as he stated afterwards, was looking for a ribbon for his daughter, when in the window of a small shop he saw some copies of the magazine *Tropiques*. He opened them and was struck by the voice of Aimé Césaire. "I could not believe my eyes," he said. "For what was said there was not only what had to be said but was expressed in the most articulate and forceful way." He asked to be introduced to him and revealed to an awe-stricken Césaire that his poetry was Surrealist. Years later, when questioned by the critic Jacqueline Leiner, Césaire confessed:

> *Quand Breton a lu les troits premiers numéros de* Tropiques *il a cru que j'é-*
> *tais Surréaliste. Ce n'était pas entièrement vrai. Ce n'était pas entièrement*
> *faux.* [When Breton read the first three issues of *Tropiques* he thought I was
> a Surrealist. This was not entirely true. Yet it was not entirely false.][9]

For Suzanne Césaire the adhesion to Surrealism was complete. Surrealism enabled her to criticize previous poets whom she despised as exotic: John Antoine Nau, Leconte de Lisle, José Maria de Héredia. After ridiculing them she states categorically: "*La vraie poésie est ailleurs.*"[10] [True poetry is elsewhere.] It is with the help of the Surrealist ideas that she constructs a poetical art. Surrealism advocated the free expression of the inner self and the destruction of the values imposed by education. Surrealism wanted to put an end to the domination of reason and logic. At the end of what can be regarded as a true *art poétique* she concludes: "*La poésie martiniquaise sera cannibale ou ne sera pas.*" [Martinican poetry shall be cannibal or nothing at all.][11] As we said before, in so doing she was the first Caribbean writer to acknowledge and rehabilitate the appellation "cannibal," once a term of opprobrium, and transform it into a symbol of a new, noncolonized self. The claim to a cannibal identity forms a part of any poetical self-birth or parthogenesis. However, in his interesting article published in *L'Héritage de Caliban* in 1992, "Cannibalisme tenace" ("Anthropophagic Fictions in Caribbean Writing"), the critic Eugenio Matibag makes no mention of Suzanne Césaire and quotes abundantly, among others, Aimé Césaire, Edouard Glissant, Alejo Carpentier, Roberto Fernandez Retamar, and George Lamming.

We can now raise these questions: Why up to very recently has Suzanne Césaire been so often ignored? Is it the fate of the women writers in the Caribbean? Is she being punished for having an independent mind? If we analyze her various writings we notice that she departs very early from canonical Négritude. Very early on, Suzanne Césaire displays an audacity which allows her to reinvent a past and propose a definition of the colonized Martinican: "*Qu'est-ce que le Martiniquais? Réponse—l'homme plante.*" [What is the Martinican? Answer—a plant man.][12] It would be erroneous to take this sentence as an expression of a banal cliché. A plant possesses a vital force; it is integrated into a cycle of fecundation, reproduction, resurrection—that is to say, eternal life. Therefore, a plant man possesses the same vital energy and power to overcome death. We can still trace here the influence of Surrealism. Surrealism advocated a new human being in close communication with the universe thanks to the dreams and the power of the unconscious. The emphasis laid on a specific Martinican identity is not shared by Aimé Césaire and the other Négritude poets who simply saw the Caribbean people as Africans who had lost the sense of their identity. For Aimé Césaire the notion *of métissage* (intermixing) simply does not exist. Fair or black-skinned, a Caribbean person is an African. Suzanne Césaire shuns this simplification and the Manichean rhetoric of colonialism and decolonization. In so doing, perhaps in spite of herself, she runs counter to the polarizing aesthetics of Négritude. According to her, Caribbean reality cannot simply be the resurrection of the African past. Africa has been obscured by the Middle Passage and the plantation system:

> *Il ne s'agit point de retour en arrière, de la resurrection d'un passé africain que nous avons appris à connaitre et respecter. Il s'agit au contraire d'une mobilisation de toutes les forces vives mêlées sur cette terre ou la race est le résultat du brassage le plus continu.* [This is not a question of turning back and resurrecting an African past that we have learned to know and respect. On the contrary, it is a question of mobilizing all the living strength of this land where race is the result of constant mixing.][13]

She emphasizes the notion of diversity. Suzanne Césaire can justly be regarded as the precursor of Glissant's Antillanité and even Créolité. Créolité is the most recent attempt to express the current state of Francophone Caribbean culture. The term emerged in 1989 with the publication of *Eloge de la Créolité* (In Praise of Creoleness) by Jean Bernabé, Patrick Chamoiseau, and Raphael Confiant. Not to be confused with the Creole language, Créolité advocates the exploration of the self and urges the writer to go beyond the process of recuperating the past. It also reaffirms the validation of multiple origins. As the authors put it: "Créolité is the interactional or transactional aggregate of Caribbean, European, African, Asian, and Levantine cultural elements united on the same soil by the yoke of history."[14]

Thus fifty years before these contemporary theoreticians, Suzanne Césaire rejects the binary opposition of black/white that impedes the multiculturalism of the Caribbean. It is true that it is not an entirely new idea. The Barbadian poet and historian Kamau Brathwaite had long before defined creolization as a way of seeing Caribbean society, not in terms of white and black, master and slave, in separate nuclear units, but as contributory parts of a whole. Throughout his career, in both his poetry and his theoretical work, it is this cross-cultural challenge that not only the diverse worlds of the Caribbean but the world as a whole must learn how to confront.

What differentiates Suzanne Césaire from Brathwaite as well as from the exponents of Antillanité and Créolité is her deep concern for the sociopolitical realities which are a legacy of the plantation system. The complex Caribbean *métissage* will not be able to mature if the difficult relationship between the Blacks and the Whites, i.e., the descendants of the slaves and the planters, is not resolved. As long as the African, European, Indian, and Asian elements are not merged, Caribbean identity will not flourish.

As I said before, Suzanne Césaire's last essay in *Tropiques* surprises the reader by its lyrical quality. Is this the same author who declared death on what she calls *"Littérature doudou"* (folksy literature)? Is this the same author who declared death on the hibiscus, the frangipani, and the bougainvillea?

At first reading, *Le grand camouflage* seems to be a celebration of the dynamism and splendor of Caribbean Nature. She starts by praising the sea and the volcano, then the hurricanes and the earthquakes, as if their violence were the sign of a profound creativity. But very soon her voice changes and she links Nature with Humanity. She surveys the complex history of the Caribbean from the days of the conquistadors to the institution of colonialism as if she wanted to illustrate the birth pangs of a new people. Thus the contradiction is only apparent. This essay disturbs only those who do not know how to read between the lines. What Suzanne Césaire wants to illustrate is how diffiicult it is for an outsider to appreciate the inner reality of the island as he is overwhelmed and blinded by its beauty. She wants, on the contrary, to establish a fundamental relationship among all the elements existing on the island. For the superficial visitor, the poverty and despair of the human beings are veiled behind the smokescreen of natural beauty.

It is clear that *Le grand camouflage* can ultimately be read as a very criticism of the celebrated André Breton. After his brief stay in Martinique, André Breton, in collaboration with the painter André Masson, wrote *Martinique, Charmeuse de Serpents* (Martinique, the Snakecharmer). In this text, Martinique is no longer seen as a real land but becomes one of those *objets de rêve* (dream objects) that André Breton and the Surrealist group were so fond of. The association of paintings and texts contributes to the mythification of the island and the eradication of all unpleasant elements. Suzanne Césaire implies that André Breton's eyes could not see, and therefore that the poet has failed his mission defined by Rimbaud as a seer and a prophet.

In her refusal of the separation of cultures in her antiessentialist way of thinking and her newfound sense of the ambivalence of cultural and racial identity, Suzanne Césaire is certainly the founding mother of all the postcolonial critics who denounce, as Sara Suleri puts it, "the simple pieties that the idiom of alterity frequently cloaks."[15]

7. *The Silent Game*

SYBIL SEAFORTH

Jessica Bright, on the eve of her thirtieth wedding anniversary, reflects on her life with her husband, Lionel. His growing silence over the last few years, and her powerlessness to break through that barrier, consumes her. She is recognizing how devastating the weapon of silence has been in the dismantling of their relationship. Day by day the strands are unraveling and she cannot mend them because, like a scythe, sharply, effectively, silence is cutting the strands and soon every strand will come undone.

Her reflection is interrupted with the arrival of a letter from Ruth, a friend who has been married for twenty-eight years. Ruth tells Jessica about the disintegration taking place in her own marriage.

In the unnamed island where Jessica resides, two other friends, Dora and Norma, are witnessing the breakup of their marriages. Dora has been married for twenty-five years. Norma has been married for twenty-nine years. The women reflect on and share their experiences. The common thread woven into the fabric of each couple's relationship is weak communication.

The women discover that conversation appears to be more important to them than to their husbands, and wonder why men are so afraid of using conversation.

Is it that they are afraid of establishing intimacy and connection? Is sexual intimacy the definition of married love for these men? The woman sought intimacy through encouraging conversation and reaped silence! Silence, the weapon which efficiently and systematically unravels the strands of their relationships with their spouses.

I don't know if it is popular culture in the Caribbean for middle-aged, menopausal men to abandon their wives after more than twenty-five years of marriage, but my experience living in three Caribbean communities over forty years has led me to think it a part of Caribbean culture. The voices of three women speak of their rejection after so long a period of married life. I am reminded of the poem "Estrangement," by Margaret Ward Morland:

> Silence is a long thin ache
> That snakes beneath the ribs
> To pinch the breath and inch beneath the diaphragm
> To clench the gut with coils of dry pain
> One word would loose the grip

In my work-in-progress *In Silence the Strands Unravel,* three women speak to the pain captured in Morland's poem. And as fiction communicates in a special way these words and sentiments, I would like to share the following excerpt in which three women reveal the depth and breadth of the experience of abandonment.

I SIT AT MY KITCHEN WINDOW with a cup of tea in hand and watch the morning sun clear mist-covered mountain peaks. This was a familiar sight to me during the more than twenty years that I had to live in La Portal. I had accompanied my husband, Lionel Bright, to La Portal five years after marrying him. And here I was this morning remembering that day in spring in a place hundreds of miles from this island, when Lionel had asked me to marry him.

It was a cool sunny day and there I sat in Munton Park dazzled and awed by the sight of clusters of bright-colored crocuses peeping up out of the dark brown earth, earth which had been covered by snow a few weeks ago. I had known Lionel for eight months and was surprised at myself for agreeing to marry him so soon after he had popped the question. That familiar line, "Give me some time to think about it," did enter my mind, but for a reason inexplicable at that moment, I felt that I would have been insincere and pretentious had I repeated that familiar line. For somehow in my heart, and in my head too, I had known for days that he was preparing to make that proposal.

There was that refreshing candor and transparency so unlike the Antillean men I had met at home. And today I am thinking, how could one who appeared so transparent, so without guile, be so transformed? I was impressed too by his seeming honesty, self-motivation, and self-discipline. He was humble though not submissive, and his manner in general convinced me, a woman over twenty-one, that Lionel possessed the essential qualities that I sought in a husband. So when I said "yes" to him I really felt that I had chosen my Mr. Right.

When Lionel expressed his wish for us to marry in Trenton, a place in which we were both strangers, bearing in mind that we were planning to return to the Cantillean region within three months I was both surprised and disappointed. I remember expressing surprise, but I concealed my disappointment. I told myself that it was a reasonable decision. For although Lionel had accepted a job in his homeland, he had not suggested that our wedding should take place there. It would be selfish of me to insist that we be married in St. Lucy to be with my family and friends. I harbored a lingering disappointment, though, that Lionel appeared to have taken matters in his hands.

So our wedding took place in Trenton on a crisp, cool autumn day. Twenty years after that momentous event, I realised that I had begun very early in our relationship to overcompromise, to be too agreeable. I had begun the dissembling of Jessica. I was adhering to the rules of the myth that for a marriage to succeed the female partner must put the husband's needs, career, and all else before her own. And here am I sitting in silence and alone on the eve of our thirtieth wedding anniversary, wondering when? where? how? could this marriage arrive at what appeared to be the total unraveling of the strands of our relationship. The strands must have begun to unravel years before. But the unraveling became apparent to me when I began to talk seriously about self-fulfillment. And began to do something about it. I was shattering the myth that a wife's primary fulfillment as a human being is through caregiving and nurturing roles as wife and mother.

When I sought to attend to my career, in my husband's view, I was breaking the rules. My affirmation of self he perhaps interpreted as competitive, an attempt to invade or share his public domain. I was about to compete in "his world," and he saw this to be incompatible with my role of wife and mother. "Could this woman," he must have asked himself, "be the same giving, yielding person that I married in Trenton?" For after he had arranged for us to be married and after a brief honeymoon, I accompanied him to his homeland, Daruba, where he had accepted a job. I felt somewhat uneasy about abandoning my career in midstream, reneging on a promise that I had made to myself earlier. But having been well schooled in the myth that a husband's needs are paramount, that it was my responsibility to support my husband's career and attend to his needs, with love for and faith and trust in Lionel I placed my career on hold.

Adjusting to life in Daruba was more difficult than I had imagined. My life revolved completely around Lionel. Within a year I had moved from an independent, single female to a wholly dependent wife. There were days when I felt like a boat adrift in Lionel's ocean. And though there was for a while a kind of calm, the days stretched out before me—long, uneventful waiting for Lionel to come home to relieve boredom and long solitary hours. I was living the myth, waiting for my Prince Charming to bring me happiness from his world.

Ten months after we came to live in Daruba, we moved to the island of Selena. It was a place where I had lived for many years and I was happy to be among relatives and friends. Within three months I had resumed my career. I was enjoying my work tremendously. I had just been offered a position that would provide deep personal satisfaction. However, at the same time Lionel accepted a job appointment in another country. I gave up my job reluctantly and not without a trace of resentment. My husband's career naturally took precedence. He was the provider! In fact, I cannot recall if I was asked if I would like to go to New Coast. It was not up for discussion. Whither Lionel goeth, I go! A wife's place is with her husband. The right to choose ended in the choice of a husband. It was my duty and it was in the best interest of the marriage, I comforted myself. The thought did occcur to me to resist the move. Brushing it aside, I said to myself: "Even if I succeeded in changing his mind about leaving Selena at this time, Lionel would hold it against me. I could be contributing to shaking the foundation of our four-year marriage!" So like a dutiful wife I followed Lionel to New Coast. I was being faithful to the myth. How painful it was for me to be told by Lionel twenty-five years after canceling out my personal goals that I was not supportive of him.

We spent twelve months in New Coast. This time, however, the initiative came from me. And I was of the opinion for many years after that he was pleased with coming to La Portal. As a matter of fact, within five years he was promoted to a very senior position. And for the next five years, Lionel received a great deal of recognition from the institution with which he was employed. Throughout all those years, my principal career was mother-caregiver-homemaker. Aware that mothering will end inevitably because of the passsage of time and not because I would necessarily have brought a piece of work to a successful conclusion, I sought to reaffirm my selfhood in choosing writing as a career. Perhaps Lionel saw in this move something that was threatening, competitive. I can only guess. What I am clear about is that the first tearing of the fabric of our marriage took place at about the same time that my work was recognized publicly. I had thought Lionel would have been happy for me, pleased with what I had achieved. For I had always shared his work, rejoicing in his achievements, and tried to let him know that I shared his disappointments. I say tried, because Lionel has never been very communicative about his feelings to me, especially when he was hurt. That's where, I think, for me the sense of alienation began. Marriage, I expected, offered an atmosphere of sustaining emotional warmth and sharing beyond sexual gratification. And in what appears today to be a crumbling marriage, I look back at thirty years in less than thirty minutes. And I think of how much I have given, how much I have invested; and I know there is nothing left because everything has been taken. The myth of female weakness has come true and the result is desolation.

And Lionel, feeling trapped in the marriage cage for thirty years, is turning away from me—perhaps to another woman. I am about to be made destitute. How well he has used silence to accomplish this desolation. A dog is barking! The postman rings! I am reminded that it's ten o'clock and that it is Wednesday morning. The postman hands me two letters. One is addressed to me and the other is for Lionel. I am looking at the postmark on my letter when I hear a car in the driveway. It is Lionel. It is the first time I am seeing him this morning. He nods and is about to pass into the kitchen.

> "Good morning, Lionel. There's a letter for you."
> "Thanks."
> "I'd like to talk with you when you have some time."
> "Whatever you have to say, say it now! I'm not into any long conversations with you."
> "Lionel, why are you so angry?"
> "If you are going to tell me about my voice and how loudly I speak to you, that's not going to change. That's how I speak to everyone."
> "But everyone is able to control the texture of one's voice. I have heard you speaking over the phone in dulcet tones to the special friend or friends you value and like, I suppose."
> "I don't have time for this kind of nonsense and I don't have to stay here and listen to you."
> "Lionel I am just trying to find out how we can communicate with each

other without the anger and the hostility, every time I—"

"You said you have something to say, speak, I am busy."

"I just wish we could remove or even begin to break down this wall of silence—"

"Just cut out the fancy words! I keep telling you, there is nothing to talk about."

"We keep screaming at each other every time we speak!"

"Look, I know you don't like my voice! It's too loud! You don't like my lifestyle, but I am not going to change."

"How can you say that? I have been living with you for almost thirty years!"

"And you have been trying to make me over, you refuse to understand that I don't wish to be anyone else! I am a simple man."

"So simple and uncomplicated that I don't understand you."

"You don't have to understand me, nor me you. I don't have a problem. I think you should see a doctor!"

"For God's sake, stop telling me that! You know I've been seeing a doctor regularly for a chronic, physical problem. Why don't you just say what you mean, that I should see a psychiatrist! You think I am mad because I try so hard to communicate."

"Think anything! I don't have time to sit around and listen to you!"

"I am just trying to . . ." My voice fades away.

"Stop trying and do something. I don't have to listen to you!" He rushes to the door; closes it firmly.

Today, in fact, is the first time in many weeks that he paused long enough to respond to me, even though the anger has increased. He'll probably be increasing the silence as well. And his silence fills the house; it coils around my body.

How well he knows the power of silence! It alienates and it is a dull lasting ache that does not go away. As I wipe away the tears, tears of depair, of frustration, I notice my letter is still lying unopened. I open the letter and am pleasantly surprised, for it is from a friend I have not seen in more than a decade. I am even more surprised at the length of the letter. For she sends me Christmas greetings once a year with a promise to write soon, and the promise has remained just that. Well, it's the month of April and Ruth has written:

Dear Jessica,

Guess what? I, me Ruth, your friend, have gone and completed a University course in History. Can you believe that? Jess, I feel like I've been reconstructed after all these years of unpaid, unrecognized housework. And just as I am rejoicing for finding or redeeming myself after twenty-five years of marriage, Milton is threatening to leave me. And I use the word "threat" advisedly. He has the power to do that, for I have never earned a cent since I married him.

*There have been times in the last few months when I cannot really believe this
. . . this tragedy is happening to me! Sure it has happened to some couples, but
not Milton and Ruth Stone! Why did I ever think we were so special? It had
happened to my mother. Dad eased out of her life after forty years. And for ten
of those forty years he never spoke directly to her. I called it the silent game.
Well, the game caught up with me about three years ago. Now I wonder how
my mother survived that terror, the silence that a man enforces on a wife he no
longer needs, the silence that makes her invisible!*

*So for economic support, even when he has long ago withdrawn every
other kind of support, the abandoned, silent woman bears the pain. And like
my mother, I, too, have become a product of a society that pressures women
into first seeking husbands, and all the other good things in life will come to
them. We have to reject that myth, that notion, that for a woman, her ultimate
goal is marriage, and that for her, getting a husband is her life's achivement.
Men seek achievement in their chosen field of endeavor; women seek theirs in
marriage. So, my life's achievement! That's what I get for projecting my ambition and my career! In the first five years of our marriage, he had asked me:
"Why are you thinking about a career? My career is for both of us." To think
that I believed him (he may have meant it at the time). But oh God! I was naive
or just in the state of being in love!*

*So while Milton worked hard at improving his career, a job that took him
away from home several times a year, I kept myself occupied with the housewife career, busy caring for and nurturing three young children, the only parent present at the children's concerts, Parent Teacher Meetings, Sport Day,
Speech Day. Even when our son won the coveted School Prize, Milton was too
busy to attend.*

*And I remember feeling angry with Milton for not arranging to begin to
participate more in our lives. Looking back, I see we had begun "arguing" even
then about his not sharing very much in our children's lives and mine. But I
told myself that when the children were older, Milton and I could communicate more. He would invite me on a few of his trips, introduce me to his colleagues, listen to what I would like to do now that the children were gone. But
the communication decreased, and even a brief conversation would end up in
a shouting encounter. It grew worse within the last few years. And the periods
of silence became longer. And when I dared to break that imposed silence, Milton would erupt! It was as if the sound of my voice enraged him. And the man
for whom in the first twenty years of our marriage I had to buy shirts and underwear, began to buy trendy shirts and underwear. The signs that I was being
traded in were beginning to appear. Then there was that day when I invited
Milton to a function. He refused (that was becoming a habit), but I was trying to break the silence that was so effectively alienating me. I attended the
function anyway, and there was Milton with this woman. His face wreathed
in smiles (something I had not seen on his face for months), their arms around*

each other! I knew then that Milton was having an affair.

And I think it began about six months ago. For it was about that time he really stopped listening to me. He would just walk away and leave my words hanging. Or a question or a comment from me would turn into a shouting competition. He would blame me for not being supportive, and he refused to give a single specific reason for his accusation. And the anger I would see in his face alarmed me: there was so much disgust, dislike. I had unwittingly become his enemy. And one does not eat from one's enemy, so Milton started to cook! Can you believe that, Jes? Milton, the scholar, who did not know—and did not care to know—how to boil an egg! He stopped sharing, stopped sitting at the table with me. He could no longer eat the food I had been preparing for over twenty-five years! Could there be a clearer statement of rejection? Milton, who has taken all that I could give, must now sanctify his love relationship with this other woman. So he eats alone if he cannot share a meal with her! I have allowed myself to be owned, controlled by him. How can one love a creature that one owns, when that creature is another human being? He has owned me so now I have no value. Beware the husband, my dear, who begins to buy trendy clothes, especially underwear! The first sign that your husband is about to trade you in is an interest in clothes, especially, a husband who was so disinterested in clothes that his wife's selection was okay. I really most sincerely hope that things are going well with you and Lionel and that your marriage will resist any takeover bid! Forgive me for burdening you with my woes. Girl, it's a nightmarish experience, but I will, I must, find the strength to survive and to surmount this seeming tragedy.

I have been invited to a Cantillean History Conference in June. Would love to spend a few days with you on my way back, if that is a convenient time for you. My address is still the same and so is the telephone number. You were such an excellent essay writer at school ! You talked about writing some years ago. Have you started ? If you haven't, START NOW!

Much love,
Ruth

I was staring at Ruth's letter, slowly turning the pages I had just finished reading. And I was thinking how Ruth's experiences in her failing marriage are so similar to mine, it's uncanny! She is as yet unaware that the fabric of my marriage has begun to unravel.

Milton and Lionel have each been married for over a quarter of a century and have apparently grown weary of their respective spouses, and it seems that neither Ruth nor I can be sure why the disillusionment! Is it for the sake of variety that men get tired of their wives and seek new women? Do they see women as commodities: select, use, throw aside or away? The shrill persistent ring intrudes on my racing thoughts. I place the letter in my pocket and walk to the phone.

"Hello, Jessica. I was just about to hang up."

"Was the phone ringing that long, Dora? I just heard three rings or so."

"Oh, that's alright, glad you are at home."

"Guess I was just totally absorbed, shocked, by a letter from an old friend."

"Nothing too serious, I mean it's not the death of—"

"Not a physical death, Dora, the dying of a marriage."

"Oh God, tell me about that! You know my story! Girl, the pain, you think it's gone, then a word, a place, a face, and the ache is there again. Anyway I am calling to invite you to dinner tomorrow evening to meet a few visitors. Remember that conference I told you about? It starts tomorrow. One of the guests is the opening speaker. Your husband is welcome if he has the time. Oh no! Tomorrow is your wedding anniversary. He'll probably be taking you out to a candlelight dinner at the Inn!"

"Oh Dora, come off it. Even in our post-honeymoon days that was not Lionel's thing or style, as he would say. But, "thank you, Dora. I will tell him, if he is in the mood to listen to me at all."

"Girl it's not easy whether the break is sudden like mine was or if it's a slow unraveling. I am looking for you anyway. Dinner is at seven-thirty p.m. See you, Jessica."

"Thanks Dora, I'll be there."

Lionel was already at home watching the news on television when I returned from the supermarket. To my greeting, he responded with a hasty nod. I had learned over the years that when he is watching a program, he is totally focused. Any comment, even on what's happening, he regards as an intrusion. I watched the news in silence with Lionel before going into the dining room. I was probably halfway through my meal when he entered. He had not shared food with me at the table for many months past. Suddenly I remembered Ruth's letter. A trade-in could be near. The thought filled me with anger, pain, and a bellyful of injustice. Lionel poured himself a drink and turned sideways.

"I am leaving for Selena tomorrow."

"Oh, that's sudden."

"Well, I could not be certain until today, when I received my travel documents."

The ensuing silence was thick with unspoken words. His back was turned toward me. He was getting ready for flight.

"When are you returning?"

"Sunday or Monday. I need a good night's sleep."

Hurriedly he left the room, having taken great care to avoid looking at me. I twisted the fork on the plate, my throat constricting, my eyes burning with unshed tears. That silence followed me as I left the table, clenching my gut. One word from Lionel, I thought, would loose the grip and ease the pain. And I thought of Dora and what she had said about the finality of divorce. There is a finality about silence too. For a stream of words, nay, even one word, would crack the silence. I did not tell Lionel about Dora's invitation. Clearly he had better things to do than to be with his wife of thirty years on our wedding anniversary. His abrupt departure was perhaps a way of denying the event anyway.

Part Two

Politics and Economics of Caribbean Life

Overview

With the exception of native populations (Arawaks and Caribs, whose history is much longer than those of the groups presently predominating in the region), inhabitants of the Caribbean—historically from another place and another culture—were compelled to adjust to new environments and societies outside of their ancestral milieu. Their histories form the backdrop of Caribbean literature and offer a special challenge to writer as well as reader. According to Wilfred Cartey:

> In a special way the world intersects at these islands, for one cannot speak of them meaningfully without speaking at once of Africa, Asia, Europe, and America. At this point of intersection, Caribbean personality has derived from symbiotic intermingling of all these cultural rootings from the history of servitude and freedom, of domination and the quest for self.[1]

The construction of identity is both a political and an economic act as it locates the subject within the scheme of existence divided by worlds—third world, second world, and first world. That division is informed as much by economics as it is by geographical space. From varied ethnicities, to varied religions, to varied geographical expressions of its boundaries, the Caribbean is a study in diversity.

In this section, writers make specific statements about and share their concerns on political and economic issues affecting Caribbean women. Daisy Cocco De Filippis explores the voices of the women in Dominica who fought for suffrage and endured during the Trujillo regime. Marie José N'Zengo-Tayo analyzes the plight of Haitian children in migration as depicted in the works of Maryse Condé and Edwidge Danticat. Marion Bethel reflects on capital punishment in the Bahamas. Lourdes Vázquez laments the passage of the popular balladeer in Puerto Rican American culture, and with biting satire, Chiqui Vicioso reflects on issues of literary production for the artists who writes from the Caribbean.

In her essay "The Politics of Literature: Dominican Women and the Suffrage Movement," Daisy Cocco De Filippis examines the life, work, and political milieu surrounding Delia Weber, an early Dominican feminist. De Filippis argues for a new reading of Weber's texts. Mother, wife, painter, poet, fiction writer, and president of the organization Acción Feminista Dominicana, De Filippis offers Weber as a case study of the challenges faced by women under the limitations imposed by the Trujillo rgime. In 1940, Dominican women were granted suffrage as a result of the Acción Feminista Dominicana campaigns on behalf of Trujillo (1934 and 1938). Defining themselves as wives and mothers, Acción's members espoused an ideology of support and benefit to members of the family and to the citizens of the nation.

The feminist struggle, then, was aligned with existing notions of womanhood. Yet under Trujillo's regime, De Filippis argues, "the family became one more piece in a machinery of authoritarian politics whose ideological structure had three manifestations: Hispanism, anti-Haitianism, and anti-communism." Hence, unwittingly, Acción Feminista Dominicana's agenda was largely co-opted by the politics of the time. Weber's rhetoric on behalf of the organization espoused conciliatory principles, while her creative writing (poems, plays, short stories) is marked by a discourse of escapism and lyricism. De Filippis offers interpretation of that element of Weber's work that would place it in the categories of psychological conflicts and fantastic tendencies. In the main, De Filippis offers that "the woman who wants to be the mother (author) of her own existence must choose flight, a getaway, or suicide, rather than remain locked-in, controlled by her mother, her biology, and her spouse."

The politics of the esthetics of subject matter in fiction is the concern of Marie-José N'Zengo-Tayo's essay "Haitian Children and Migration as Seen by Maryse Condé and Edwidge Danticat." N'Zengo-Tayo asserts that the Haitian boat people migration (especially the plight of the children) has less literary appeal to writers than sugarcane migration because of the "impossibility of transforming this reality into a meaningful metaphor." She also says that there is no tradition of childhood novels in Haitian literature as there is for the rest of the Caribbean, and those childhood works written were largely written by women until quite recently. N'Zengo-Tayo examines Condé's novella for children *Haiti Chérie* and Danticat's bildungsroman *Breath, Eyes, Memory* in an effort to focus on the writers' use of children as a mouthpiece on Haitian popular migration. In sum, N'Zengo-Tayo maintains that both writers use children to question injustice in the world economy, social abuse, and economic exploitation on the one hand and issues of estrangement, adaptation, and social promotion related to migration on the other.

The concern for children continues in the essay, "I'll Fly Away," in which Marion Bethel reflects on capital punishment in the Caribbean. The politics of capital punishment is very much a feature of the debates currently raging in the Bahamas. Speaking to the preponderance of violent symbols, Bethel asserts that hers is a community "where young men use guns and their penises in the same manner and in the same breath—to overpower and destroy—in order to overcome and avoid the terror in their own lives." She calls for the community to name the fear in its own voice, affirm its existence, and she adds that only then will solutions lie within its control for "[o]ur children will not forgive us for the quick fix of the gallows." Her remarks are based on an actual hanging which led her to the understanding "at a powerfully emotional level how we, the descendants of enslaved Africans in the Caribbean, creatively combine and adapt different forms of beliefs and practices to accommodate our experience and reality." Life-and-death issues, she says, carry her back to the elusive security of the womb and bring into sharp focus her need to deepen her spiritual life and to tap wildly into her creative capacity.

Similarly, writers in this section turn to popular culture as the source of creative impulses.

In "Of Popular Balladeers: Narrative, Gender, and Popular Culture," Lourdes Vázquez provides a personal narrative, a remembrance of her uncle, a singer who was a member of the nucleus group of Puerto Rican musicians and singers in New York. Vázquez uses the occasion to simultaneously comment on the writing process:

> And why have I started to write memories? the writer asks herself. It's not just me, but all women in my country. From Rosario Ferré who writes and rewrites the story of her family and friends, up to Ana Lydia Vega who writes about the daily life in Rio Piedras. This may be our response to an auctioned national history written in remnants. It is our history by gender.

Using the technique of cinema to capture the act of writing and remembering, she records the disappearing world of the *bolerista* which, as the twenty-first century approaches, will be supplanted in her memory by other concerns—drugs, and other elements of counterculture.

In her essay "Between the Milkman and the Fax Machine: Challenges to Women Writers in the Caribbean," Sherezada (Chiqui) Vicioso defines the difficulty of writing in the Caribbean and offers comical treatment of the regulations governing her visit to Florida International University to participate in the 1996 International Conference of Caribbean Women Writers and Scholars. Vicioso highlights the difficulties of literary production for those who do not live in the metropolis. Such women live "without a fax, without a credit card, without dollars, and generally without electricity." Her essay speaks of disruptions, silences, technical difficulties, and North American insensitivity—in short, she exposes the conditions under which she labors. To conclude she offers reflections on eight propositions offered by Edouard Glissant for writers of the Caribbean.

Accordingly, the essays in this section evoke the inextricable connection between politics and economics as they affect Caribbean life and culture. Because of its diversity, Maryse Condé believes that the construction of a Caribbean identity is caught up in many contradictions. Condé reminds us that "[t]he Caribbean, although sharing common historical founding experiences, erupted into a collection of social orders with distinctive features." With such diverse topics as Dominican women and suffrage, Haitian migration, capital punishment, Puerto Rican balladeers, and the difficulties of writing in the Caribbean, the essays featured in this section demonstrate the very real connection between politics, economy, and cultural productions. The essays provide readers with a myriad of historical, political, and economic realities which explicate Condé's ideology of the vast but contradictory and distinctive lives of the peoples of the Caribbean.

8. The Politics of Literature: Dominican Women and the Suffrage Movement Case Study: Delia Weber

DAISY COCCO DE FILIPPIS

> *Mystery was beginning to take shape . . .*
> *Dora's eyes would become vague and her*
> *image divine; she wanted to become*
> *the mother of her own existence and*
> *that her life would be as a poem,*
> *without an ending. . . .*
> —DELIA WEBER

Delia Weber's life (1900–1982) and art present one of the most interesting case studies of what it means to be a Dominican, mother, wife, painter, poet, fiction writer, and feminist in the earlier part of this century. Delia Weber's interpretation of the role of women in the Dominican Republic, her active political life as president of the Acción Feminista Dominicana, and her creative life as a first-rate painter, poet, and fiction writer offer valuable insights on Dominican womanhood and woman's creativity when faced with the limitations imposed by a patriarchal society. To the extent possible, this paper will endeavor to present her life, filled with the contradictions between her public activities and political compromises and her deep spiritual beliefs as a student of eastern philosophies, as well as a new reading and interpretation of her literature, born of the dissonance between her ideals and the practical political compromises she was forced to embrace during the Trujillo regime.

Delia Weber was born on October 23, 1900, in the old Santa Bárbara part of town, in Santo Domingo, where she spent most of her life. The daughter of Enriqueta Pérez de Weber and Juan Weber, a jeweler, Delia Mercedes Weber Pérez spent her childhood playing in the shade of the venerable arches of the courtyard of the church of Santa Bárbara, one of the oldest religious edifices in the Dominican Republic, founded in the middle of the sixteenth century by Padre Antonio. Until the year 1972, the church of Santa Bárbara enjoyed the right of granting ecclesiastical asylum to political dissidents. A childhood and a life spent in such surroundings, with images of present ruins of past colonial glories, filled Delia Weber's eyes and, we can only speculate here, marked her existence, encouraging her to lead a life of reflection, interest in the arts and letters, religious questioning, and political action.

Delia Weber attended the Universidad de Santo Domingo, where she studied philosophy and Latin and Greek. A mother, community organizer, and teacher, Weber took the valuable lessons received in the ateliers of Abelardo Rodríguez Urdaneta and Celeste Woos y Gil to her classroom in La Escuela Normal de Santo Domingo, where she taught painting for many years. Among her many responsibilities, Delia Weber's role as director of the Biblioteca Nacional de la Secretaría de Educación, Bellas Artes y Cultos, is remembered for her service with distinction. Most official chroniclers of Dominican culture and life, however, point to Doña Delia's role as one of the most prominent fighters for the rights of women in the Dominican Republic.

Her responsibilities to her family (by the time she reached middle age, she had given birth to four children, Rodolfo, Enrique, Antonio, and Salvador Coiscou Weber, and divorced their father, the writer and historian Máximo Coiscou Henríquez), her teaching, and her political advocacy did not keep Weber from painting (her "After the Tear" won Fourth Prize in the E. Leon Competition of 1970), or from her commitment to creative writing. By the time of her death, Delia Weber had published *Encuentro* (1939), *Ascuas vivas* (1939), *Los viajeros* (1944), *Apuntes* (1949), *Los bellos designios* (1949), *Dora y otros cuentos* (1952), *Espigas al sol* (1959), and *Estancia* (1972). She left unpublished "*El mundo sin fronteras*," "*Salvador y Altagracia*" (a three-act play), "*Albores*" (poetry for children), and "*Vocabulario*" (poetry), as well as other manuscripts. Thanks to the diligence of her son Rodolfo Coiscou Weber, we are still able to find some of her publications and enjoy the fine opportunity to view her paintings.

In her eighty-two years of life, Delia Weber participated actively in all facets of Dominican life. A self-defined feminist, she was for many years a member of the executive board of the association Acción Feminista Dominicana, and was its president as the association lobbied, struggled, and waited until women's suffrage had become the law of the land; that position provided Weber the opportunity to study the condition of women, and to take a stand on behalf of women's rights, a stand whose long-term judiciousness we must now begin to question. Whatever insights we might have in hindsight, we must recognize that the situation of the organization's leaders was a precarious and very difficult one. According to Abigail Mejía de Fernández in her *Ideario Feminista*, the organizers of Acción Feminista Dominicana often met with male criticism and ridicule in their early years. According to Angela Hernández, these women were often called "*impreparadas, impertinentes, insuficientes, ñoñas, agachaditas . . . y otras yerbas*" [untrained, impertinent, inadequate, whiny, false . . . and other weeds].[1]

Despite severe opposition, those women, mostly daughters of the middle class who had managed to be educated, understood the need for their involvement in the women's movement. The decade of the thirties marks the high and low points of politics on behalf of the rights of women in the Dominican Republic. Delia Weber, in her capacity as member of the board of directors, and at times its president, found herself in a very difficult position, one that with the passing of the years we can begin to try to understand.

In her *Historia del feminismo en la Republica Dominicana*, Livia Veloz points to the precarious condition of women during the first decades of this century:

> As far as instruction is concerned, it is a given that the daughters of well-to-do parents or even those of the middle class, would receive an instruction adequate for the times and their social and economical condition. This was the minority of the women. The majority, the daughters and women of the masses, the poor and lower classes, could not count on any opportunities. The little ones would go to the neighborhood school where they would learn to read and write poorly and to create some manual crafts at the same time that they were taught some catechism. Later as adults, life changed them radically. They had to work, some as housekeepers, others knitting and embroidering for pay . . . For women there was only one road once they reached adulthood: marriage.[2]

Given the situation described, the members of Acción Feminista Dominicana understand that in order to gain authority and to have the support of the rest of the population, they must speak from the platform of authority provided by a definition as wives/mothers. Therefore, part of their political platform points to a definition of education and rights of women as the base for the advancement of the family:

> Feminism will tend to create the happiness of women by preparing them so that they always marry for love and not for necessity and in a hurry, with the first to knock on the door, out of fear of facing life's necessities. It [feminism] will work to have laws passed that favor marriage and the stability of the home.[3]

The women of the Acción Feminista Dominicana take the traditional parallelism home/homeland and use it to present feminist struggle as an act of support and benefit to members of the family and to the citizens of the nation. As a present-day aside, we note with alarm the imagery used in a number of advertisements launched in the early 1990s by feminists in the Dominican Republic, in which two halves of an orange are used to indicate that a well-balanced home fosters a well-balanced *madre patria*. Furthermore, the women of Acción Feminista Dominicana use male-accepted arguments to demonstrate support of family to be, after all, synonymous with being a patriot.

The effort to maintain what they called "that delicate balance," however, immersed the leaders of Acción Feminista Dominicana into the murky waters of Dominican politics under Trujillo. In her seminal monograph *Emergencia del silencio: la mujer dominicana en la educación formal*, Angela Hernández explains the situation of women during the thirty years of Trujillo's regime. According to Hernández, the

family became one more part in a machinery of authoritarian politics whose ideological structure had three manifestations: Hispanism, anti-Haitianism, and anti-
communism. Women, as the lighting guide of the family and in their traditional role
as mothers, were granted a public voice as motherhood acquired legal status when
procreation was rewarded with the Premio Julia Molina de Maternidad, decreed as
law 279, on May 22, 1940.[4] The irony is apparent here. In 1940, as women gained suffrage, they were subjected to a massive campaign designed to encourage procreation,
and thus perpetuate traditional roles, in order to keep women at home.

Acción Feminista Dominicana's history is caught in the midst of this political
wave, and its development is co-opted by the politics of the time. The movement had
begun in the early 1930s as a result of a number of activities that had taken place the
prior two decades. Officially, however, by the closing of its May 14, 1931 meeting, the
women of Club Nosotras declared their intention to form the first feminist group in
the nation. Some of these women had been studying and writing about the condition of women for publication in the journal *Femina* since the 1920s. Their main
goals were the betterment of women's intellectual, social, moral, and legal condition.[5]
Their specific agenda, however, is much diffused, since the fifteen members of the
founding board also indicate their interest in fighting alcoholism, prostitution, and
drug addiction.[6] And although there is an attempt to be inclusive, requirements for
membership include literacy, in a country with a high index of illiteracy. As Hernández points out, a clear sense of solidarity based on gender was also accompanied by
a certain maternalism, based on the privileged position of many of its founders.

The implications of having such a movement take hold of the nation's educational and cultural centers was not lost on Trujillo's regime, and co-optation began
with a speech pronounced by *el generalísimo* on the first anniversary of Acción Feminista Dominicana. Trujillo's speech was peppered with compliments to a number of
the women in the group as well as vague promises of support for women's suffrage
in the Dominican Republic. The strategy, as Hernández points out, was to incorporate these women into a much more conservative political movement that included
as a centerpiece women's role in the home as wife and as mother. In the elections of
1934 as well as the ones in 1938, the women of Acción Feminista Dominicana cam-
paigned on behalf of Trujillo's reelection, believing his promises of support for
women's suffrage. Finally, by 1940, Trujillo made good on his promise and women
were granted the right to vote. As a result, by 1942 the Acción Feminista Dominicana
joined El Partido Dominicano (Trujillo's Dominican Party) as it issued a proclama-
tion inciting Dominican women to vote in support of Trujillo's reelection, thus form-
ing the feminine wing of the party.

In 1943 the Primer Congreso Feminino took place. Its main agenda was to propose the formation of mothers' clubs in each city. The tasks to be performed by each
of these mothers' clubs included but were not limited to the following:

1. Scheduling of talks centered on social issues, i.e., hygiene, religiosity,
   housework, drug and alcohol rehabilitation;

2. Designation of days to be occupied in charitable activities and to practice housework, i.e., mending, sewing, knitting, etc.;

3. Cooking and household management lessons.[7]

It is discouraging to note how closely this agenda resembles the description of
women's education in the first two decades of the century. By the early 1940s, the
women of Acción Feminista Dominicana found themselves sacrificing all to obtain
suffrage at the price of working for an agenda that would perpetuate the role-
stereotyping that had kept women out of all spheres of power except, of course,
within the confines of their homes. It comes as no surprise that the original board
quickly dispersed. Individuals like Abigaíl Mejía and Petronila Gómez, vigorous
champions of women's rights, found themselves walking away from Acción Feminista Dominicana. Early on, a group of women refused to sign on as supporters of
the regime, among them the distinguished educator Ercilia Pepín, who was eventually dismissed as principal of a public school in Santiago. Others, who rose to promi-
nence by supporting the regime, were rewarded with cushy overseas appointments.
Such is the case of the much honored Minerva Bernardino, one of the original sign-
ers of the U.N. charter, who continues to receive accolades, including honors granted
not too long ago by the Clinton administration. In fairness to the women, we must
point out that the co-optation of Acción Feminista Dominicana was not an isolated
instance but a way of life in the Dominican Republic of the time, where institutions
were either assimilated or destroyed.

By 1948, Delia Weber's rhetoric reflected the need to accommodate to circumstances as well as to express some of her fundamental beliefs about life. In her talk,
"*La nueva mujer,*" Weber elaborates the home-centered theme as well as introduces
a number of philosophical ideas with regard to nature and the environment that
would be pretty much a part of the world of esoteric religions she was beginning to
enter. As far as the definition of women is concerned, Weber reiterates the official
theme when she states: "In synthesis, I sustain that there is no such thing as a new
woman. Nor such feminism . . . Nor 'masculinism' that would threaten our tran-
quility. . . ."[8] She continues: "This informed woman will comfort, consolidate the new
home, and will know how to better love her child and her husband because she will
have educated better her child by then. . . . Dramatists will no longer be able to create Doll Houses as the genial Ibsen had done where the home collapsed because of a
lack of understanding."[9]

As she reflects on the condition of this woman whom she deems neither new
nor feminist, Weber also considers the history and the world women are called upon
to inhabit, and she notes:

We observe through History that the values of civilization in any given moment: Morality, Rights, the State, Religion and the Arts, the Fatherland,
Humanity, are problems relative to the human ability acquired up to that

moment. That is to say, always dependent on its time and circumstances, and apparent changes. And in truth, everything is related, dependency, fusion, unity, harmony.[10]

Weber continues to examine the human condition in an age of technology and alienation from nature where love for material things appears to take precedence, in particular, in North America:

> Today civilization is the development of innumerable necessities. Absolute technical control over nature. Man believes himself triumphant by defeating the obstacles nature places before him. But this is the true sense of western civilization, drunken with industrialization, mechanism, whirlwind ideas. Western man, North American man to a high degree, with the astounding development of industrialization, shows that he defends himself and defeats nature as he would a hostile enemy.[11]

Arrogance, hostility, and disregard for nature are the qualities Weber finds when she looks at Western civilization. Throughout the essay, as a refrain she cannot let go of, Weber repeats the phrase "*somos hijos de la tierra* [We are children of the earth]." As the essay develops, the weaving of the official and the unofficial discourse becomes more evident. Weber is expressing ideas about women she is expected to repeat. Yet, the essay is taken over by her concern with a philosophy that is to take her quite far from her immediate surrounding reality. Escapism and lyricism begin to mark her discourse, as Weber arrives at a precise delineation of difference:

> The goal of the life of man in the west generally is to acquire. First, the employment that would allow us to save enough to own a beautiful little house. Pretty furniture. To be followed by more expensive commodities. A refrigerator. An electric kitchen. A car. A house in the country. Or an apartment house to rent out and be able to live ever more comfortably. . . .

> The goal of the life of man in the east is generally dispossession. True possession derives from meditation and understanding the secrets of nature. And the sense of life is the search for truth. The answers to the important questions: Where does this eternal rushing of human endeavors lead us? What is the truth about human existence?[12]

With the passing of time Delia Weber would get more involved in her studies of Eastern religions. At different points in her life, Weber was the director of the Rosacrucian chapter Amorc Filial of the Great Lodge until it changed from chapter to lodge. She was also the founder and director of the Great Universal Fraternity, an institution dedicated to the study and promotion of yoga in the Dominican Republic. A follower of Rabindranath Tagore, Weber wrote an essay on his philosophy. In his introduction to the posthumous publication of this essay, Rodolfo Coiscou Weber, her son, indicated:

> We allow ourselves to add to the heretofore unpublished essay written by our dear mother, some poems of Rabindranath Tagore and by Delia Weber, as a simple proof of the spiritual affinity between the Dominican poetess [sic] and the Hindu poet, as if they both emerged from the same essence.[13]

As we study Delia Weber's literature, we can make the following generalizations: For the most part, the poetry seems to have been the space where religious considerations and philosophizing could be expressed. In the short stories as well as in the plays, Weber re-creates a poetic world, mystical and full of escapism, where women act in a manner quite different from the ideals enunciated by the Acción Feminista Dominicana. It is as if, with her literature, Weber found a way to insinuate many of the beliefs her position did not allow her to articulate.

A reading of Weber's three one-act plays, *Lo eterno, Los bellos designios* ,and *Los viajeros,* written in the 1940s, as well as her short story collection *Dora y otros cuentos,* published in 1952, illustrates this theory by introducing a number of women characters who show their unhappiness with their lot as women by either leaving or running away from home. In *Lo eterno,* Weber introduces the theme of appearances versus reality. As we read the play we become convinced that one woman, an actress, has chosen to commit suicide as a solution to her problems with her lover. In "reality" this is not the case. Nothing could be further from the woman's mind than to succumb to the opinion of others or to despair. In *Los viajeros,* a young woman about to be married runs away to a mountain in order to collect flowers. The further she ascends, the less likely she is to return. Ultimately, the young woman decides to settle down on the mountaintop, closer to heaven, whence she sends back rose petals to her admiring traveling companions. In *Los belles designios* the same imagery of a runaway bride-to-be is repeated, except that here while in flight the young woman meets the son of her much older bridegroom who also falls in love with her and is quite willing to give up his "kingdom" for her love. Quite certain that her lot is to set an example for the woman of the future, Dulce Maria (Sweet Mary) concludes the play by pronouncing: "In my nuptials with silence, on the top of the mountain, I will engender a new conscience."[14]

The image of a fragile, poetic woman who nevertheless defines her future by her flight is also reproduced in Weber's short stories. "*Para una descripción temática del cuento dominicano,*" published in *Eme-Eme* in 1975, is the only critical essay on the stories of Weber published to date, with the exception of my own introduction to *Combatidas, combativas y combatientes* (1992). In their study, Norma Reyes, García Rodríguez, and José Enrique catalog Weber's stories as examples of psychological conflicts and fantastic tendencies. In their analysis, these critics conclude that in Delia Weber's short stories:

The psychological predominates by their quantitative order; all of the stories studied present in their plots conflicts of a sociological nature; these
being imaginary conflicts that emerge as intellectual creation of their author.[15]

As the title of their essay indicates, Reyes and her coauthors offer only a description,
not an interpretation of the elements that constitute Delia Weber's work. And although Weber's complete works are worthy of further study that the present essay
does not offer, I will endeavor to analyze this "fantastic tendency" in Weber by means
of a careful reading of one of her stories. In "Dora," the story that provides the title
for the collection, Dora is a young woman who is languishing in her room; she is kept
company by her mother's vigil and Lucilo's visits. At no time are readers told about
her ailment nor of the need for her confinement, although we are told of her disquiet:

> Mystery was beginning to take shape. . . . Dora's eyes would become vague
> and her image divine: she wanted to become the mother of her own exis-
> tence and that her life would be as a poem, without an ending. . . .[16]

Dora wants to become her own mother, although she does not want only to create her own image but also to create the elements that make up her world, which like
a poem or nature is to have no end. This story, labeled "psychological" by critics, presents us with a world in which the mundane details of everyday existence are of little consequence. The plot can be summarized as follows. Dora, a young and beautiful
blond woman, remains confined to her bedroom. Kept company by her mother, who
reads in a corner of the room, Dora spends countless hours reflecting on the nature
of life and love. Lucilo, her husband, betrothed, or lover (we are never told), pays her
a visit once in a while. Dora is not satisfied with a love that at some times appears to
be infinite and at others goes out like a candle besieged by a storm. One day, when
Lucilo tells her that he has given María the flowers he had intended for her, Dora offers to cut flowers for María herself. She leaves the room and disappears forever. Years
later, Lucilo, who is still awaiting Dora's return, approaches the shores of a sea whose
waves grow as Dora's name is mentioned. Lucilo allows himself to be enveloped by
the waves and he too disappears.

The complete absence of realistic details and the disappearance of Dora, perhaps
a Dominican ancestor of that Remedios la bella of García Márquez's fame, force us
to look for another explanation or the subtext of the story. If Dora's health is in a precarious state, and at one level the text appears to suggest it (the mother's vigil, Lucilo's flowers to María, Dora's sister, the other virgin?) then the story can be read as
another case of young love destroyed by illness and lovers separated by death à la
María of Jorge Issacs fame. Nevertheless, the separation is only temporary because in
the wave, another rebirth of spring, the young lovers are reunited in a new territory
chosen by the woman, in a permanent manner and without the limitations imposed
by morality.

Perhaps in this interpretation we could find Weber's interest in Eastern philosophy. Another possible reading, and that is what is being proposed here, is that the woman who wants to be the mother (author) of her own existence must choose flight, a getaway, or suicide, rather than remain locked in, controlled by her mother, her biology, and her spouse.

In her essay "*Crítica feminista: apuntes sobre definiciones y problemas*," Gabriela Mora points to an interpretation of literature written by women which supports the interpretation of Weber's story offered here:

> The examination of the writings of women authors has brought us, as we might suppose, to the discovery of the repeated use of certain tropes and images that encapsulate poetically ideas central to the text. Thus, for example, we have found numerous repetitions of images expressing the concept of enclosure and escape . . . (Mora: 5-7)[17]

A reading of Delia Weber's works brings us necessarily to a reconsideration of the themes espoused by Acción Feminista Dominicana, to Mora's reflections on the characteristics of women's writings, and to the conclusion that Weber's texts require another approach, another reading, another interpretation. We also understand that despite public reconciliatory pronouncements, Weber's stories and plays betray her grave disappointment with the condition of women of her time.

9. Children in Haitian Popular Migration as Seen by Maryse Condé and Edwidge Danticat

Marie-José N'Zengo-Tayo

There is a popular saying in the Caribbean that "children must be seen but not heard." This saying seems even more true in Haitian migration and fiction. It is not until 1979 and the dramatic turn in Haitian boat people migration that the media became aware of the presence of "unaccompanied" children among the illegal migrants. That same year, examining Haitian popular migration in the Bahamas, Dawn Marshall stated:

> The profile is one of a man from the rural parts of the North West, a man because three out of every five migrants are men. He . . . is likely to be young, less than 30 years old; and he is illiterate.[1]

However, her study was to show that Haitian women were also migrating in the Bahamas, usually alone, leaving their family (husband and children) behind. Similarly, in 1981 Jean-Claude Charles, reporting on the Haitian boat people in Miami, indicated that children were a hidden part of the treatment of Haitian migrants.[2]

In the background of this paper, there is the assumption that fiction and other creative writing reflect in one way or another (apology or denial) the tensions and the preoccupations at work in the society. For quite a long time, popular migration (of sugarcane workers) had been used in Haitian literature as a form of protest and means of creating a political awareness among readers. In comparison, it can be said that the Haitian boat-people migration does not seem to have the same literary appeal. I have argued elsewhere that the reason for this "absence" can be found in the impossibility of transforming this reality into a meaningful metaphor. So far, very few Haitian writers have dealt with this topic (compared to that of sugar cane migration) in fiction.

Concerning the presence of children in the boat-people migration, it can be said that there is "invisibility" of these children. As stated by Jean-Claude Icart in his research on the Haitian illegal migrants in Miami (boat-people migrants), it is very difficult to obtain testimony:

> *notre rôle de témoins serait parsemé de silence et d'absence. De trop de silences, de trop d'absences. Plusieurs intéressés refuseraient simplement de deposer; d'autres ne pourraient pas être rejoints, ni même approchés: ministres du gou-*

vernement haïtien, financiers de Miami, trafiquants, etc. Il nous faudra donc inférer à partir des informations que nous aurons pu obtenir, essayer de reconstituer le puzzle à l'aide des éléments fragmentaires dont nous pourrons disposer.[3] [. . . our part as witnesses would be broken down by silence and absences. Too much silence, too many absences. Many of those concerned would simply refuse to testify; others could neither be found nor met: Ministers from the Haitian Government, Financiers in Miami, Traffickers, etc. We shall infer from information we were able to gather, to attempt to reconstitute the puzzle with the help of fragmented pieces we will obtain.][3]

Before Icart, Jean-Claude Charles (1981) had stressed his difficulties in trying to access information on Haitian children who had illegally migrated to the United States. On the other hand, there is no tradition of childhood novels in Haitian literature as there is for the rest of the Caribbean (i.e., English-speaking Caribbean, French Overseas Departments in the Americas). Interestingly enough, for quite a long time stories of childhood were written mostly by female writers. It is only recently (in the 1980s) that male writers have started to write about their own childhood (Laferrière) or organized fictions with a child protagonist (Ollivier's *Mère Solitude*, Trouillot's *Les Fous de Saint-Antoine*). Female writers had done so a long time ago (Marie Chauvet's *Fille d'Haïti*, Colimon's *Fils de misère*).

This paper seeks to examine two stories written by female writers, one Guadeloupean, one Haitian, about Haitian children's experience of migration. It must be said that the texts do not have the same literary value. The first one, *Haiti Chérie*, by Maryse Condé, is a novella for children. Its brevity does not allow for a full comparison with Danticat's *Breath, Eyes, Memory*. My interest, however, focuses on the writer's use of children as a mouthpiece for Haitian popular migration. I will devote more space to Danticat's novel, and eventually I will make a brief mention of Danticat's short story "On the Floor of the Sea."

In the case of Condé's story, the targeted audience and the rules of the genre make it hard to assess fairly and fully. Though Condé's narrative techniques can be recognized, there are many "lapses" in the text. Time contraction and "skips" significantly alter the credibility of the story. However, this weakness of the narration is what gives strength to the author's "message" in this novella. *Haiti Chérie* traces the plight of a young peasant girl sent to the capital city as "*restavek*" (a servant child) because her parents cannot provide anymore for their family. The life of the family and its neighbors is marred with forced migration toward the cities and the Dominican Republic. The protagonist's brother has left for the Dominican Republic and nobody has heard of him since then. At a quick pace the adventures of the young protagonist Rose-Aimée unfold until she is faced with the alternatives of being arrested or leaving the country.

Haiti Chérie examines, through the experience of a young girl, the push-pull factors at work in Haitian popular migration.[4] Condé rewrites the themes of children's abandonment and "fugue" (the runaway kid), so popular in children's literature since the second half of the nineteenth century. However, in *Haiti Chérie* Rose-Aimée is forced to leave her family by circumstances beyond her control and starts what could be termed *une descente aux enfers* (a fall in the abyss), since she experiences one blow after the other. Condé examines the various aspects of children's exploitation—from households to business places—and demonstrates how children end in the streets of large and inhumane third-world cities.

In contrast with the cruelty of adults, she portrays solidarity among children. Interestingly enough, when Rose-Aimée loses her money, there is no hint that the money might have been stolen by one of the children with whom she was playing on the beach. On the contrary, all of them feel sorry for her and try to help her to search for it. When they have to accept the fact that the money is lost, they arrange for her to have a free ride back to Port-au-Prince:

> *La bande accompagna Rose-Aimée au tap-tap expliquant au chauffeur ce qui venait de se passer. Le chauffeur, bon bougre, accepta cette petite passagère qui ne pouvait le payer et la coinça entre un ballot de panders et une padre de pores braillards.*[5] [The group accompanied Rose-Aimée to the bus and explained to the driver what had happened. The driver was a good chap; he accepted this young passenger who could not pay her passage. Thereafter Rose-Aimée was stuck between a cast of baskets and a pair of grunting pigs.][5]

Similarly, when Rose-Aimée hears another street person crying in the night, she feels sympathy and tries to comfort her.

> *quelqu'un vint s'allonger contre elle. Et bientôt s'éleva la musique des sanglots. Emue par ce chagrin égal au sien, Rose-Aimée se redressa sur un coude.*
>
> *Ecoute, ce n'est pas la peine de pleurer ainsi. Est-ce que demain n'est pas un autre jour?*
>
> *Les sanglots redoublèrent et Rose-Aimée, étendant une main protectrice, toucha l'épaule de sa voisine, la forçant à se tourner vers elle.*
>
> [. . . someone came and lay down at her side. A little while later, sobs raised whining in the air. Moved by this sorrow similar to hers, Rose-Aimée sat up on her elbow.
>
> Listen, there is no reason to cry so much. Isn't there a saying that tomorrow is another day?
>
> As the sobs increased, Rose-Aimée stretched a protective hand to touch her neighbor's shoulder, forcing the latter to turn around toward her.][6]

Migration is presented as the last resort after everything has gone wrong. From the plush bourgeois household where she is treated as a slave to the streets with the homeless, Rose-Aimée discovers how ordinary people are deprived of their fundamental rights.

Rose-Aimée savait déjà que son pays était un des plus pauvres de la terre. Cependant, elle ne se doutait pas que fant d'hommes et fant de femmes n'y possédaient pas ce bien auquel tout homme devrait avoir droit: un toit' au-dessus de sa tête. [Rose-Aimée knew already that her country was among the poorest of the world. However, she never thought that so many men and women did not own what everyone should be entitled to—a roof above one's head.][7]

Haiti Chérie allows for a questioning of factors leading to migration. The protagonist considers migration as a forced expatriation whose causes should be found in the world's economic inequalities.

Pourquoi? Pourquoi des peoples sont-ils riches, et d'autres si pauvres qu'ils doivent alter chercher hors de leur pays natal des moyens de subsister? Rose-Aimée eut beau tourner cette question dans sa tête, elle ne lui trouva pas de réponse. [Why? Why are some populations so wealthy and others so poor that they have to seek their means for living outside their native land? Rose-Aimée thought over and over about this issue but she couldn't find an answer.][8]

Migration is presented as the only way to escape ill-treatment, exploitation, abuse in the home country. This perspective is reinforced by the image of the United States as a land of opportunity. According to Lisa, Rose-Aimée's companion in Port-au-Prince,

Aux USA, pas question d'âge. On peut travailler dès que l'on peut se tenir debout. On peut cirer les chaussures, manoeuvrer les ascenseurs, laver les voitures, porter les paquets à la sortie des supermarchés et tout cela procure ces billets verts qui ouvrent la porte du bonheur. Les dollars! [In the U.S.A., age is not a problem. One can work as early as he or she knows how to walk. One can work as a bootblack, an elevator-boy, a car-washer, a delivery-boy carrying packs for customers coming out from supermarkets. All these jobs bring these green bucks that open the path toward happiness. Dollars!][9]

Condé's story recalls the myth of America as the promised land and signals Haitian misconceptions concerning this country. It also evokes the dream of the migrant who wants to help his or her family with his or her remittances. The protagonists imagine that reaching the United States will bring an end to their plight. They choose to ignore negative information about this country: they either dismiss those who warned them or keep secret information they have about the risk of the journey.

In *Haiti Chérie,* Condé uses the child protagonist as a mouthpiece to question injustice in the world economy, social abuse, and economic exploitation. As the young protagonist "discovers the ways of the world," she is struck by its "mis/dis-functionment" and exposes it.

Danticat presents another aspect of children's experience of migration. In her first novel, *Breath, Eyes, Memory*, she addresses issues of estrangement, adaptation, and social promotion, among other issues related to migration. Danticat's novel is a very complex one and this paper examines only one aspect of it (and only one section of the book). One of the most interesting issues in this novel is the impact of migration on the mother-daughter relationship.

The narrator/protagonist, Sophie, is left in the custody of her Aunt Atie while her mother migrates to the United States. She is torn between her love for the aunt that she considers a true mother to her and the desire to know her mother. This ambivalence toward the absent mother is expressed through a dream:

> I only knew my mother from the picture on the night table by Tante Atie's pillow. I sometimes saw my mother in my dreams. She would chase me through a field of wildflowers as tall as the sky. When she caught me, she would try to squeeze me into the small frame so I could be in the picture with her. I would scream and scream until my voice gave out, then Tante Atie would come and save me from her grasp.[10]

In addition, at Mother's Day, the protagonist Sophie makes a card for her aunt: when the latter decides that the card should go to its true owner, Sophie destroys the flower (a daffodil) that adorns it, amputating the card's love message. In this reaction we can see a silent protest against what is understood as abandonment by the young child. Though Sophie would like to love her mother, she cannot relate to the blurred image she has of her. The first encounter will be disappointing as the mother does not resemble the image Sophie had of her.

> She did not look like the picture Tante Atie had on her night table. Her face was long and hollow. Her hair had a blunt cut and she had long spindly legs. She had dark circles under her eyes and, as she smiled, lines of wrinkles tightened her expression. Her fingers were scarred and sunburned. It was as though she had never stopped working in the cane fields after all.[11]

However, the sacrifice of the mother is for the sake of offering a better opportunity to her child. Migration offers the means to expand the "limits" that bring to a stop the mother and aunt's dreams of intellectual promotion (to study, to become doctors, engineers):

> You have a chance to become the kind of woman Atie and I have always wanted to be. If you make something of yourself in life, we will all succeed. You can raise our heads.[12]

The attraction of the United States is constantly justified by the "opportunities" it offers to people. Migrating is presented as a rite de passage. The day following

Sophie's arrival in the United States, she has the feeling of growing older:

> I looked at my red eyes in the mirror while splashing cold water over my
> face. New eyes seemed to be looking back at me. A new face altogether.
> Someone who had aged in one day, as though she had been through a time
> machine, rather than an airplane.[13]

Migration represents a challenge thrown at the child in terms of adaptation. As she
prepares for the start of the school year, the young protagonist learns about the first
hurdles that she will have to overcome:

> My mother said it was important that I learn English quickly. Otherwise,
> the American students would make fun of me or, even worse, beat me.[14]

The narrator understands all prejudices Haitian children have to face in American
schools, including racial prejudice and rejection based on popular stereotypes. Adjustment to American society means confrontation with rejection.

> Outside of the school we were "the Frenchies," cringing in our mock-
> Catholic-school uniforms as the students from the public school across the
> street called us "boat people" and "stinking Haitians."[15]

The experience of migration is also the experience of learning another language.
Mastering the language to become "unnoticeable" is an important objective for the
young migrant. More than adult migrants, migrant children do not want to "stick
out" in their adopted country:

> After seven years in this country, I was tired of having people detect my ac-
> cent. I wanted to sound completely American, especially for him.[16]

Children coming from popular migration have to bear the "responsibility" of knowledge.

> My great responsibility was to study hard. I spent six years doing nothing
> but that. School, home, and prayer.[17]

Through the experience of Danticat's protagonist, we can recall most of the West
Indian attitude toward education in North America (e.g. Paule Marshall's *Brown
Girl, Brownstones*). Access to higher education is one of the main objectives parents
keep hammering in the head of their children. As Joseph (Sophie's old boyfriend)
brings it out of her, Sophie's plans for the future are dictated by her mother:

> "What would Sophie like to do?" he asked.

That was the problem. Sophie really wasn't sure. I had never really dared to dream on my own.[18]

The experience of migration increases the gap between parents and children in terms of culture clash (Haitian culture versus American culture; tradition versus modernity). Sophie's mother is able to identify the problem through male attitudes in life as she examines the characteristics of potential Haitian suitors for her daughter:

> "It is really hard for the new-generation girls," she began. "You will have to choose between the really old-fashioned Haitians and the new-generation Haitians. The old-fashioned ones are not exactly prize fruits. They make you cook plantains and rice and beans and never let you feed them lasagna. The problem with the new generation is that a lot of them have lost their sense of obligation to the family's honor. Rather than become doctors and engineers, they want to drive taxicabs to make quick cash."[19]

One advantage of migration concerning traditional values is that social promotion is more accepted even if people still think in terms of family clan. One of the positive elements of the American society appreciated by Haitian migrants of popular background is the possibility for upward social mobility and praise for those who raised from humble origins.

> She said that in Haiti if your mother was a coal seller and you became a doctor, people would still look down on you knowing where you came from. But in America, they like success stories. The worse off you were, the higher your praise.[20]

This possibility offered by the American society seems to be one of the most valuable to Haitian migrants and plays a major role as a "pull" factor in Haitian popular migration.

Migrant children are in a very difficult position since they are crossing cultures and borders. They invite redefinition of nationalism as they contribute to the emergence of new notions such as transnationalism, transculturalism, and multilinguism. Haitian children are straddling the cultures (see Carolle Charles's "Haitian Migrants in New York City" in Nina Glick Schiller, Linda Basch, and Cristina Blanc-Szanton's *Towards a Transnational Perspective on Migration,* 1992). This is illustrated in Danticat's novel when she describes the group therapy:

> There were three of us in my sexual phobia group . . . Buki, an Ethiopian college student, had her clitoris and her labia sewn up when she was a girl. Davina, a middle-aged Chicana, had been raped by her grandfather for ten years.[21]

In addition, the therapist, who is an African American, is a Santeria priestess who was initiated in the Dominican Republic. I find this interesting as Danticat seems to advocate for this miscegenation of cultures and moreover a blending of traditional cultures in the midst of American technological society.

[Children "are the reward of life," declares Sophie's mother. On becoming a mother, the protagonist will make sure that errors are not repeated with her daughter, even though by naming her after her grandmother, Brigitte Ifé, she indicates also that her American daughter will not reject her mother's heritage.]

Comparing Condé's and Danticat's visions of children in migration reveals the difference between internal and external response to Haitian popular migration. While Condé shows more interest in the "push factors," Danticat stresses the "pull" ones. Condé emphasizes the tragedy and suffering of the poor people. Danticat acknowledges the harsh conditions of the people but at the same time emphasizes their resilience and resistance. While Condé's Rose Aimée ends tragically, sinking in the abyss of the Caribbean Sea, Danticat's Sophie becomes the mother of an American girl who will assume the positive elements of Sophie's mother's culture.

10. *I'll Fly Away: Reflections on Life and the Death Penalty*

Marion Bethel

DeeDee really believed he could fly away. As he guided me through the Book of Esther, Revelations and various Psalms, DeeDee made me believe he could really fly. "I alright," he smiled. "I be free soon, soon. Jerusalem waitin for me," he said with no apparent anguish as he gently held the bars of his cell. Then we sang, "Like a bird from prison bars has flown, I'll fly away."

DeeDee's belief in his capacity to fly away was an extraordinary and moving experience for me. His story immediately connected me to the numerous slave narratives and spirituals which speak of captive peoples flying away at will. I gazed at DeeDee as he effortlessly summoned up the mystery and the magic of the capacity to fly away. I bowed my head as I envisioned our foreparents in the same circumstances and in the same spirit exerting this same power over the slave master and the overseers.

He was about five feet five and had tamarind brown skin. Inquisitive, unschooled, tea-brown eyes were set in a broad, boyish face. His smile was equally broad, revealing a "governors gate," distended top teeth and two missing front teeth at the bottom. Curled hairs sprinkled his upper chest. His large hands often drooped in prayer through the prison bars. DeeDee wanted to be a car mechanic. He loved to dance. He had been on the street since the age of ten and felt that it was only Jah that kept him safe from being killed or actually killing someone himself. He had owned four handguns including a .357 Magnum, and by his own admission was a terror on the streets. He said he needed to protect himself from bigger boys who would threaten and tease him. DeeDee said that he could never be certain that his gun was the one that killed Brian Ferguson. During the incident there had been a general shootout with other armed young men.

At the age of eighteen DeeDee was charged with murder. He became a Rastafarian a year later while on remand and practiced his faith initially with other inmates but without the dignity of dreadlocks. On death row for just under five years, he religiously read the King James Bible and actively rejected the religious platitudes of the prison chaplaincy. During this time he chanted and prayed without a community.

I met Dwayne McKinney for the first time on the evening of Monday, March 11, 1996, some thirty-seven hours prior to his first State appointment with death. He was communicative, alert, resigned to his destiny, and certain that he did not want any further legal action on his behalf. Above all, he was extremely peaceful. Dwayne smiled and thanked us graciously for coming anyway. He shared with us his absolute readiness to die. He conveyed an uncanny sense of well-being and a clear desire to be in Jerusalem on Wednesday morning. I sensed that a part of him was already absent.

In the days to follow, Dwayne's dignified composure, clarity, and deep faith took me to the extremities of my own terror, awe, dread, wonder, despair, and hope. I began to feel alive in ways I had not experienced before. I began to touch and name the emptiness and powerlessness I had been feeling since the issue of Dwayne's death warrant one week earlier. My eight-month-old commitment to move my writing to the center of my life and to deepen my spirituality gained a blazing momentum of its own. I felt intoxicated. I began to access my desire to experience and feel in this life the rapture of being fully alive and my desire finally to die with grace.

State officials and citizens, Goliath-like, were ready and poised to execute Dwayne McKinney and Thomas Reckley at 8:00 a.m. on Wednesday, March 13. There was a palpable excitement and anticipation throughout the community. The rough, shallow graves in the State-owned pauper's cemetery had been dug days in advance. This, however, was not Dwayne's appointed hour or time. The public had to be satisfied with the hanging of Thomas carried out within the privacy of the prison and witnessed only by State officials. DeeDee's victory in Jerusalem was postponed due to a last minute stay of execution.

During the following two weeks of his life, Dwayne shared with me and Glenys, his attorney, the roots and creation of his redemption song. We saw him for the last time on Wednesday, March 27, at 5:40 p.m. Glenys brought for him a large collage, made by her brother who is a Rastafarian, of a picture of Haile Selassie, Rastafarian emblems, scriptures, and Nyabhinghi festivities. She had secured a promise from the superintendent to allow Dwayne to have this collage in his cell throughout his final night. Ordinarily, the cell of a person about to go to the gallows is stripped naked.

During our last hour with Dwayne we sang, as we had done on other visits, "Redemption Song," "By the Rivers of Babylon," "Because He Lives," "I'll Fly Away." DeeDee sang by himself Rastafarian songs which we did not know. I was initially surprised that one of Dwayne's favorite songs was "Because He Lives." I remembered singing this hymn as a child on Easter Sunday. I, too, loved and identified with the suffering and joy undergirding this song. It took on a special meaning for me as Dwayne, Glenys, and I sang it together. "Because Jah Lives, I can face tomorrow," DeeDee belted out, "Because Jah lives all fear is gone, because I know Jah holds the future, and life is worth the living just because Jah lives." Throughout the two weeks with Dwayne I continuously experienced the ways in which we, the descendants of enslaved Africans in the Caribbean and the Americas combined, shaped, and creolized African and European religious beliefs and practices to accommodate our experience and reality.

At 8:00 a.m. on Thursday, March 28, DeeDee walked swiftly and bravely, I was told, the short distance between Babylon and Jerusalem. I was also informed by one of his fellow prisoners on death row that Dwayne had chanted through the entire night. Long before the clang of the gallows reverberated throughout the prison walls, long, long before the public heard the news, Dwayne had released his soul, crossed over, yes, flown away to Jerusalem. The vivid memory of Dwayne's deep faith, his lusty singing and tone-deafness, along with his unwavering courage, brought a welcome smile to Glenys's face days later. At the age of twenty-four Dwayne had answered for himself questions concerning life and death, questions to which I have barely given shape, unformulated questions. More often there are simply the question marks preceded by blank spaces. Dwayne's belief was that the Book of Revelations was coming to pass. He felt that some had to die in order that others may live. Even as I reflect on life and death issues as a consequence of just plain living and as a part of my writing craft, nothing, with one exception, has exercised my mind, engaged my emotions, tormented my soul so deeply and unashamedly as the hangings of Dwayne and Thomas.

The other experience where life and death issues had confounded and nearly trounced me concerned the second, third, and fourth months of both my pregnancies. On these occasions, I experienced an extreme twenty-four-hour nausea and severe vomiting and was extremely depressed. I nurtured thoughts of death, not suicidal notions as such but just wanting to die. I thought of terminating my pregnancies because there seemed to be no relief in my reach. Lying in a fetal position, I agonized over the meaning of life, my powerlessness, emptiness, loss of faith, my desire to die, my desire to live.

Both events, Dwayne's execution and my pregnancies, carried me back to the illusive and elusive security of the womb and childhood and brought into sharp focus an ever present drive to deepen my own spirituality. I am trying to understand more fully my community's response and my own to State executions and, in particular, Dwayne's hanging. I am increasingly aware that his death has renewed my desire to live this life fully, to locate and heal my own bruises, to live my freedom responsibly, to live my desires courageously, and to meet the challenges with a deep faith. Dwayne's dying has created for me a yielding, living, fertile space within which to rediscover, reinvent, and renew this gift of life. He also shared with me the real possibility of dying with dignity and grace even under extraordinary and oppressive circumstances. I feel blessed on this journey with life and death as ever present constants, with regeneration as an ever present possibility.

We are angry. We are very angry, hurt, frustrated and in pain, unnamed and unidentified. Our anguish takes on the faces of Thomas and Dwayne as we grope to identify, locate, and embalm the pain. These young men dared to play god, to appropriate for themselves the power of the god, and ironically dared to act on the human fear in their souls. There is no balm in the gallows, no quick fix to our problems. A brutally broken neck cannot be our highest response. A ravaged throat and a spilled, dead tongue can no longer help us to tell our story, give shape to our collective voice, sing the sad and hopeful songs of our vision. Dwayne's attempt to empower himself with a gun, to have the power of the god at his fingertips, to play out a young man's right of passage into manhood. How was that drive created?

We live in a community where young men use guns and their penises in the same manner and in the same breath—to overpower and destroy—in order to overcome and avoid the terror in their own lives. What are the creative and imaginative possibilities of manhood? Too many of our young men's eyes are ahistorical; their tied tongues, semiliterate; their hands, penises, destructive.

We have to name that anger, that wound, or it will forever have the face of Dwayne or Thomas or some other convicted person. Call it the shame of not knowing who we are, the fear of emptiness, the void; call it the pain of neglect and abandonment; call it the bruise of sexual abuse; call it cultural domination, economic powerlessness; call it self-hatred; call it slavery. Just name it in our own voices, affirm its existence, and the journey, the possibility of healing and renewal, is within our reach.

Our children will not forgive us for the quick fix of the gallows. They will despise our lack of creative possibilities; they will hate our legacy to them: a culture of destruction and death void of life-giving properties. What will they make of the gallows, the official State slaughterhouse? What will our youth feel about this display of State manhood? The naked, omnipotent, unexamined violence of the State is in some ways shockingly similar to Dwayne's posture on the street and in other ways dissimilar. This staged, orchestrated, and deliberate annihilation of youthful possibility! Must we remain within the master's paradigm, eliminating what we fear and hate, what we judge to be of no value, what we pretend not to understand, what we ourselves have created? The gallows cannot ease our anger and pain, cannot define the color and shape of our bruises, cannot illuminate our path to the healing waters.

We move with such ease between negotiations with Disney World, establishing a Stock Exchange, servicing the tourist trade, going to church and sending our youth to the gallows. Or do we? It all appears as one indistinguishable event, very easy, safe and comfortable. It is so much harder to face the void, the emptiness—the pain of the legacy of slavery, the loss of spirit, the impotence in the face of Euro-American domination. And so we try hard to manage the State efficiently for the safety and prosperity of the foreign investor.

As much as I would like to disassociate myself from the State's license to kill and claim no responsibility for this action, I cannot. In the same way and for the same reasons that I bear responsibility for the spiritual and cultural devastation of our community, I claim a part in bearing witness to and contributing to creative alternatives to a culture of destruction, despair, and hopelessness.

On the morning of March 13, Thomas Reckley was hanged, the first execution after a twelve-year moratorium. The crowd's palpable excitement outside the prison walls, our spontaneous cheering and apparent celebration of the execution of Reckley were interpreted as junkanoo and carnival behavior. What I witnessed, however, were the fragile emotions of a people, naked, exposed, vulnerable, releasing, trying to let go of an unidentified pain. Simultaneous with the cheering, there was the unmistakable and identifiable chorus of a grieving community as we broke into "It's Alright Now" and other redemption songs. This ambivalent feeling contained the communal awe and powerlessness in the face of the power and authority of the State; it revealed the deep-seated anxiety and frustration of a deeply wounded people unable to imagine life-giving solutions. A community confronting the terror of gun-toting youth was reaching for a sense of primal gratification as well as a divine answer to the hurt. What I experienced essentially was a people overtly crying out for retribution and at the same time unashamedly longing for spiritual sustenance in the wake of a fellow human being's death by hanging.

It is always painful to grapple with the reality that our community (evolving from a history of slavery) can so readily affirm both corporal and capital punishment with little reflection on the possibility of human redemption through living, healing, and faith. While I fully accept the moral agency and personal responsibility of the individual, I also affirm the responsibility of our community to develop and create institutions and facilitate ways of being that would heal instead of destroying further. Dwayne was hanged the week before Good Friday and Easter. I could not reconcile what appeared to me to be a contradiction for a self-professed Christian community.

On the eve of Dwayne's death I leaned against the bathroom wall and called on the god of my childhood to save him from the gallows, to spare our community and myself this piece of pain, destruction, and violence. I lay awake the whole night either in fetal position or stretched stiff in complete terror.

On the morning of Dwayne's execution, I joined with Glenys, her mother, and three young children, Madeleine, and a group of persons in protest outside of the prison. There was also a small crowd of onlookers present including Dwayne's mother. At 7:59 a.m. there was a spontaneous silence. I wept singing "Redemption Song" and "By the Rivers of Babylon" with Glenys, Madeleine, and other persons. "He's in Jerusalem," I said to Glenys. She nodded a pained smile.

We continued with our protest. Glenys, Madeleine, and I made several emotional statements to the news media. The parts which spoke of Dwayne's courage and deep faith were never aired or printed. Glenys took her children to school and returned home. Madeleine and I drove to the cemetery to witness Dwayne's burial. There we met a large crowd of people standing behind barricades in the presence of several armed policemen. At about 11:00 a.m. a small convoy of State officials and a hearse entered the cemetery. There was a lone wailer, unknown to me, who was inconsolable as Dwayne's coffin was lowered into the grave. Dwayne's burial was bare and undignified. The prison chaplain performed a brief ceremony.

I do not know the nature of death, post-life, or the life hereafter. I don't know the meaning, if any, of life itself. What I do know, however, is that during my sojourn with Dwayne I was being invited by him or through him to seek with urgency the experience of being fully alive, to feel the rapture of this life. This was Dwayne's gift to me. I also know I experienced with Dwayne his pure effort to redeem himself and to die with dignity and faith. He had looked beyond the crossover, that illusive and elusive bar between life and death, to life in Jerusalem. He had accepted the consequences of his actions on the street and had prepared himself to pay the State's price for the death of Brian. I also know that I saw him drawing on that sustaining reservoir of ancestral spirituality which runs deep in our popular culture. Dwayne had made peace with Jah. When he reached through the bars to smile peace and love to Glenys and me for the final time, I touched his wings.

The prison chaplain stumbled over his hollow, prerecorded voice and his robotic feet as he tried to keep pace with the whispered chant and rhythmic, strident bop of DeeDee. "Make the gallows redemptive, my Son! Jesus loves you; died for you. He lives; He forgives. You, too, will live!" DeeDee sustained his chant on this final walk in Babylon, his eyes focused on Jerusalem. Standing on the trapdoor, he turned to the prison chaplain and said, "I aint fer dat, Sir! Rastafari! Jah know I's a innocent man. Haile Selassie I, the living God. Freedom in Jerusalem. Jah forever!"

DeeDee could fly for true true.

11. *Of Popular Balladeers: Narrative, Gender, and Popular Culture*

Lourdes Vázquez

The camera enters an empty room. The walls and the floor have a soft color to the eye. There are some electrical outlets placed discreetly in the walls, where you can hook up the wiring, the telephone, and the appliances. In the center, a table with a writer as its only animal. With furious instincts she types on a computer, recreating family experiences. She writes.

When one refers to devoted love, I always think of my grandparents' living room in Villa Palmeras, Puerto Rico, full of women boleristas with enslaving bodies and shameless backs. They would go to that house to look for my uncle the good-looking singer, and to practice the tunes of boleros. Women who would control its rhythm in an intuitive way that was almost genetic.

Villa Palmeras was a neighborhood of teachers, nurses, cabinet makers, housewives, musicians, singers, and drunks. We lived close to Ismael Rivera and Cortijo, two famous salsa singers. I never went to Cortijo's performances, since our social territory was my grandfather's house, although we would hear him sing every Friday afternoon. From the backyard we could see Gilberto Monroig, our neighbor and magic bolerista, and his mother, who would go looking for him every time he disappeared; when we wanted to listen to Cortijo up close, we would climb up to the roof since the sky has better acoustics. My uncle had sung along with the birds ever since he was young, and sometimes he would sing duos with them. The birds would look at him surprised at having as an accompanist a singer who was so human. He would spend the day imitating Pérez, Cortijo's saxophonist with the shrieky voice, or he would climb up to the roof and sing a duet with Gilberto, a neighbor who would sing from his balcony. We girls would spend our time listening not only to that duo in outer space, but also to the seagulls that would gather on the electrical wires.

Up to now the memory is a rabid instrument, and when it fails in its narrative function all action comes to a stop and the act of writing ceases. The writer will have to get up from the machine, do a lithe exercise, look out the window and watch how the snow falls. The writer enjoys a moment of cold weather and listens from any part of this beloved New York, to Marc Anthony, singing a delightful salsa. She becomes absent from the present and remembers. The writer remembers that she also loves our music and on weekends she goes out to dance in the nightclubs of the great city. And she says great city because she understands that the principal city for Puerto Ricans is New York and not San Juan, as the official history says. In fact, listening to today's salseros, she remembers her uncle and starts to narrate this memory. The writer has been writing memories for seven years. What they told her, what she saw, what she heard, what she read. And she thinks that this text will close a cycle of memories. She sits down once again at the computer. The camera moves along with her figure. She gives thanks to the Pachamama, who has nothing to do with the Caribbean, but for all intents and purposes works in the same way, and she continues her narrative.

My uncle joined the army and once he finished his enlistment, he stopped in New York and started to sing with other musicians, singers, and composers. That's why my family says that my uncle left the army singing. In the city of New York the trios and quartets would organize and reorganize themselves, especially in the Puerto Rican neighborhoods. These small groups would sing with each other, would exchange songs, would argue and get angry, and would make amends and sing together once again. My uncle was part of this nucleus of Puerto Rican musicians and singers, who moved around the city. One day one of my aunts, who lived in New York, heard a recording on the radio that seemed like her brother's voice. She called the radio station and confirmed that, sure enough, it was her brother who had recorded a 45 record. Immediately she notified the family by letter.

The writer gets up from the table once again, the camera moves slowly. She walks around the large table and stops in front of the electrical outlets. CLOSE-UP. The camera knows exactly what this writer is thinking.

Through these walls there must be dozens of cables, telephone lines, wires, and insulation, and I am hooked up to them like the widow of a train conductor to its rails. That's why I can't stop writing. I go to the keyboard looking for a magic cure, looking for a hidden answer.

The writer returns to her computer and writes. The camera remains still.

Now my uncle was heard in Panama and on the rest of the coast, thanks to the endless number of sailors who stopped in New York, and meanwhile he worked as a dishwasher, barber, and cook, like all good Puerto Ricans. Once he worked in a funeral parlor and he started to collect the hooks on the flowers that they would leave on the tombs of the dead, filling up all of the closets in the funeral parlor. When they started to run out of them in the city, my uncle resold them at a higher price. Two or three years later he returned to Puerto Rico. From then on my grandparents' living room turned into a constant coming and going of musicians, composers, arrangers, singers, and above all the women, the bolero singers, singing to love, invoking the shadow of passion, accompanied by guitars and maracas, or accompanied by orchestras, in daring and intensely provocative dresses.

At that time couples would go out to dance on Saturdays at Te-Danzants or nightclubs. Sometimes my grandmother would give parties in the living room, and she would rent a juke box and they would dance the guaracha, the mambo, the son, the danzón, and above all the bolero. My uncle hooked up with the Montaner trio and later with Los Hispanos, and meanwhile he sang, in the shower, in his room, in the yard, and in the serenades that he gave throughout the neighborhood. My mother, a big fan of Libertad

Lamarque, worked as a clerk in the Miramar store in Old San Juan, and my grand-mother would take care of the grandchildren. After the afternoon siesta the procession of singers would begin. Listening to the singers, but above all to the women boleristas, I un-derstood that there is nothing that expresses all of our feelings like the singing of a good bolero with unbridled passion. My uncles' five sisters would stop doing the housework and would sit in the balcony to form the chorus. As an adult I was told by my aunts that from there my uncle continued his procession, singing at the house of Sylvia Rexach, the composer, while they stayed behind, washing and ironing the eleven thousand shirts that were consumed daily.

And why have I started to write memories? the writer asks herself. It's not just me, but all women in my country. I see examples of the youngest women writers, who go out on the streets in search of stories, and with their extraordinary judgment they take them and describe them exactly as they are. This may be our response to an auctioned national history written in remnants. It is our gender history. The writer does not believe in a dilettante myth of official writing, because women's writing in Puerto Rico is not written by one or two women, but rather by all of those women who write and who write about themselves in newspaper accounts and in dentist's offices with their Hola in their hand. It is taking one's memory and anointing it on popular culture like the makeup that we learn to use since we were little. It is to do the same thing as Basquiat—use painting to disintegrate the official image.

She sees her marvelous colleagues write, and she remembers Basquiat in the par-adigm of the ritual of reconstruction of officialdom, in order to enter in a ritual of recovery. She also remembers Matilde Basquiat—confined to an asylum for possess-ing the same knowledge as her son. It is impossible to return to the text without an explanation. The writer sees her daughter making up other faces in order to repaint her emotional structure, and she sees herself remembering, because memory is also entering into a familiar landscape that is no less painful. The writer cannot get her cigarette and inhale it, because she does not smoke, and never has smoked. The writer continues her narration.

At Christmas, my family's parties were a kind of live concert with piano and every-thing. They practiced a bunch of times and the rehearsals included not only professional singers organized by my uncle, but all of the neighborhood. Once people found out that we were organizing a parranda, they would join in the procession and sometimes there would be fifteen or twenty cars until sunrise and the kids would doze off in any corner. Then television arrived and they started to sing along with it. They sang on national hol-idays and the international tours were constant. They sang all over America and in front of Queen Elizabeth, and I wonder if the queen had the special sensibility to understand my uncle's falsetto voice. I have always thought that the experience of listening or danc-ing to a bolero is an intimate one, without intellectual, erudite, or scientific interference. It is just the message in the words and how we join this message to our own experience of love, loneliness, and gambling—everything, in the space of one or two minutes. This intuition is developed over time, and when my uncle sang in front of Queen Elizabeth, I thought that it was a wasted effort. I do not believe that Anglo-Saxons can understand the soul's intense passion in this melody.

The writer takes the risk, accepts the adventure of her own subjectivity expressing a language as frank and direct as the message in a telephone line between Tokyo
and New York. The writer has conflict with some critics, who, like government bu-
reaucrats, delineate different genres in order to understand what writing is about.
What does the writer want except to learn the business so that she can later write
about Las Vegas showgirls and how much they pay them to exhibit their boobs in
public. The writer asks. The writer interviews and constructs her own questionnaires
and compiles a new set of statistics. The writer writes. The camera follows her.

*As an adult I decided to interview the bolero singers who had passed through my
grandparents' living room, and I came to the conclusion that it was an impossible task.
The few times that I tried it, I ran up against a wall of Chanel No. 5, and then they would
invite me into a world of photo albums and interviews, or they would invite me to listen
to their recordings, or better still to listen to them live in an upcoming nightclub performance. I, in the meantime, try to describe my uncle's voice registering endless variations,
or making fun of the young boys and girls of our neighborhood because we preferred the
triple register of rock & roll. Like all good Puerto Ricans my uncle returned to New York
and again sang among the Latin community, and in small and large dance halls in the
city. Rock, soul, and soneros ran wild but the boleristas kept singing the traditional ca-
dence of the bolero.*

The writer proceeds to interview a bolerista. First telephone call.

"Doña Carmen, I would like to ask you some questions. I am the niece of Char-
lie the singer. I would like to interview a number of boleristas." *Immediate cutoff.*

"I am not interested in interviews. Have you seen me sing?"

"Well, yes, on television and in my grandparent's house, when I was little."

"You have to see a bolerista on stage. Come by the Caribe Hilton next Saturday
and see what it means to sing a bolero. You won't need an interview."

The telephone questionnaire ends and the writer is at a loss for words. The writer
heads to the Tropical salon of the Caribe Hilton Hotel in San Juan, Puerto Rico. The
bolerista sang in front of her, for her, knowing that she was everything in that powerful audience of realtors with their latest lovers. In order to construct an immense
glow, the writer packs her bags searching for refuge in a dark city, where anonymity
is the norm and where she can go by any streetcorner without running into anyone
she knows, no one who will smile at her, no one who will greet her or who even knows
her name. The writer finds herself on the brink of a new precipice. She writes from
the other side of the sea. She writes:

*I have been in New York for a while and each afternoon when I return home, I run
into an endless number of singers, jazz and concert artists, on every sidewalk, but most
of all in the arch of Times Square. Sometimes I run into a bolerista who strums the strings
of the guitar with a knowledge that affects me deeply. He is an old and fat man who sings
with a feeling based on experience. This bolerista's guitar clashes with the walls of that
tunnel, giving the impression that there are a thousand microphones, when in reality it
is only a bolerista who sings about unrequited love from any corner of the station. I have*

asked him about my uncle, and he says he remembers him. He says that the two of them worked as dishwashers in the same restaurant where a couple of boleristas, now old and sickly, still kept singing, until they were "suspended from work and pay" for singing so much in the kitchen; they went out singing in the streets of the neighborhood and they walked in a cold winter evening, waking the bums and old ladies who were already asleep, and who opened their windows to applaud or to hum the words of some bolero. They finished the evening in the house of some singer friends of theirs. Sunrise arrived between the singing and talking, and they found themselves unemployed once again. This bolerista has become my favorite singer. When I get off work, I hurry to listen to his performance in Times Square, totally free ladies and gentlemen, while he is surrounded by an endless number of caribeños who like me take the train every evening.

The memory ends here and the writer has decided that's enough of memories because the twenty-first century is almost upon us. Now she is more interested in the different components of popular culture and the monopolistic net of drug trafficking on a worldwide scale. She is now interested in following the streetwalkers in Cuba named Zuleidi and asking them how they determine their workday itinerary, and what it feels like to fornicate with some stranger whom you're not attracted to. The writer lies in wait for her son the rapper, who maintains a silence learned in jail. She spies on her daughter who already has three tattoos on her body, trying to find the answers for the future. The writer spies, observes, and jots down on pink paper, and then writes. Still yet the writer inquires about the homosexuals of this city who constantly transform popular taste, and thanks to the sadomasochistic style—s/m all Latins have to possess a leather jacket. The writer studies the feminists and their culture of difference, and the old republics, which is politically correct. The writer is interested in these significant moments, such as: "Shop Puerto Rico by telephone or mail." The writer gets rid of the reminder, but condemned to maintain the memory, she now has a virtual screen on which she writes, transcribes, and breathes the written word in a white-blue perspective, because completely white damages the eyesight. The writer finishes the sentence. She turns off the computer, but not before saving the work. She picks up her purse and goes out to the street. The camera follows her steps. New York and its snows . . .

12. Between the Milkman and the Fax Machine: Challenges to Women Writers in the Caribbean

SHEREZADA (CHIQUI) VICIOSO

(Translated by Daisy Cocco De Filippis)

My name is Chiqui—not Chico. Vicioso—not Viscoso. And I hang on to my name because I cannot understand the contours of this reality if I am not constantly reminded that we are at the end of the century.

I search in the generation of Spanish literary luminaries closer to the Dominican intelligentsia, its sorrows and questionings, in order to see if they match my own and I find Pro Baroja and his proposal for a Republic of Intellectuals and I discard it, not because it was used to promote a dictatorship of the "intelligent ones," but because I imagine it a rather boring dictatorship and boredom is, among contemporary ailments, one of my own.

Some of the items proposed in the Manifest of 1901 of the so-called "Regenerationalists" (or The Generation of Disaster) of 1898, in Spain, written by Pro Baroja, Azorín, and Ramiro De Maeztu, seem to have been drafted for the Dominican Republic of our days.

I pour a cup of coffee and serve myself a papaya salad and I prepare for this moment of transcendental reflection, when the phone rings and a voice requests that I connect the fax. . . . The first assault of modernity, for which, happily, I had prepared by investing part of my meager savings in a machine that has blown off of the map for poets the need to wait for the mailman.

I turn the fax on automatic and I return to my reading of the Regenerationalists, or regenerated, and of some of their principles, which could be used as content in the present Dominican electoral campaign in order for us to avoid taking ourselves so seriously:

1. One of the typical traits of our time is the fast digestion of ideals. There is, in the moral ambience of this period in which we are living, an energetic ferment of discomposition, be it dogmas, utopias, metaphysical formulas. All that is not based on positivism and exactness, albeit born healthy and strong, is digested by the ambience with unbelievable speed.

2. The Philosophers of our day, the most important ones, have tried to prove the relativity of absolute ideas.

3. We are witnessing the bankruptcy of dogmas; many of those that years ago appeared as beautiful utopias, today have been cracked, modified; they would accrue interests, they would serve to defend what has been created, but they lack the character of stability.

4. A wind of disquiet reigns in the world. Given the intellectual laxity of the country (it refers to Spain but it has its applications in its ex-colonies), given the national loss of a sense of morality, the most logical conclusion is to assume that the youth, following the steps of the majority of men of the previous generation, those fortunate ones will join political parties, and will live in the atmosphere of amorality of our public life; the failed ones will go on vituperating against country and governments from the forgotten corners of their offices or from the tables of a café.

The phone rings again. Yes? That I should please disconnect the fax so that I can receive a phone call? I run to disconnect the fax. . . .

"I regret to tell you that the university is not going to pay your hotel stay right away."

"Why is that?"

"Because that is the only way the State of Florida can protect itself against corruption."

"How is that? Does the University know that we are professional women writers (in saying this I take care to use my most severe of tones) and that in the past we have been invited by other institutions, some of them Ivy League schools! Those institutions paid us quite well and we did not even break a dish or a leaf in their property!"

"I am sorry. I really have nothing to do with this and if I charge your hotel to my credit card, I will not be reimbursed. Those are the laws of the State of Florida. But not to worry, we will refund your expenses by mail."

"How did you say we would be reimbursed?"

"By mail."

"Does the State of Florida realize that in this country mail tampering is not a federal crime?

"Does the State realize that in this city letters take more than six months to be delivered because our mailmen work on foot and do not visit streets where people don't write and they tend to accumulate the correspondence and to deliver it in large quantities twice a year?"

"You must be kidding."

"Kidding? This, my friend, is the Caribbean where a woman is trying to write, but I know, this has nothing to do with you."

I return to the Regenerationalists (by now sharing their pessimism):

5. Can one believe that the strength of all these useless people [they refer to the youth], without purpose, has nothing of value?

6. Can one believe it possible to love a country like that?

7. No, we ought not love a country for what it is, because it would continue to be thus eternally. But what it is ought not to move us not to love it. To love the country as it is would be horrible; not to love it the way it is would be horrendous. We need to love it ARBITRARILY, like (finally we women show up in these reflections) mothers love their children and like women love men. We must love it with a transcendental love.

Manifiesto Regeneracionista, Spain, 1901

The recipient of such capacity for transcendental love, which I imagine must also include the love for writing, or this craft so poorly appreciated, I begin to recover my spiritual strength when I receive another fax. This time it is sent by the travel agency.

"We need your credit card number in order to be able to make reservations in the hotel and to make sure you pay one day in advance, before your arrival."

Hell! Now, besides assuming we Caribbean female writers are North American, they are assigning us a class status. A credit card? Where can a woman writer today dig out, in these islands where college teaching is paid at a rate equivalent to four dollars an hour, five thousand dollars to deposit to get a credit card to charge dollars, without having to pay a high rate of monthly interest?

"Do the Cuban women have a credit card?"

"No, and they will not be able to come."

I return to pour myself another cup of coffee and to reaffirm my pledge of transcendental love for the craft of writing in order not to send the university and the State of Florida to hell, and I rush to write about the topic that has been assigned to me for my presentation, thinking that brilliant ideas are worthless if the women writers who are to get together don't understand the way we live and the conditions under which we labor, those of us trying to write in these lairs. Without a fax, without a credit card, without dollars, and generally without electricity. In Santo Domingo we experience fifteen to twenty hours black-outs, because the solar lighting system that can be purchased in Miami costs ten thousand dollars here, and the small converter we have is not capable of accumulating sufficient voltage to ensure us at least three hours of light to sit under to read or to write.

What is the challenge to the woman writer of today in islands such as ours? Some fundamental theorists such as Edouard Glissant have already posed the question in a much more lucid manner, and the poet Derek Walcott, awarded the Nobel Prize for Literature in 1992, has summarized this in three verses:

> I have Dutch, nigger and English in me,
> and either I'm nobody
> or I am a nation.
>   Derek Walcott, *The Schooner Flight: 1-Adios, Carenage*

And, if we were to think of ourselves as a nation, beyond the specific issues related to gender that frame us, which would be some of the essential challenges before us? Edouard Glissant has formulated eight propositions for reflection for writers of the Caribbean which I offer for discussion:

1. THE CONFLICT BETWEEN SIMILARITIES AND DIVERSITY
Cultural similarities or "sameness," in this context, means the encompassing cultural world which the West imposed on our fragmented diversity. The weight of this similarity tends to interrupt the efforts of the human spirit to transcend a "universal" humanism which tries to assimilate all our national peculiarities. And, I add, there would be nothing wrong in it if it were not for the fact that *definitions of that* UNIVERSAL HUMANISM WERE ALSO GIVEN TO US BY THE WEST. Which are our own definitions? To answer this question represents the first conceptual challenge for Caribbean women and men authors.

2. THE CONSTRUCTION OF DIVERSITY
A diversity that is not synonymous with sterility and chaos but is the creation of cross cultural relationships by individuals searching for an answer. Not by persons who are absorbed or swallowed by the predominant notion of culture, but by individuals who intend to create new relationships. Cultural similarity or "sameness" demands "imitators," "supervisors," and "disseminators." Diversity establishes BECOMING, OR TO ARRIVE AT BEING, as a fundamental principle. Is our creation a search for becoming or a search to succeed? To succeed as what?

3. TO CONFRONT CREATIVELY THE TRANSITION FROM THE WRITTEN TO THE ORAL
The written is understood here as the result of the universal influence or the "sameness" and the oral as the ORGANIZED MANIFESTATION OF DIVERSITY. It seems, Glissant says, that the written acquires, each time and with more frequency, the role of ARCHIVE, and it is reserved for the very few. How are we dealing with the challenge to FEED THE ORAL INTO THE WRITTEN TEXT? The dream of Mallarmé of the universe becoming a book falls to pieces before the creative fragmentation of the Caribbean.

4. THE CREATION OF A NATIONAL LITERATURE
I know that when I mention the word "national" (living in an island that is open and in a world practically without frontiers) some would think I do so in the old sense of ethnocentrism, chauvinism, or insular neurosis. To me, to make a national literature

is to create a space for the emergence of new voices and new people, precisely those individuals left out by cultural similarity or "sameness." It means expressing that which characterizes us, that is to say, a system of relationships, under the aegis of diversity, without falling into regionalism, or into folklorisms that reflect only what a culture has been or was.

5. TO UNDERSTAND THAT A NATIONAL LANGUAGE IS THE LANGUAGE PRODUCED BY THE PEOPLE OF A GIVEN CULTURE

This means understanding that a national literature emerges when a community "whose collective existence is threatened" tries to define the reasons for its existence. If cultural alienation has an impact on the structure of literary creativity, should not the writing or the literature that seeks to express national idiosyncracies be attached to the SEARCH FOR AN IDENTITY WHICH IS ALSO THE EXPRESSION OF THE DIVERSITY that frames us?

6. TO BEGIN TO DEFINE WHAT REALLY DEFINES US AND THE TECHNIQUES OR FORMS OF EXPRESSION WHICH OUGHT TO EXPRESS IT

I espouse the same questions as Glissant when he demands: Is the sonnet, with ends that both summarize and transcend the meaning of the poem, a form for the expression of orality, for the apparent synchrony of the songs of the black population? Is the novel, conceived as an individual act, "set aside from the poetics of the group," a means in societies where the community plays a central role in the artistic production of its inhabitants? What are the genres we could call our own? What is the feminine specification in that "own"?

7. THE CREATION OF A CROSS-CULTURAL POETICS AND OF A SENSE OF CARIBBEANISM

I also espouse the reasoning of Glissant and Derek Walcott when they affirm: Our place is the Caribbean, and although our first stubborn reaction against the generalized universality is to remain where we are, our intellectual challenge is to create and to define a notion of Caribbeanism. Caribbeanism is a dream that frees us from the unilateral alternatives of a nationalism impossible in such small islands as ours and at the same time introduces us to a cross cultural process that modifies a stricken nationalism without undermining it. What are we really, Glissant asks us, but a series of multiple relationships and interrelationships, an opening that paradoxically encompasses us and defines us? Is this "we" the same for men and women of the Caribbean?

8. TO EXPRESS IN A PARTICIPATORY MANNER THE DIALECTIC OF WHAT IS FROM WITHIN AND FROM WITHOUT

The expression of the dialectic between what is within and what is without, WITH THE PEOPLE AND FROM THE PEOPLE: their orality, their music, their painting, their sculpture, their dreams, their sorrows, is our greatest challenge and a topic of

much discussion in literary conferences today on the role of women and men writers in the contemporary Caribbean.

The other challenges and problems to the women writers of today, those related
to physical survival, social uncertainty such as "class," the difficulties in disseminating our work, the pros and cons of professionalization, the absence of a feminine and
feminist criticism of our work that would project in all its dimensions our writing,
are the same old problems that have had an impact on our lives since writing began,
and although fundamental they are equivalent (in their challenge to our craft) to
those related to the creation of a culture: a national culture that would mean the
LOVING integration, the transcendental love we women are supposed to embody,
of all of the voices we are today.

Part Three

Beryl A. Gilroy: World Griot

Overview

To date, Guyana-born writer Beryl A. Gilroy has to her credit seven fictional works, a volume of poetry, several children's books, and an autobiographical account of her experiences as the first female Black teacher in London. A writer, teacher, and clinical psychologist, Beryl A. Gilroy is the most prolific female writer of the Anglophone Caribbean. Her works have been translated into German, Danish, and French. She describes her writing as "fact-fiction," drawing a picture of contemporary reality through her characters. Gilroy explains:

> In my work I try to capture the essential differences between us and other people. I use emotion to unite people. I try to incorporate a feeling of the poetic into the language I use. It is not easy to express how much my interior life is defined in my writing. I am hypercritical of my work and perfectionist in my expectations, and yet I exist in all my worst characters, even in Token (from *Frangipani House*), who has learned the callousness of the acquisitive society.[1]

It is her insistence on rendering the experiences of the Caribbean, in Guyana and in London, that qualifies Gilroy for the title "World Griot." Her Guyana is as small as the village and as extensive as London. Wherever her characters go, they take with them parts of their home, for better or for worse. And the language they employ is the sign of their connectedness to the village.

Even within the village itself, language renders information on connectedness. In Gilroy's *Sunlight on Sweet Water* (1994), the narrator describes a chemist who sets up shop in her village:

> He had not bothered to learn our ways and started shouting to Orchro [the village crier] to stop the noise he was making and to move his "ugly self" from outside his shop. He behaved like a white overseer. He had never ever admitted to himself that he, too, was a black man, like all the other black men in our village. He used white-people words too. [2]

Like other Caribbean writers, Gilroy sees vitality as well as the potential for healthy resistance in the oral cultures of the Caribbean. Resistance is a healthy response to colonial domination as well as a preoccupation of the community griot. In her essay "The Oral Culture: Effects and Expression," she explains: "We British Guyanese were a simple people, able to laugh when someone wrote 'De cow jump over de fence with defeat before details,'" i.e.. an attempt to use words in ways that showed the futility of linguistic imperialism.[3] For the writer, Gilroy admits that the choice of Creole informs cultural traditions. Specifically, "[t]he oral tradition lays down its own scripts and it is this script that makes dialogue and characterization possible."[4] The creation then is a function of language, which is tied to culture.

Additionally, Gilroy is very interested in cross cultural psychology and the interior lives of the characters who people her fiction. As Richard Daveson observes:

> A country doesn't, of course, necessarily become independent by becoming Independent; and in the same way it is hard for the literature of an ex-colony to avoid being ex-colonial. The political past lives on, a factor in the intellectual present. The writer is very likely an exile, in Europe or America—at any rate, an advance guard of decolonization, an outsider looking in. And yet the past has receded all the same, and the writer, besides looking in, may also turn out to be looking back. Separation, if it isn't turned to artistic account, can breed both nostalgia and distress.[5]

Yet Gilroy manages to escape the impulses of both nostalgia and distress as writer because she has never undergone the process of complete separation in spite of her long sojourn in England. The key to her success rests with her function as educator. The best educators are psychologists, surrogate parents, entertainers, and disciplinarians rolled into one. Gilroy confesses that

> Caribbean writers in Britain have to deal, when writing about the Caribbean, with a retrospective and increasingly unrepresentative view of the reality of the place they call home. My view of Guyana, British Guiana, had been set in the precolonial era, which in my opinion was a less punishing time. To justify this remark, I would say that there was a model of education which, though unsuitable, was established in all schools. Priorities did, in my time, include a concern for young children. As the years passed, my awareness of the issues became located in the new environment, Britain. How could we, I wondered, demand the inclusion of a Caribbean sonnet in the literary music that was being nationally orchestrated? We were expected to write certain books; hence, *Drum* of the fifties, *To Sir, With Love*—a benign book of patiently endured racism, *Journey to an Illusion*.[6]

As educator, Gilroy was privy to the generations of Caribbean immigrants who descended on London beginning in the 1950s, and she continues to witness the reality of the "new British" subjects of today.

Her life as an inhabitant of a small village and as a citizen of London is tied intricately into the stories she tells. As such she becomes like the women of her works who guard and recite information about the village, the community griot.

In July 1995, the Vice-Chancellor and Chief Executive of the University of North London wrote to Dr. Beryl Gilroy to invite her to accept an honorary doctorate degree. He explained:

The award is offered in recognition of the major contribution you have made to education, and in particular, the way in which that work fully reflects this University's ethos and mission. We would be honored if you were to accept the award.

Additionally, Gilroy has received the Inner London Ethnic Minorities Prize (1983), the GLC Black Literature Competition Prize (1985) for *Frangipani House,* and the Guyana Historical Fiction Prize (1992) for *Stedman and Joanna: A Love in Bondage,* among numerous other awards. The honorary doctorate, like the myriad other honors she has received over the years, is a testament to the life of an amazing woman who in her writings and daily work posits education as central to her existence. A keen observer, Gilroy explains," I write that whatever the conditions of my life, my spirit would lead me on in my desire to converse with others. When I write I say that I have never for one single moment of my life seen myself as a victim. I express my identity in the craft of writing."[7]

Beryl Alnwich was born in a small village in British Guiana in the West Indies in 1924. She and some thirty cousins were raised by her grandmother. She did not attend school on a regular basis until the age of twelve. Beryl resisted formal education with a vengeance, rejecting the regimentation of it all. Her aunt, who was a teacher, was thus compelled to teach her at home. Yet Beryl loved to read and write. She was forever making up stories for her younger cousins. At the age of five, she won a creative writing competition and received a much valued prize—a genuine silver sixpence.

She earned her first class teachers diploma in Guyana in 1945 and an advanced diploma in child development psychology in 1954. She later earned a Froebel trainer's diploma and a diploma for English as a second language from the University of London. She earned her academic diploma from the University of London in 1958. She earned a diploma in food science in 1959. In 1980, she earned an M.A. in Education with distinction from Sussex University. And in 1987, she completed a Ph.D. in counseling psychology from Century University.

Her occupations have been numerous and varied—class teacher, head teacher, educational counselor, parent development specialist, and lecturer. From 1946 to 1951, she worked as a lecturer at a training college for UNICEF. In 1953, Dr. Gilroy made history by becoming the first Black female teacher in England.

At present Dr. Gilroy is a clinical psychologist who counsels women under stress and children with behavioral problems. She continues to write and is currently working on a book about Black women in history. Education (the reader's as well as her own) is for Dr. Gilroy a lifelong endeavor.

Her writing career engenders a symbiotic relationship with her educational career. She has to her credit a number of educational and children's books, including *Carnival of Dreams* (1970) and *Nippers and Little Nippers* (1970). In 1976, she published the autobiographical work *Black Teacher,* which chronicles her experiences as Britain's first Black, female teacher. *Black Teacher* was republished in 1995 to wide acclaim. A collection of short stories, *In for a Penny,* was published in 1980, and her much celebrated *Frangipani House* was published in 1986. This novel was followed by *Boy-Sandwich* in 1989 and *Steadman and Joanna* in 1992. She published her first volume of poetry, *Echoes and Voices,* in 1990. Gilroy also published *Sunlight on Sweet Water* in 1992.

In 1996, concurrently with the 1996 International Conference of Caribbean Women Writers and Scholars, Peepal Tree Press published three new titles by Gilroy. These novels, *In Praise of Love and Children* (written in 1959), *Inkle and Yarico* (written in 1985), and *Gather the Faces* (written in 1995), form a tribute to memory. The rural women of Gilroy's Guyanese village tell stories that are

> fables, full of proverbs about how to deal with life, but they [are] also the means whereby the women [act] out their personal feelings through tone of voice and gesture. I . . . put my deepest concerns down on paper.[8]

The narrator's authority to commit to paper, like Gilroy's efforts in the three works, is informed by the experiences of storytelling derived from such women as these. Not only does Gilroy solidify the literary tradition of Guyanese women, she offers a form for examination of times past with an eye to the realities of existence today. The effect is a celebration of memory as much as it is a celebration of storytelling.

Inkle and Yarico and *In Praise of Love and Children* posit tribalism in the form of chauvinism and classism as central to the challenges faced by Gilroy's Caribbean characters. *Gather the Faces* is a love story which suggests that not only can you go home again, but that you can also grow from the experience. Gilroy celebrates the historical and communal, illuminating cultural impulses. In sum the works suggest that the "tribe" can be as empowering as it can be restricting. Her themes are rich and diverse. Recurring themes include the threats of the class system, the beauty of the village, the sisterhood of women, racism, and power relationships. According to Gilroy:

> My main interest is cross-cultural psychology. I want to explore the fantasies and dreams of women who change cultures. I am also interested in the perceptions of old age in different cultures, and I am keen to observe— through art and bibliotherapy—the behavior of old people who are living in a chosen culture.[9]

Excluding the publications written for children and young adult readers, Gilroy's works might be grouped according to the following scheme: works on education: *Black Teacher* (1976) and *In Praise of Love and Children* (1996); works on the exile experience: *Boy-Sandwich* (1989) and *Gather the Faces* (1996); works on the village: *Frangipani House* (1986) and *Sunlight on Sweet Water* (1994); works on historical personages: *Stedman and Joanna* (1991) and *Inkle and Yarico* (1996).

Gilroy began writing children's books to encourage her students to read because, she says, "[t]he school readers bore no relationship to their lives," and subsequent talks with children suffering post-World War Two trauma allowed her to enter "the lives of the children; in time our homemade books, which reflected their experiences, became therapeutic and meaningful to them."[10] Ever the psychologist, she notes: "The social familiarity of the texts released a desire to read. Cultures must be made explicit." Making culture explicit is Gilroy's lifelong writing project. Her works are entertaining, educational, deeply reflective; and above all, they celebrate culture in its myriad forms. Like the village griot's, her works are a tribute to the history of the community/village. That tribute celebrates the characters who remain inside the village in the Caribbean as well as those who venture out to the metropolitan areas. The experiences she records are expansive, important, and, above all, they ring true to the ears. According to Gilroy, "A writer's work is cast in time. No writer can cover all contingencies and all the nuances of culture and awareness that develop over time."

In her essay "*Frangipani House:* Beryl Gilroy's Praise Song for Grandmothers," included in this section, Australia Tarver reveals the heroic tradition of Mama King, the protagonist who does not acquiesce to abandonment. Tarver places *Frangipani House* within the tradition of the African praise-song, elevating the central character of Mama King to the level of the heroic. Such a comparison situates Gilroy within a tradition of Diaspora writers who select from an arsenal of creative forms to render their messages. Tarver explains: "Gilroy is the bard or singer who brings her characters to life by connecting aging to personal triumph and by celebrating the power of the mind to heal despite age."

Joan Anim-Addo, Gilroy's biographer, contends in her essay "Anguish and the Absurd: 'Key Moments,' Recreated Lives in the Narrative Works of Beryl Gilroy and the Emergence of New Figures of Black Womanhood," that Gilroy portrays women from the perspectives of authorial intent, historical context, and intertextual relationships. Anim-Addo asserts that Gilroy's fictional women "assume the circumscribed roles available to them as Black women" while resisting stereotypical roles. Anim-Addo explores the relationship between the array of Gilroy's Black female characters and the part they play in the author's individual struggle for cultural production. Together, Tarver and Anim-Addo speak to Gilroy's construction of figures of new womanhood—accounting for places of residence, external influences, and internal conflicts.

The final essay in this section contains the reflections of the "World Griot" herself. Gilroy analyzes her position as a woman and writer within two cultural perspectives: the island nation of her birth, Guyana, and her adopted "homeland," Great Britain. Gilroy begins the essay with questions received from young people who read her works, mainly, "Why did you write it?" The piece ultimately takes the reader on a journey through Gilroy's life and life's work.

13. Frangipani House: *Beryl Gilroy's Praise Song for Grandmothers*

Australia Tarver

Although Beryl Gilroy does not suggest it, her grandmother, who lived to be almost one hundred years old, could perhaps be a prototype for Mama King, the central character in *Frangipani House*. This grandmother, Gilroy has explained, was the savior of Gilroy's childhood, the inspirer of her youth, and the long-distance voice exhorting her against a poverty of spirit as she struggled to situate herself in England.[1] One could infer from the heroic portrait of her grandmother that the spiritual seeds for Gilroy's use of the praise-song technique in *Frangipani House* occurred long before she created it. Mama King is celebrated like the heroes in such African, male-centered songs as those of Sundiata, the powerful hero of Mali, or like the praise poem of Mnkabayi, the aunt of Shaka, the Zulu warrior.[2] There is a similar parallel to some types of praise orature in Gilroy's effort to account for Mama King's past history. Also, Gilroy's identification with Mama King can be viewed as what Isadore Okpewho describes as the praise singer's use of "authorial empathy."[3]

The heroic in *Frangipani House* is measured by the forces which operate against Mama King from the beginning. Frangipani House, named for the trees surrounding it, is a waiting station before burial for Black elderly women. Mama King's consignment to this house reflects the changing value system of a class of Americanized West Indians who leave elderly family members to fend for themselves or who believe that leaving the elderly in expensive homes is a substitute for love. These depersonalized homes are West Indian Bantustans where the soul is left without spiritual vegetation. Folk in the community view the house as fearful and distant: "Over-yonder—Frangipani House! People dies out dere! They pays plenty to die-out inside dere!"[4]

Dying inside is a major force against which Mama King must fight. External forces, such as the owner, Olga Trask, and some of the nurses, are not so powerful as annihilators as Mama King's own despair at being confined. At one point, Mama King refuses food, tears her clothes, and remains confined to her room, "[c]urled up like a foetus" (35). Her observation of the impact of sun and rain on small objects is a metaphor for her sense of helplessness. Looking from her window, Mama King observes a picture card, "waterlogged and disintegrating," pushed by the rain. She says, "That card like me. Going where rough water push it" (31).

Like the praise singer, Gilroy highlights Mama King's adversaries in order to further illustrate the conditions under which she strives for her own survival. Mama

King's first adversary is her own family, who have placed her in Frangipani House assuming that she would be attended to by whites, whom the daughters equate with competence and efficiency. In addition to two daughters, Mama King has reared five grandchildren. Faced with taking Mama King back to America or leaving her in Frangipani House, Token and Cyclette, the daughters, want her to remain. Although Cyclette admits that children and grandchildren "took [Mama King's] strength" (97), Token feels "sickened" by her mother's "low goals" and concludes that Mama King is "[w]orn out—worked for nothing" (98). To her family Mama King symbolizes a past they have discarded. She is the island they left; as one grandson puts it, "She was young and fine and strong. Now she's just a heap of old age. She is so poor. It's hard associating with poverty to this degree" (98).

To further compound the obstacles against Mama King, Olga Trask, the matron of Frangipani House, behaves as if she is acting as an agent on the family's behalf. She is Gilroy's "queen of the world of dependency and infirmity."[5] Matron, as she is called, is rewarded well for operating a home which incarcerates the elderly, causing their hopes and dreams to "disintegrat[e], leaving faint smudges" (2). Gilroy describes the Matron as a "honey-brown predator of a woman" whose part-European ancestry encouraged her "eager, seeking hands that would confiscate the copper pennies on the eyes of a corpse" (2). This image of her is suggested somewhat in Mama King's imaginings of a crow eating the eyes of her cat, Brownie. Under Matron's control, Mama King has no freedom over her personal self. Her teeth are taken and she is made to eat sausage without them. Matron gives Mama King drugs and does not mail her pleading letters to Token. Gilroy uses humor to reemphasize the Matron's misplaced values and her indifference to the group of women under her care. Matron treats her dog better than the women. Mama King accepts the dog's antics philosophically: "It can't help itself. None of us in here can help ourself. Poor Dog. You wouldn't like it if Matron own you. You will act stupid just like the dog" (23).

By compounding the negative forces against the hero, Gilroy prepares us, by implication, for the ability of Mama King to muster her will to challenge them. Mama King's name suggests empowerment and dominance. Gilroy demonstrates this power by assuming the voice of the praise singer at the height of celebration. Like Sundiata, who grows a leg where there once was none, Mama King, the narrator tells us, reconstitutes herself by making choices which did not seem apparent before. She had always been a risk taker and a hard worker. Frangipani House seemed to deny her the choice of hard work.

There are also religious allusions associated with Mama King's transcendence. Mama King chooses to escape the house on a Friday, rising from the prospects of having her corpse placed in what the Matron calls the "dead room" and also rising out of her own decomposing spirit. The language used to describe Mama King's rebirth reflects celebratory orature. After having walked away from Frangipani House concealed by a company of beggars, Mama King is described as "never more moved to contentment and happiness" (60). Her life with the beggars resurrects her, but when she is beaten by a group of market youth for money, she is taken to the hospital unconscious. Gilroy has described some of her writing as "prose poetry."[6] This description fits well with the epic quality of a praise singer portraying Mama King's suspension between life and death, two forces which want to possess her. In this passage Mama King is the object of contention, mother of twin forces and the sexual prize:

> Even as she lay suspended between being lost and the coming of her destiny, Mama saw Death and Life, both children of the same father, both legitimate. Death, dominant and conclusive. Life uncertain and accidental, friable as dry earth, malleable as clay, and finally fragile as gossamer in the hands of Death. . . .

> Death came close—blacker than black. Life's eyes explored her like a reluctant lover while Death reached out for her hand. . . . She retracted her hand like a turtle its head. . . . The shaft of light streaked across the bed, its phallic form touching all that was vital in her—magically reconstituting and reawakening her—making her whole again. (79)

Gilroy attributes Mama King's rebirth to her ability to recall her past and use it to sustain her in moments of distress and loneliness at Frangipani House. Gilroy shows her respect for Mama King by balancing her interior and exterior worlds. To the Matron and some of the nurses, Mama King appears mad, a condition they equate with the elderly. But Gilroy allows us into Mama King's private world. Retaliating against the Matron's judgment of her, Mama King shouts: "Since I come here I look, but all I see is what past and gone. You have now. Go and count you money. It got old people blood on it!" (16).

In these recollections Gilroy is able to explore the strengths and weaknesses in Mama King's character. Mama King's recollections alternate between desire and reality. We learn about her extraordinary strength in supporting a family. When Danny, her husband, disappears, Mama King takes any job she can manage physically, including breaking bricks and carrying heavy loads on her head. She struggles with children and grandchildren through their illnesses and death. When her children give Mama King grandchildren to rear, she regards the grandchildren as gifts, while her children see leaving them with her as being relieved of a burden. Taken for granted, Mama King exalts her husband in her dreams and blocks out the reality: that he was a wife beater, a drunk, and a womanizer. In Gilroy's hands, Mama King's memories are not mere babblings; they keep her sane and safe from the dehumanizing power of Frangipani House and they are a resourceful substitute for the physical action she is denied by not being able to work.

Isadore Okpewho's term "authorial empathy" mirrors what Gilroy does in identifying with the struggle and transcendence of Mama King. Okpewho defines authorial empathy as language which suggests that an African oral performer sees himself as part of the action of the performance he is giving. Of course, an oral performance is improvisory and a written text is fixed. However, it is the very consistency of the narrator's voice in this novel which emphasizes her devotion and allegiance to Mama King. As Lucy Wilson implies in "Aging and Ageism in *Praisesong for the Widow* and *Frangipani House*,"[7] Avey Johnson receives more respect from family members than does Mama King. But Gilroy does not waver in her appreciation of Mama King. Taken together, Gilroy's utterances comprise a singular praise poem. Mama King rears her grandson Markey with "commitment, courage and compassion" and a "hard-wearing spirit"; her strength is described as a "germ . . . lying deep inside her [taking] root and rapidly [growing] into a towering plant" (50) and, finally, the value of the elderly is unquestionable, for, like Mama King, "they like the backbone in the fish and the thickening in the soup" (50).

Gilroy's philosophy seems to reflect that of Zede, the grandmother in Alice Walker's *The Temple of My Familiar:* "we *are* our grandmothers."[8] In discussing her approach to writing, Gilroy explains that her attention to the old has to do with the struggle for identity or "the fear of being forgotten, of failing to resist the anguish of indifference, rejection and betrayal."[9] Gilroy presents Mama King as having overcome such failures. Gilroy is the bard or singer who brings her character to life by connecting aging to personal triumph and by celebrating the power of the mind to heal despite age. She invites the reader to extol Mama King's highest virtue, "the ability to choose" (53), when Mama King decides to remain on the island rather than go to America with her grandchild. Another tribute that is paid to Mama King is the intergenerational bonding she is able to complete by witnessing and helping in the birth of her great-grandchild. Gilroy's tribute to her own grandmother is similar to the one she makes to Mama King throughout the novel:

> Gentle as a breeze her love. Its power all enduring.
> It touched which ever spot was sore and instant was the curing.
> There dwelt in her a little child who always showed resilience,
> And understood that success came through hard work and persistence.
> Thoroughness was her delight, it made for sure survival,
> To act in anger was a blight that hindered joy's survival,
> Yes, soft and gentle was her love yet strong and heart-enriching
> As certain as a raindrop's touch and equally life-giving.[10]

14. *Anguish and the Absurd: "Key Moments," Recreated Lives, and the Emergence of New Figures of Black Womanhood in the Narrative Works of Beryl Gilroy*

Joan Anim-Addo

Beryl Gilroy's early narrative works, *Frangipani House* and *Boy-Sandwich* recreate, like many texts from the region, generational Caribbean figures as culture bearers.[1] Gilroy herself writes of culture as

> customs, artifacts, values and behaviors that identify a people, even if they have been contaminated with European values and cultural patterns through colonization, contact and economic domination.[2]

Mama King, the elderly protagonist in *Frangipani House*, recalls, at a moment when the oppressive conditions at Frangipani House, home for the elderly, forces her into a reassessment of her own life, the critically influential "values and behaviors" of her own parents. That assessment leaves her distinctly uncomfortable.

> Me mother dead with sod in her hair. Me father dead with rice grass underneath him. And me I sittin' till me bones get sore waitin. (*Frangipani House*, 54)

In the light of such comparison, Mama King finds her own inaction unacceptable and resolves to escape Frangipani House.

Gilroy's fictional women, such as the grandmothers, Mama King and Clara Grainger, and mothers, Lucinda and Janey, as well as the younger character Adijah, in *Boy-Sandwich*, who is interested in choices other than motherhood, assume the circumscribed roles available to them as Black women. Yet, so many of Gilroy's characters resist stereotypical roles as Victim, Strong Black Woman, Bitch, or other variants familiar to readers of Black women's literature.[3] It is the relationship between the array of Gilroy's Black women characters and the part they play in the writer's individual struggle for cultural production that is interrogated here, revealing, at the same time, characters portrayed between anguish and comic irony, who resist easy interpretation.

The reading of Beryl Gilroy's fiction offered here is, unlike poststructural readings, positively interested in authorial intent, historical context, and intertextual relationships.[4] Such a reading does not deny the significance of uncovering a plurality of possible (even competing) meanings.[5] Rather, the objectives are first, to play, in the Barthian sense, with meanings suggested by the author, and second to foreground the Caribbean woman writer's project through an exploration of Beryl Gilroy's.[6] Significantly, a twofold pleasure derives from the production of meanings in this instance and relates directly to the writing of the text. First, the recency of the phenomenon of African Caribbean women's publication of fiction and the growing diversity of this field of literature contribute to my pleasure as a Black woman critic engaged in the making of meaning. Second, and as significant, is the relative rarity of having meanings suggested by African Caribbean (women) authors, who also interpret their work. Further, it may be argued that such meanings are "more or less hidden" as a result of the politics of publishing, which ascribes to the literature and its author-interpreters a multiply-marginalized position.[7] In addition, credence may be given to the authenticity of Beryl Gilroy's meanings in view of her professional expertise at the center of which, as a practicing ethnopsychologist, is a trained understanding of human motivation and situations which her nonfiction writing indicates is consciously applied to the characters she creates and their situations. Gilroy states the following about her intention as author:

> Following the search for identity, however false or fragile, allows me as an author to explore the key themes of existentialism and to build characters around them.[8]

The concepts referred to, "*identity*" and "*existentialism*," offer a frame of reference central to the present discussion. Black women critics and interpreters constantly have a struggle which, to borrow from Gay Wilentz, concerns the need to "use literary criticism which is neither racist, patriarchal, nor Eurocentric."[9] I am interested to add to the critical debate by placing an African Caribbean woman writer's intention at the center of a critical reading.

Beryl Gilroy's lead directs critical search toward two overriding concerns already indicated: identity and existentialism. I explore the latter mainly through "key moments" in the lives of selected women characters, moments which reveal the anguish of specific characters and, at times, the absurdity of their situations. The former concern, identity, is discussed specifically in relation to Black, that is, African Caribbean womanhood, itself a problematic of identity.

Mama King, in *Frangipani House*, for example, "independent and determined" (3) to the last, insists on her identity as a mother and asserts, "I am Mama King. Mama mean mother" (4). Accordingly, she demands that Matron acknowledge the significance of her maternal identity, a sign, within the culture, of a woman deserving respect. Yet, Mama King's experience as wife and mother, effectively a single mother, has been both exacting and, at times, painful. Mama King's survival and that of her family has depended upon her resourcefulness, the goodwill of others in her community, and her willingness to undertake a host of menial jobs: "I use to do plenty work—bake, wash, sell, scrub, domestic work" (11). However, despite the circumstances of her life, material poverty, abandonment, and single motherhood—Mama King does not fully conform to the stereotype of Black woman as Victim. She does not "surrender," but rather remains, overall, "her own woman" (71).

How does the writer achieve this? I suggest that part of the wider vision which Gilroy's particular writing project inscribes is an awareness of a distinctive spectrum of women characters who demand articulation. Contemplating the project, Gilroy states:

> Creativity, like history, like moments of existence, like everyday experiences, differs according to what we strive to retrieve from the chasms of experience to record with passion and integrity.[10]

The trope of "retrieval" may similarly account for characters such as Janey in the later publication, *Boy-Sandwich*,[11] a text which further strives to extend the range of women characters retrieved. For example, there is the minor character, "capable and ambitious" (35) Janey Grainger, Tyrone's mother, whose source of pain and anguish is, like Mama King's, her husband. Possibly an enigma to contemporary readers, Janey pursues her academic independence and succeeds in gaining the degree for which she studies, but remains to the end in a marriage with an unfaithful husband whose mother, Clara Grainger, colludes with his infidelity. Beryl Gilroy explains:

> As women writers we attempt to show whether we are empowered or not by expectations, chicanery or deceptions which lurk within the parameters of group, tribe, function or nation only to forestall our self-liberation and autarchy—or political coming of age.[12]

It is in *Boy-Sandwich* that Adijah is framed, and one of the earliest new figures of Black womanhood emerge in Beryl Gilroy's writing. Adijah's character, described as "warm and soft and rational" (92), is pivotal to the discussion. Ironically, the description is that given by Tyrone, Adijah's lover and the central narrator, who is himself doubly voiced, ultimately by Gilroy, the female author. Adijah's portrayal is interesting not only for having been constructed through female-male, author-narrator prisms. Adijah is also a positive young Black woman figure whose choices are not limited to gender roles, and consequently she appears set to realize the goals of her choice.

Tyrone the Man, the latter-half-cum-sequel to *Boy-Sandwich*, remains as yet unpublished. The manuscript reveals several Black women characters who, like Adijah, may be described as new figures of Black womanhood. What is new about such characters? Principally, they are women of real choices whose lives are not inextricably linked to material poverty or negation. They are essentially articulate women, accepted as equal to their menfolk and equally able to assert, "It's how you feel about love and life that either destroys or elevates" (92). Or, "Shut bloody up!" (116). As yet, such Black women figures remain largely absent from the literature, not because they are absent from the vision of Black women writers but because the prevailing ideologies of literary production exclude them from the definitions of "Black women."

So, given the conditions of cultural production restricting publication of Black women writers generally and Caribbean women writers specifically, what are the mechanics employed by Gilroy to resist the prevailing definitions of Black womanhood whether as Strong Black Woman or as Victim? I suggest that it is in Gilroy's ironic treatment of the anguish of Black women characters, particularly in her juxtaposition of anguish and the absurd, that the mechanics central to an understanding of her portrayal of characters may be understood. In addressing this, I refer also to the text *In Praise of Love and Children*.[13]

An examination of the existential struggle of women characters in the texts focuses particularly on the way in which differences in generational figurations are revealed in portrayals such as Mama King, Grandma Clara Grainger, and Julietta, on the one hand, and Adijah, Lucy, Dorothea, and Candyetta, on the other. The latter characters are portrayed in *Tyrone the Man*. In addition, Melda, the central protagonist of *In Praise of Love and Children*, offers a particularly interesting problematic of Black womanhood examined here.

Existentialism

Existentialism, the philosophy which informs Gilroy's writing, is not to be equated with the atheistic French school of thought characterized by the works of Jean Paul Sartre.[14] Beryl Gilroy's use of the term describes less a "total philosophical system" and much more a general appropriation. She states:

> I consider any creative work depicting the human condition to be existential—coming out of the inner life, as emotional rhetoric, to liberate us from fears and nightmares. Existentialist language has its limitations but the older one grows, the more everyday experience forces one to reflect and revise one's agenda and forgo remembering and nostalgia....My conception of existence is both mental and metaphysical because that has been the nature of the historical experiences handed down to us.[15]

Existentialism, in this context, denotes an emphasizing of the existence of the individual while referring generally to the human condition. Beryl Gilroy in her "existentialist" writing is antideterministic. The women characters she portrays need not be "of a type." Their psychology influences the choices they make, as does their material condition despite the author's palpable awareness of the absurdity of the universe which she writes into situations encountered by her characters.

"Anguish" and "the absurd" are key concepts of existentialism, or rather, part of the existential language to which Beryl Gilroy refers. Existential philosophy attributes to human beings freedom as "the true nature of man,"[16] bringing with it responsibility and therefore "anguish" in the wake of that responsibility. Anguish is, then, bound up with the individual or character deciding for herself the meaning of her being and actively taking responsibility for it. As backdrop to such a way of being in the world is the understanding or concept of the universe as "absurd." To illustrate, Melda, the protagonist/narrator of *In Praise of Love and Children* and Trudi, her German sister-in-law, cannot transcend the racial chasm which divides them. The mindset of each and the historical understandings held make an appreciation of the "other" impossible. When Trudi presents herself in Melda's ancestral home, by Melda's account:

> The very next day a woman visited us. But none of us had bargained for what we got. She looked so peculiar it was not difficult to recognize her. It was that woman—no matter how she tried to pretend. She wore her hair in such an unreal way it had to be a wig—black and tightly curled, and her skin darkened so she looked like a being that had lived in the tropics. But she could do nothing about her eyes. They were as blue as summer skies. (118)

Humor: "The Zone of Maximally Familiar and Crude Contact"

The absurd is the material of humor in Beryl Gilroy's writing. Juxtaposition of the two concepts, "anguish" and "the absurd," recorded through narrative action and a focus on particular characters, form the basis of the humor peculiar to Beryl Gilroy's narrative fiction. I draw on the writing of Bakhtin in his discussion of the seriocomic to further illuminate Beryl Gilroy's characteristic humor. Referring to seriocomic genres, Bakhtin offers the following observation:

> Everything that makes us laugh is close at hand, all comical creativity works in a zone of maximal proximity. Laughter has the remarkable power of making an object come up close, of drawing it into a zone of crude contact where one can finger it familiarly on all sides, turn it upside down, inside out, peer at it from above and below, break open its external shell, look into its centre, doubt it, take it apart, dismember it, lay it bare and expose it.[17]

Beryl Gilroy's fictional narrative treats serious themes: Black elderly in contemporary society, racism, family and community relationships, immigration, and other issues central to the lives of her Black characters. Yet, carefully juxtaposed against her observation, recording, reconstruction, and retelling of levels of poignancy in the processes of Black lives is her sharply observed rendering of comic elements in situations which she presents. The overlapping which results brings into relief the seriocomic elements which contribute to Gilroy's style and takes the reader into the "zone of maximal proximity" referred to by Bakhtin. Within that "zone of crude contact," insight may be gained about the inner workings of specific characters. "Key moments" or "flashes of individuation or self-realization,"[18] are often humorously depicted, a skillful technique allowing the reader to hold both the serious and the comic together. Thus Trudi's blue eyes and grotesque disguise belie the sincerity of her approach to being accepted even as she accuses Melda of prejudice.

Mrs. Mabel Alexandrina King, or "Mama King to all who knew her," is the overworked protagonist of *Frangipani House* discussed earlier. A decisive or "key moment" for Mama King is when she is found hiding in the latrine of the home to which she has been assigned in old age by her daughters. Mama King has carefully preselected the location of her hideout. Prepared for that moment, she wears two dresses, one over the other. She removes one of her dresses, drops it into the latrine, and watches it disappear. A child walks in with her frock raised ready to relieve herself.

The moment is one of pathos crystalizing Mama King's despair at being locked away, compounded by having her final days controlled by the reductive practices of the "home" against the old women. It is a poignant moment when Mama King drops the discarded dress into the latrine, for she is also discarding her lifelong pattern of being in the world, waiting for key individuals, principally her husband, to act on her behalf. The anguish in Mama King's hiding in the latrine is reflected in the account given of her inner thoughts and emotions followed immediately by narrative action:

> They were leaving now. Would they pass her way? Would a nurse dawdle by the window? Her heart was as tremulous as a leaf in the wind. They took the curve that brought them close. A child lifting her ragged dress entered the latrine. (58)

Within the "zone of crude contact" is drawn the innocent child with her dress lifted to relieve herself, no doubt, on Mama King's dress. Also drawn in is Mama King, elderly woman, African Caribbean grandmother, with whom respect from young people is associated. Such respect would be antithetical to the child's relieving herself on the grandmother figure's frock. The effect is comic irony. It is a crude situation evoking her laughter, however briefly.

> Laughter demolishes fear and piety before an object, before a world, making of it an object of familiar contact and thus clearing the ground for an absolutely free investigation of it.[19]

Part of the irony of the situation lies in the taboos associated with grandmother figures such as Mama King, but the juxtaposition of the humorous episode with fear for Mama King's safety gives rise to overlapping effects. Laughter, having briefly demolished "fear and piety" for the old woman, is soon replaced by concern. Toward the end of her days, Mama King's roles have been principally "mother, wife, negated woman, patient, and resident in a home."[20] Ritualistically encircled, not by family and friends, not by "caregivers," but by a band of beggars and strangers who appreciate her as another human being in need, Mama King is elevated from the "zone of crude contact" which provokes laughter.[21] She is once more the matriarchal figure who has given all in nurturing others: husband, children, grandchildren. An irony perceived in the "crude contact" underlines the absurdity of the situation in which the elderly woman's protection can be secured only by a band of beggars.

The "zone of maximally familiar and crude contact" is one within which many of Beryl Gilroy's female (and male) characters may be viewed. Like Mama King, in roles as mothers, wives, negated women, or at times just as younger generational figures without these complications, the existential struggle of women is played out. Though many themes addressing Black lives are treated in the literature, a great many women characters are nonetheless portrayed within "the plane of comic [humorous] representation."[22]

The Existential Struggle of Women: Some Key Moments

The existential struggle of women is marked, then, in seriocomic key moments in much of Beryl Gilroy's fictional works. *Boy-Sandwich*, set in postimmigration London, and its sequel, *Tyrone the Man*, allow further exploration of the existential struggle of women portrayed in Beryl Gilroy's works. The latter particularly signals the emergence of new figurations of Caribbean womanhood.

Paradoxically, and despite the novel's central focus on Tyrone, the boy sandwiched between cultures, many women are portrayed in *Boy-Sandwich*. Of these, Clara Grainger, like Mama King and the slightly drawn Julietta, may be perceived as "generational" figures, that is, representative of their generation. Clara Grainger is a grandmother figure who, as might be expected, has absorbed and maintained the values of her island home. An immigrant to London, "cautious Clara," as her husband refers to her, proved competent and skilled in her working days. Retired and dispossessed of the home the couple worked so hard to purchase, Clara Grainger, seen through her grandson's eyes, in the home for the elderly is an altered individual.

Clara's identity is pieced together by Tyrone. He contrasts the Gran, whose personal history he was familiar with, to Clara the inmate. The reader learns that, "in her salad days Grandma was the captain of the village rounders team and the champion chequers player" (63). It is Clara's vigilance as a younger woman which leads to the child Tyrone's rescue from the neglectful child minder (35). In contrast, placed in "The Birches" following eviction, Clara sits clutching her bag full of possessions, "the tools of her trade," thimbles and pinking shears and tape-measures (11). She carries her identity with her in her "linen bag full of Island earth" (13), her "burden bag" (57). Clara's behavior, like her life, has taken on reductionist elements not just because of old age, but through being confined in the home for the elderly. In the void of existence which The Birches represents, Clara calls to her remembered cat, ritually feeding the absent pet under the table.

A key moment depicting Clara's anguish in the situation of The Birches is when, caught up in her own inner world, she begins to sing as she would in her own house. The act of singing in the public space of the sitting room in The Birches provokes a shouted response. "Shut up, Clara. You people are too noisy." Implicit in the reference to "you people" is the racial stereotyping which underscores the racialized meanings intended by the unidentified old woman (50). When Clara continues singing "in full flood" she unleashes the stinging "Shut up, you bitch!" The abusive response is partly to the volume of Clara's singing, but it is within the song itself that Clara engages in battle with her colleague. Immediately following the old woman's first verbal attack, Clara, who had been singing of "love's tender lessons," shifts to lyrics referring to "haughtiness" and "cunning," obliquely referring to her attacker. Called "you bitch" in response, she shifts again, addressing in her song "angry words" which "soil de lip."

Life in the "home" does not allow Clara a way of dealing with such an attack so as to leave her dignity intact; it is an absurd situation. Equally absurd is the way in which it is Clara's religiosity which provides the ammunition she needs so that on one level she is innocently singing hymns and on the other she is engaging in verbal battle with an assailant.

Clara Grainger, as she appears at The Birches, seems to fluctuate between frailty and strength, at times appearing to her grandson "even younger than my mother" (94). What Tyrone perceives as life threatening to both his grandparents in that situation is the danger of forgetting "who they are and what they were in their long span of years" (30). In The Birches life is a long, drawn-out form of identity crisis exceeding that faced by so many immigrants in metropolitan areas like London. Yet, when Tyrone accidentally finds the financial means to take his grandparents back home, it is Clara who, contrary to his expectations, is ready immediately to return to the island.

While Clara's relationship with her husband suits her needs, the minor character, Janey Grainger, a generational figure younger than Clara, lives out her days in London in a rage. The identity mismatch constantly threatening immigrant women like Janey contributes to her anger, but she also carries overwhelming frustrations with her marriage. Married to Clara's son Robby, Janey finds her life in England a bitter contrast to the one she had previously known as wife of an island politician. England means loss of status for her in addition to living with her husband's infidelities. Janey holds to her personal vision though it requires her to work in the day and study at night. Only when the couple have been able to buy a house does she show some visible signs of "contentment." Janey's identity, as Robby's wife, remains important to her and she perceives no choice but to stay with him so that by this means, her identity becomes highly dependent upon her unfaithful husband's.

Gilroy's discussion of identity sheds welcome light upon characters such as Janey. Identity, she states:

> is the fear of being forgotten, of failing to resist the anguish of indifference, rejection and betrayal, and of being unable to fuse all the expressive moments of life into a panorama of reality that could be called authentic. Identity is having the strength of will to love deeply, and this struggle to love is an intriguing part of the human existence.[23]

In Gilroy's works, it is within "the struggle to love" that many women and men reveal significant aspects of identity, at times at odds with a public facade they have set in place. Janey's is the respectable woman in complement to her husband's earlier role within the community.

Identity, then, is not determined in a vacuum, and significant to identity is historical context. The contexts which concern the texts explored in this paper are post-1950s Britain and postcolonial, postindependence Caribbean. Both British and Caribbean contexts provide settings for the three main texts examined here. Homi Bhaba's caution that "to frame the problem of identity leads inevitably to being caught athwart the frame, at once inside and outside" is useful in considering the problem of identity for figures like Claire and Janey Grainger.[24] Reared in the Caribbean and having migrated to Britain, such women are often painfully "caught athwart" the identity frame; they are at once outsiders and insiders in both national spaces. Further, the cultural values they carry to the exclusion of others are often a source of personal pain.

Black Women's Identity

In part the women's difficulties represent "a certain problem of identification between nations and cultures, between foreign and floating signs."[25] For Janey and Clara, as for Mama King, significant "floating signs" are woman, wife, and race. To be woman and wife is to be dependent, if not financially, then emotionally. Julietta and her daughter, Lucinda, like Janey are trapped in the need for "respectability" which informed their early socializing, as girls. A male relative of the Graingers, Herod, describes Lucinda as a "handsome girl with dirty tricks." He further explains the fatalistic outcome of her several marriages as "She like she got a conjure on her, man after man, marriage choked dead time and again" (61). It is Adijah who reports on the wedding of Lucinda. The joyful occasion of this "conjured" or "bewitched" woman's latest wedding takes place, as planned, in a prison, since the bridegroom is himself a prisoner whom Lucinda had met in the hospital. A key moment for Lucinda at her wedding is when, among congratulation cards, she receives also one of deepest condolences. Lucinda, it appears, suspects Janey of this. The moment is not necessarily one from which Lucinda learns much, though the marriage ends as abruptly as the relationship began.

Black Womanhood

Black womanhood, from an examination of Gilroy's works, has its share of women as losers. I refer to African Caribbean womanhood, an identity deriving from heritage regardless of the character's location although in this instance it is postwar immigration Britain. The initial impulse of this trend, post-1950s migration, would prove to be significant to the emergence of altered perceptions of girlhood and womanhood as reflected in Gilroy's portrayal of younger generational figures. Another generation, therefore, has taken on a qualitatively different identity. In *Frangipani House*, work-weary Mama King epitomizes one generation; in *Boy-Sandwich*, Adijah signals another. Adijah is no victim stereotype despite the horrific racist incendiary attack which leaves her scarred. In Adijah may be found the beginnings of a "radical departure" from prior fictional characterization of Black women in Britain. It is to be remembered that depictions of Black womanhood and specifically African Caribbean womanhood in an English setting are still rare enough at the end of the 1980s, the dates of the two publications mentioned above.

It is from the generation represented in Gilroy's writing of women after Janey Grainger, Tyrone's mother, that new figurations have emerged. Adijah, for example, like Tyrone, has not undergone the "total body world adjustment" coldly known as immigration.[26] The "petite and pretty" Adijah who has a strong sense of self commands both love and respect from her partner, Tyrone; he describes her as his friend, who is "full of fun and good sense" and who "belongs to life and I'm allowed to walk beside her" (62). Tyrone confides also the quality of his feelings for Adjiah when he states, "I would have liked to confine her inside my heart, like a rare and beautiful gem" (68). It is in characters like Adijah that new African Caribbean womanhood may be glimpsed, for though she seems to be all that Tyrone perceives, Adijah is also portrayed as highly independent and prompt to act upon her own needs while being perceptive to those of Tyrone. Adijah also bears the culture; she holds traditional African Caribbean values enough to visit Tyrone's grandparents in The Birches even when visiting has become burdensome to Tyrone himself.

In *Tyrone the Man*, a range of new figurations of Black womanhood emerge, their "newness" linked to representation in the literature depicting African Caribbean womanhood in Anglophone novels. What *Tyrone the Man* makes clear is that the confident, independent, balanced, and clear-sighted women figures emerging are constructed out of a sense of new "Britishness" or biculturalism in Gilroy's novels. Like Adijah, the young women are, generally, born to Caribbean parents in Britain. Migration, then, appears to be a key part in the process of the constructing of new womanhood grounded in bicultural experience, one which offers new choices to young Black women.

Beryl Gilroy writes: "I snake into the interior of my characters, give their feelings the validity that relates to Black experience and weave a tale around those feelings."[27] The feelings of the younger women are significantly shaped by their bicultural experience. Figures like Candyetta, Lucy, and Dorothea act very differently in the world than many women of an earlier generation. They are of different social backgrounds and unburdened by child care or oppressive male relationships through the choices they make. Candyetta, from a working class background, and Lucy from more privileged circumstances, are similar in their independent and outspoken mode of acting in and upon the world.

It is Candyetta whose behavior is perceived as distinctly unconventional, or, "for a girl child, a disgrace." When Candyetta physically confronts her assailant, Robby, the reader grasps a moment of insight which simultaneously reveals the absurdity of gross patriarchy within the society. Robby's masked sexual desire parades as moral vigor entitling him to physically punish the female, Candyetta, as an act of ultimate authority. Robby acts to "right" a situation by beating a young woman, but when

Candyetta matches his physical aggression, it is the depth of Robby's own wife's store of repressed anger that is briefly unmasked. Unexpectedly, the situation reveals the hidden, deep seated feelings of Janey, the long suffering wife who momentarily drops all pretense, abandons her wifely facade and yells for the younger woman to "kill him," baying for her husband's blood.[28] It is a moment which depicts Janey's anguish, Robby's "come-uppance" and Candyetta's sense of being equal to anyone in the world. Unlike Wanny and Stephy, who begin their lives with expectations of being outmaneuvered and manipulated, characters such as Lucy, portrayed as independent and liberated, indicate a new African Caribbean womanhood emerging in the literature.

A problematic of the new Black womanhood is Melda, protagonist of *In Praise of Love and Children*.[29] Melda arrives in postwar London as a young woman aware of a strong sense of freedom which she feels "for the first time"(12). She is fired by ambition to prove herself through "work, as generations of black women had done" (12). Melda's painful childhood is behind her. She had known what it was like to be worked "like a donkey from dawn to dusk" and to regularly attract irrational punishment, "an unexpected cut with a stick" (15). She had understood about being unloved without comprehending why. Schooled to silence—"speech is silver"—Melda does not demand answers (49). Melda's story of a childhood incident, ostensibly about Mama Tat, an older woman of the yard, equally reveals young Melda's own anguish and confusion.

A key moment in the child Melda's story follows Mama Tat's explanation to the young Melda about the making of a "rose bedspread" by the women of the village for a wedding. The bedspread, described as "a thing heavy with love," contrasts painfully with Melda's acute feeling of lovelessness. Given the explanation for the bedspreads being made, Melda bursts out. "I will never have one! Everyone hates me. They all hate me. God never even gave me a mother. . . ." Mama Tat, trying to console the hysterical girl, hugs her close, but Melda, noticing Mama Tat's hairy armpits, spitefully pulls out some of the hairs. As a result, Melda, in turn, leaves Mama Tat yelling, "Gal, you so bad. Gawd pretect me liver from you!"(152).

Melda's learning is guided by the perceptive schoolteacher Mrs. Penn, whose "generous bequest" allows the young woman in her midtwenties to visit London in order to train as a teacher. Melda's independence in London is hard won because of the spiritual adoption of Mrs. Penn. Melda proves herself capable of determining her own lifestyle despite her unpreparedness for the racist context which finally contributes to her decision to leave teaching. Like other "independent" women characters discussed earlier, as the narrative unfolds, the adult Melda determines her own agenda. Among the wealth of understandings guiding her life are the following: "to be a proper woman I had to suffer" and "my life had taught me to love women." Perhaps because of those, Melda turns to work, accepting: "I have work. There will be work and me together forever." Is the price of Melda's independence repressed sexuality? She turns to her brother initially for adult male companionship and, when that fails, she singlemindedly fosters children. From the latter she gains emotional fulfilment: "joy, pleasure, fellowship" accepting with it the inverse "ingratitude, suspicion and resentment" (128).

Melda's character is not "new" in the sense of newly conceived. On the contrary, Beryl Gilroy asserts that the manuscript of *In Praise of Love and Children* was written in 1969.[30] Its publication in 1996 raises issues about the politics of publishing and African Caribbean women's writing in Britain. The literary history of British based Black women's writing is patchy indeed. I have written elsewhere of the gap between key nineteenth-century publications of Mary Prince and Mary Seacole and twentieth-century longer fictional works by writers such as Sylvia Wynter and Merle Hodge. Between Mary Prince's publication in 1833 and Sylvia Wynter's silence-breaking publication *Hills of Hebron* in 1962 are over a hundred and thirty years of Black women's silence shattered finally in the latter decades of the twentieth century. Beryl Gilroy's twenty-seven-year wait for publication in this instance is indicative of African Caribbean literary history, as well as of Gilroy's unique project.[31]

Educational mainstream publishers within the Caribbean region have played an invaluable role in allowing African Caribbean women's voices to be heard. Publications of this nature nonetheless brought constraints related to the education market and limitations in terms of the portrayal of African Caribbean womanhood. Homi Bhaba's location of the problematic

> between history and literature, where the authoritative power of naming is undone by the political and poetical conditions of its meaning; where the language of the self is disseminated in the hybrid tongues and traditions that determine the place from which one speaks—as other,[32]

is pertinent to this discussion. The "political and poetical conditions" of literary production have precluded and, to a large extent, continue to constrain the African Caribbean woman's "naming," whether through lack of publishing resources, prescriptive practices excluding or limiting the use of the Caribbean demotic, or the favoring for publication of new stereotypes or myths of Black womanhood such as woman as "victim" or sex-motivated "bitch," over and above the range of characters so far examined. Recent myths, like their precursors, have served to deny the sheer range of possible characterization of African Caribbean womanhood.

New Black Womanhood

Beryl Gilroy's depiction of "new" Black womanhood redresses the balance through characters such as Adijah, Candyetta, and Lucy. In portraying such self-determined women, Gilroy's writing highlights the complex nature of Black womanhood she has observed. Alongside less powerful, more passive characters, nuances of the common humanity of African Caribbean women are presented. Issues of race, gender, and class are articulated without recourse to familiar stereotypes. Further, Gilroy allows to be revealed the untold story through which the Black woman subverts past and present myths in order to bring about cultural change affecting the choices she makes. Gilroy says of Mama King, for example: "She is the resourceful, rather than the 'strong' African Caribbean woman. She is, in fact, a cultural feminist able to use the semiotics of the culture for her own ends."[33]

It is in problematizing and developing the "semiotics of the culture" that major themes within Gilroy's writing arise. Within these, the "new" women's voices emerge speaking clearly to their own needs in relationships and in their acting upon the wider world.

In conclusion, the fictional works of Beryl Gilroy privilege Black womanhood in its varied guises. The texts discussed, like Gilroy's larger writing project, engage continuously with the constructing of new and emergent Black feminine identity. Gilroy's fictional strategy, which produces figures of new womanhood, derives from an impulse interested in the "existential" condition of black men and women. For many of the characters portrayed, identity is as dependent on the Caribbean as on their place of residence in Britain. Migration is key to much of that identity, to its constraints, and to the conflicting material of recent influences leading to cultural change and impacting upon younger generations of Caribbean women. For the younger generational figures, "accumulated negations" are offset by contemporane-ous choices less shaped by material poverty or narrow religiosity, less shaped by rigid-ity. In other words, they share a differentiated vision of reality. Gilroy defines this part of the project thus:

> These are different times. The textures of the cords that bind us must be un-raveled and inspected. And we could do this with our words in writing . . .[34]

15. *Women of Color at the Barricades*

Beryl A. Gilroy

I would like to answer some questions asked in the letters I receive from young people who read my work, which I always feel I would like to rewrite one last time before publication. I think most writers feel that way because each momentary shift of the head changes the view of the world as we would wish to describe it. The first question concerns the writing of my autobiography. "Why did you write it?" they ask. I can't answer that question fully but I can say what motivated me to do so. The fifties were my time, but by the sixties I was involved with enjoying my children: watching them grow, nurturing their curiosity, and encouraging them to discuss and debate without anger. It was also important to teach them to resist the inclination to personalize discourse or argument.

By the end of the fifties, a rush of economic migrants had arrived in London and made the mistake of thinking that the conditions they found on arrival had always been there. The conditions might not have been what they were led to expect of a Welfare State, and so youth lost no time in vilifying us, the older generation, for, among other misdemeanors, "taking crap" and "eating dirt," charges hugely resented by us. The "Pandemonium People," as they came to be known, were mostly fleeing their newly independent homelands, preferring to protest about home miles away from home as if the representatives in Britain cared at all.

We had marched, argued, and shouted for independence and freedom, and we did our bit to win both for those back home and for ourselves. We danced along with them when the flag was lowered and the new one fluttered. Like the beneficiaries, we did not realize that independence meant having no one to blame for the state of the nation state but ourselves. No one realized that society as we knew it would break out in running sores. Of course we still had the eternal whipping boy, colonialism, as a way out of the economic morass which gave rise to another kind of immigrant, no better off than those of the fifties. Like the war-displaced we were concerned with survival and with getting from place to place without too much interference from racists. No one was clear as to the true nature of independence.

I arrived in Britain, as one of two thousand professionals, many years before independence had been given to many other West Indian colonies. Black had not yet become beautiful. I started writing for my own biracial children to give them history of "the other." Books did not show Black people in a good light, but to preempt racism I read them books that would encourage them to recognize and dispute stereotypes with themselves.

My very good friend and critic the late Andrew Salkey, along with Barry Reckord, encouraged my writing of fiction for children, and after a lot of thinking I produced *Sunlight on Sweet Water*, *In Praise of Love*, and articles in *Parents*, *The Manchester Guardian*, *The Teacher's World*, and many other magazines. I also talked from time to time on programs such as "Woman's Hour" and "Calling the Caribbean" and was a publisher's reader, editor, and textbook reviewer for London University Press.

The Empire was still intact although slowly decaying, but we were being written about by high-principled liberals. There were books such as *The L-Shaped Room*, set in Nottinghill, *To Sir, with Love*, *Flame in the Streets*, and *Sapphire*, a pathetic story about a girl passing as white who is murdered on Hampstead Heath. These books were filmed, but no one ever showed Black men being the butt of unspeakable practical jokes. We could still buy Golliwogs and tickets for minstrel shows, which was our "tradition," as was so often said. By the middle fifties, the Reprint Society had run its course and the publishers had begun to produce material for the West Indies as they had done before the war. They were in effect offering their own kind of determinism and theology to schools. I wrote some stories.

When my work was sent to the male writers from the West Indies to be read, these men, in order to prove their erudition, turned to the idiosyncratic and the fastidious. My works, they said, were too psychological, strange, way-out, difficult to categorize. "Fine," I replied. I didn't have to clothe or feed my manuscripts and other texts or write for a slice of bread, so I kept them. Attitude, conviction, and experience count, but I enjoy writing different, yet emotionally accessible and truthful books in which I allow characters to talk from within themselves. My life allowed me time to write, but many Black women worked two jobs simply to feed and clothe their families.

The fifties saw the first meetings between publishers and Black women on an unequal yet semiequal footing. The publishers, editors, and other occupants of the inner literary sanctum had been raised on various forms of stereotypes and could not see beyond them. That brought discussion of my work to a dark and barren place. The class-education of those men had not prepared them for encounters with colonial thought or our forms of creativity. Mine had been damaged but did not die. Yet I gave up writing and began to read, to take courses to help me sense the unwritten norms of this society. I had to educate myself across a wide canvas.

Yet my hopes were lost in a fumarole of doubt and chaos. My carefree self had become a shadow without substance or circularity as I fought to absorb the special features of this new place. A child at the Back of Beyond, I had sworn to write books, and one day I decided to reconstitute my will. I had something to say, and say it I would.

In a final attempt to regain my identity as a writer I began to attend a gathering in the company of a liberal friend. Once a month, for the price of a guinea, we took tea with an author. Formidable women they were. Iris Murdoch, Margery Allingham, Denise Robins, Marghanita Laski, Noel Streatfield, and many others spoke of the novel from a great height of intellectualism. I have a very good memory and I have thought long and very hard indeed about those times of exclusion, which I remember clearly. Not one of those women ever made eye contact or talked to me, not even to ask me where I learned my English, a popular question at the time.

I was the little black ant looking up at the eagles at the top of the steeple. Sometimes men came, men of distinction, savants and nonbrothers to be sure. I was swallowed up by erudition and drowned in its waves. My confidence in my ability was once more like a fire deprived of fuel, and for a time nothing, not even the gentlest breezes of assurance and encouragement, would allow even a cinder to glow.

I still wrote poetry but that was not enough. Poetry has since the sixties come into its own. From the way people spoke of Blacks, we would be accommodated along with the exotic and the anthropological in the tradition of Joyce Cary's *Mr. Johnson* and *Aissa Saved,* both popular socio-anthropological novels of the time. Sadly, their siblings all had baby photos but they had none. Documentaries about Dr. Barnados and other Homes have verified the history of these children and it is touching to see reunions of siblings—one white, one black, linked by the blood of the mother. The students were kept apart from the workers. Women students were chained to their studies, while the economic migrant women were busy earning crusts and trying to make sense of British food, money, social behavior, and more— with a few of the homeless wondering where to bed down for the night. Leisure and contemplation were rare privileges available only to the middle classes of the fifties.

When Black children subsequently came to Britain and went to school all with different surnames, women and men had to be persuaded to marry. Marriage among immigrants became the trend. That took some doing, but marriage meant respectability. Little did these women know that the sixties would start to swing right back to the "help-your-self" loving of the slave plantation. The nuclear family had begun to lose its hold and new patterns of family had begun to emerge.

With the publication of their novels the Caribbean male writers became advisers and opinion addicts. They had access to more ears and hearts, could share more of the untrammeled world of men, and some did so forcibly and ably, although the reviewers were selective and biased. The mystified world of the novel was a middle-class monopoly at the time. They had more than our colonial experience to reveal and share. If we were written about, the text was invariably put through a civilized, outdated British cultural filter. They still believed that Britain ruled the waves.

Writers of earlier times, like Mittleholzer who used to be the customs officer in my village when I was a tot, wrote books about biracial Guianese, and for whatever reason set himself on fire on Hampstead Heath. There has to be an audience for the colonial experience or life within the culture of poverty. Our work has only just begun to occupy a place in contemporary writing. Edgar Mittleholzer had written all his life and limped around the margins of success. Perhaps it was despair that killed him.

Even in a population of two million immigrants in Britain there are few takers for our work, the white man's burden. What could we say that they would hear? They set the standards by which we measured our civilization and encouraged cultural mimesis. There were also the psychological and material aspects of change, of gaining familiarity with the feel and the demography of this new place. Writing calls for the use of familiar social tools, but first we must recognize them and understand their effectiveness.

Then there were the patterns of communication within the particularities of Euro-culture. New forms took the place of language, when coming to terms with our new subjective, emotional, and cognitive selves or the stigmatized, objectified, or labeled self. Labeling is a very potent, distancing strategy. In our villages, time is measured by conscious or intrusive rhythms and sounds of work. Immigration meant a change to other time-rhythms, a reorganizing of concepts of place and space, interpreting representations of applied time, as in the use of timetables, and marrying mechanistic time with the new climatic forms and applying whole new choreographies to everyday toil, everyday racisms. Everyday sedimentations are also stressful aspects of change.

When one is visible and invisible at the same moment, one loses internal as well as external landmarks, and this causes identity to become insubstantial and amorphous. At that time, I wrote to assert my sullied identity. Writing for me is therapy and nourishment. I write in the name of resistance. I come from Berbice, famous for its slave uprisings. To resist injustice is in my nature. As children we were fed stories of our moments of historical rebellion. Black women helped the war effort. But they found scant fitness in the services and the society when it was all over. The men stayed behind and found women to service and care for them. We, the women, were trying to categorize, define, and understand our own needs, so similar to those of our brothers pattering away on their typewriters.

Believe it or not, within these relationships some created works of great humor, truth, and relevance. I remember to this day one young man saying definitively, "I can be different with them." And the children of these liaisons? Stigma and rejection caused more than a few to be concealed in private homes and nurseries. Years later some were to desert their offspring after hatching them. It is said that no adult mallee fowl has ever been seen with her chicks. Our critics ignored the fact that whereas animals behave instinctively, we had to survive oppression, sedimentation, and chronic hostility by considered cognitive responses to our economic situation and forget how to be anything other than the source of supplies and so of living. Difference in appearance was perplexing and needed to be nuanced and investigated.

Children crossed the road to ask us the time to discover if we spoke words or simply made noises. We were hooted at, taunted, and if foolish enough to be out when the pubs emptied, good for a quick grope or two from teddy boys in "winkle pickers" and the army boys in chukka boots. In the tradition of Black women who write to come to terms with their trauma, or alternatively to understand the nature of their elemental oppression, I wrote to redefine myself and put the record straight.

And to answer the second question: Yes, depending on the limitations of the word, there were women writers in the fifties. They were mostly students doing scholarly work. Our relationship with this country had been circular: home, Britain for a fixed period, and home again. Until World War Two, not many people of color lived in contemporary England, a place of individualism and restraint, maturity, and live and let live. We did write. But we were not all like Jean Rhyses, whose God-given cloak of privilege brought her all the considerations she needed. Poverty is, and was even then, relative. And she, lovely woman, wrote from within the culture but outside of the true African-derived self. What is remembered in the body is well remembered. Interpretation is by thought alone.

Scholarly women like the late Elsa Goveia and Lucille Mathurin-Mair were researching and writing our history. Sylvia Wynter, respected for her scholarship, was writing plays of great power and perspicacity to be performed on radio. Black women had written about their lives all through the years that their bodies served others. They began during the nineteenth century after literacy came to hand through Mary Prince. I followed in that tradition to show my tolerance of ignorance, yet never to forget its agitations and bewilderment. Writing can be a vehicle for disseminating social ideas about the human condition, but we were colonials. Concerned people did not share the decision making with us. By doing things for us they encouraged helplessness and dependency. There were fixed ideas of woman and womaness and Black womanhood in particular. We were the concupiscent daughters of Ham and his wife. (I was then told that Ham had no wife and so was forced to make his children out of mud.)

Ignorance was rife. Few homes had television and nothing existed to counter the stereotypes offered by missionaries, travelers, mercenaries, carpetbaggers, explorers, sundry do-gooders, and spirit thieves. The society, secure in the various race theories that imperialism and slavery had spawned, ignored what our history had forced upon our progenitors. They had to ensure survival of their children and themselves and needed to infiltrate and occupy the economic pathways blocked to our men.

Black women worked in the cane fields alongside men and as stevedores, brick-layers, and stone masons long before it became fashionable to do so. Our antecedents replaced the men who had died too early, or were incarcerated, or dismissed for not being and acting "boy." In the name of our children we adventured abroad alone and worked long lonely hours, forgetting self-love in the process. In the name of the survival of our children we showed them the basic principles of resistance. In the name of their innocence, and with the help of our mothers, we taught them self-preservation, which sometimes failed to save them. We were the first feminists because we had been forced to think, serve, and do for ourselves out of bald necessity. We were the first active, unremitting feminists. Black feminism is a historical and experiential process.

Slavery and colonialism had fostered a culture of communalism through which all experienced community care. People in villages shared what they achieved by endeavors of the self. In Britain coworkers, although objecting to nation talk, marveled at the independence of Black women, sometimes equating the fact that we left young children to others, or on their own. I still wrote poetry and was asked to submit one to James Berry for a collection, his first. He told me it was excellent but pulled it as it would have been the only one by a woman in the collection.

This brings me to a point which I want to make with considerable force. The sixties were a reaction to the historical and generalized oppression of women during the previous decades. Whether we were wives, mistresses, courtesans, concubines, field laborers, or favorite slaves, we were controlled by men who ran the world. Those women who helped to win the war were seen as honorary men, and the rest, decorative objects or incubators to gratuitous inseminators. Women stayed married whatever the consequences. There was no refugee status for those fleeing desperate marriages. We moved screamlessly from sufferer to martyr to saint after death.

Lively women who "voiced off" were fiercely punished by the status quo and today it is overwhelming to hear survivors talk of experiences in the world of men: the workplace, the courts, and society in general. Many did not possess the language to express abuse, betrayal, rape, or domestic terror, hidden or sugarcoated in the novels of the period.

Wifehood was for some a torment and a descent into shame and sin. Women's bodies served as a graveyard for feelings of lovelessness, arid sufferance to cause sicknesses of the self, depression, madness, cancer, and chronic irritability. The sixties emancipated women.

The war had taken women into factories, compelled them to do men's work, and abolished the territoriality, dependence, and gender biases of the forties, but at the end of the war, the women were dragged, screaming and kicking in some cases, back to the primitivism of the past to reinstate the weaker sex—the dependent, subservient, unpaid homemaker and child-factory (although back street abortions took their toll).

Women everywhere were peripheral to the world of men, and as Black men roamed the fringes of the world of the white bosses, so, too, were we expected to behave with respect and humility to white women set over us, thus giving the power-hungry among them the regard they did not get from their class-ridden society. And Guyana. I was born and bred in colonial times. All my principal family values and instincts lie in the need for self-sufficiency, self-reliance, and the rainy-day mentality colonialism fostered in mostly all its offspring.

The "Empire Windrush" had brought some war veterans back to be housed in Brixton, which thereafter was under siege each weekend to be kept "white." Then we had come as the first wave of intellectuals—the crème de la crème of our countries—to gain and learn in their names. I lived at the Oval. It was an unpleasant experience. Mercifully I found digs in North London, Highgate to be exact. It was easier to reorient oneself and think. It was easier to access evening classes. My panic attacks disappeared. I was no longer waylaid and innuendoed.

Unless a student was paying her own way, or had a stash hidden, we were forced to rely on the Crown agents and the Colonial Office to arrange places in universities and transfer cash from home. The British Council provided entertainment and education as to the British way of life. We were thoroughly vetted before being allowed to leave British Guiana. I had hoped to continue my work with UNICEF, five years after the birth of the United Nations, and worked assiduously to do just that. However, destiny intervened, and several of us found ourselves wives to be and mothers.

Some students returned home. Others sought distant lands, and after excruciating and consuming frustrations, I began teaching.

This period of my life is well documented in *Black Teacher*, reprinted after eighteen years. It is a unique book—the only one that tells the woman's part of the tale of our recent coming. Blacks had been in Britain since Roman times and twice commanded to leave the realm by Elizabeth I.

I subsequently left teaching and moved out into darkest Toryland, among a population with an eighteenth-century worldview and vocabulary. For the greater part they wore their xenophobia with pride. Many were class-conscious, mind-armored flat-earthers. Apart from a family of Sikhs, we were the only nonwhites for miles around. Everyone knew us, the bearded man with the Black wife who spoke English and the baby who wore spectacles.

A trained developmental psychologist, I found time to monitor what was happening to me, as a displaced and isolated person. There were moments of depersonalization, fraying of the rock to survive. Racism is subterranean and protean in London. It has a cosmopolitan and multicultural dimension. Overworked Black women of the fifties had other concerns—concerns with living in overcrowded space, worrying about the mood of the childminder who took care of the children, about sharing beds, toilets, and other intimate spaces with scores of others. It was the unbelievable experience of Black children who were minded by uncaring alien women that caused the laws affecting childminders to be changed in Britain.

They worried too about the folks back home and about their self-indulgence and need of accretion.

We were not settlers as yet, and to write about a society one has to know its temperaments and its voices, its undergarments and their style, odor, and color. To find an audience we have to be comfortably certain of the message we are offering. Prior to the sixties, not many people had use for colonial voices of protest and discontent. One could not slip into a country still bearing the scars of a hard fought war and set about assumedly "leisured" work such as writing.

After immigrating, the ability to develop new forms of internal dialogues and select effective functional values has to emerge. The ability to do this varies from person to person, but we were supposed to know. Had we not been colonized for four hundred years?

Not many people viewed us incoming West Indian women as anything other than derisive, semi-mimetic intruders and job snatchers. Remember all those theories offered by the scientific racists, the phrenologists, teleologists, social Darwinists, and other purveyors of ethnocentrism widely disseminated as scholarship to this day? We are trapped inside that waspish scholarship, virulent and endemic as it is, but we can use the pen to destroy it. We need not concern ourselves with the pathology we are supposed to contain. Ethnocentrists have scrutinized, researched, and gutted us for centuries, and in spite of all the visible and invisible barriers we must surmount, we have survived as a people. Like the phoenix we will always rise out of the ashes of disregard and hate.

We have survived reductionism and minimalization. In time to come it is our writing that will challenge all such attitudes. Let us stand together at the barricades of the intellect and destroy those who seek to diminish us whether we are descendants of the biblical Ham or the mythological Chus, who begat both white and black children and sent them off to different parts of the globe. We have always been there, cutting the barbed wire, rocking the pickets, weakening the structures, clambering over the stones. We must continue the struggle so that we can stand beside the great women of fifties London—women who tore down the barricades of inhumanity and negation. They pushed against white tribalism, hyperconservatism, ethnarchies, hierarchies, and plagues of stereotypes offered as tradition.

Women opposed racism, hypocrisy, and bigotry of all kinds. We have a history of orality effective in expressing our emotions. At this point I will mention some of the women I knew in the fifties. I name the late and memorable Claudia Jones, who tried to bring cohesion to the lives of the working class West Indians through her newspaper *The West Indian Gazette*, and was responsible for the genesis of Europe's most important festival, the Nottinghill Carnival, the first of which was held in a school hall to mend fences between Blacks and whites in Nottinghill after Kelso Cochrane was stabbed to death on his way home from work.

I name Pansy Jeffries, who started and ran effectively the first Citizens Advice Bureau for West Indian women in Paddington, London.

I name Sybil Phoenix, who founded a refuge for children in distress. Jessica and Eric Huntley, who started their publishing venture. All those wonderful women entertainers: Louise Bennett, Winnie Atwell, Nadia Cattouse, and Carmen Munroe, the first to mainstream on TV. Pearl Connor, who helped to get Black actors work, and Pauline Crabbe, the first magistrate. Linda Robeson, who wrote one of the earliest history texts. Anklesaria, the one student from India who spoke with patience of cultural relativity and forced cultural dominance to defend itself.

I name Rita Redhead, who worked to rescue children labeled "Educationally Subnormal." Mrs. Morgan of Birmingham and Gloria Cameron, who ran the first all-Black nurseries. Leila Phillips and countless other young Guianese and West Indian nurses who opened the way for others, and all of us who came to do one thing and stayed to do another. There are numerous other women abused and unsung who contributed to Britain's recovery. We salute them all today.

Those who came to Britain later found the barricades weakened enough to be pushed aside, and they could cross over in more numbers than could ever have been imagined, to reach those places previously forbidden to us. They did not bring all and every consciousness of injustice or the impending emergence of the third world with them.

It is surprising that only a few attempted to discover what was there before they came to Britain. They did not even have to shout a prayer or sing, or murmur, "Deep River Lord. I want to cross over into Camp Ground"—a place of safety and continuing endeavor.

Let us also think of our sisters where the barricades are invisible, in Germany,

Australia, Holland, Portugal, Spain, and Austria, to which I vowed never to return. Racism is like currency, negotiable in all corners of the world with mammonism, self-hatred, and ignorance as its guardians and preservers. In Britain no one admits to being a racist, but they can all identify a neighbor as one.

We must continue to write with full knowledge of our history and so inform our children of their heritage. It is through the stories we tell that they will recognize those ancient bloodstains on the pages of the past and find the moral energy to erase them. And if no one walks beside us, then as person and people we must walk alone.

As colonials we knew one another even if by proxy although colonial education had much that united the oppressed, e.g., the curriculum, its delivery, and the need to invent language that would exclude the oppressors. When I came to Britain, I had not met a Jamaican, a Cuban, or an African except through the stereotype of the school text. Of course, I knew our next door neighbors, but interisland travel had virtually ceased during World War Two.

We had not then learned our own history—much less explored other histories except of course that of the country of colonization. Let us try to concentrate on our similarities. A rabid racist has suggested to our government the selling of British passports to Hong Kong people and then repatriating West Indians with the money, since their admission to Britain has failed the country, the schools, and the society. But people do not fail in a vacuum and such statements must be thoroughly discussed and debated by all who will be their victims.

Like Black men everywhere we have need to fight for affirmation, regard, and survival. It is said that young men do not conceal either their mortido (aggressive energy) or their libido (sexual energy). At one time they were valued for it by the same people who now fear it and condemn it.

Such beliefs affect all our children. Yet it is the youth who should be protected from the follies of the time in which we live, and from the tragedy of our historical experience. After all, ninety-five out of every hundred slaves were prisoners of wars encouraged, financed, and underscored by the politics of colonialism.

Part Four

Expressions: Literary Theory and Exile

Overview

What theories best define or embody the experiences rendered in literature by Caribbean women? What are the pitfalls of theorizing from an external—postcolonial—vantage point? In what ways does the metropolis affect the insular space of women writers of the Caribbean? Lizabeth Paravisini-Gebert identifies the risk to Caribbean writing (and particularly to women's writing) as that of being lured away from their own creative spaces into the niche open to Caribbean writing by the various strands of postcolonial theories.

What are the implications of exile—of writing and living in exile? Is the idea a divisive one? In the construction of a Caribbean identity, what politics impact the writer in exile? As it would appear more expedient to write in the centers of metropoles, for whom does the writer ultimately write and what techniques/codes are used to signal the group on whom the work is centered? The essays in this section are connected in their insistence on the fidelity to the region. The authors pose questions such as "Can a theory external to the body of literature adequately account for features of that literature?" and "Can a writer living outside of the neighborhood account for features of the neighborhood?"

Lizabeth Paravisini-Gebert questions the use of postcolonial theory in relation to understanding Caribbean literature. Elaine Savory describes "ex/isle" and exile in varied terms, while Astrid H. Roemer engages Peter Nazareth in her analysis of the use of the "master's language," to represent the world of her Surinamese counterparts. Patricia Powell discusses her most recent literary production, *The Pagoda*, which examines the lives of the Chinese immigrant in Jamaica. Leda Maria Martins explores stereotypical representations of Afro-Brazilian women in Brazilian literature as she deconstructs the images of "the Black mammy . . . the Black maid . . . and 'lascivious' *mulata*."

Lizabeth Paravisini-Gebert, in her essay "Women against the Grain: The Pitfalls of Theorizing Caribbean Women's Writing," asserts that throughout the history of women's orality and writing in the Caribbean, there has always been "a fluid space in which women have defined the centrality of their bodies and voices through a deep connection to the specificities of our insularities." She decries postcolonial theories that would forever posit the Caribbean (and by extension its peoples) as marginal, "perpetually condemned to reaction." Writers who choose to respond to "a multicultural, postcolonial market" serve external interests by "reassuring the reader that he or she understands the Caribbean without having to penetrate its multifarious realities." She asserts that the work of Caribbean women writers is in peril of being "coopted, seduced away from its glorious insularity . . . into postcolonial, postmodern, transnational space." For example, Paravisini-Gebert argues that "Caribbean women writers . . . 'read' and 'write' the female body, from a materiality grounded in the specifics of history that sets Caribbean writing apart from Euro-American theories of the body as text." Moreover, she claims that tensions stemming from profound class and race differences, as well as from intragender relations, fall outside the purview of postcolonial theoreticians' interests.

Exile can occur by means of canonicity (exclusion or sanction), by means of genre (marginalizing texts through the imposition of culturally or politically determined criteria), and through forced as well as voluntary actions.

In her essay "Ex/Isle: Separation, Memory, and Desire in Caribbean Women's Writing," Elaine Savory seeks to resolve the divide caused by the opposition of regional writers versus overseas writers. She asserts that "wherever you live in the world, if you live in a space which is connected to the Caribbean and you recognize Caribbean cultural sovereignty, you write within Caribbean space." Whether that space is defined linguistically or culturally, the "desire for coherent identity works on fragments of memory: language itself becomes desire, and that is what brings the commitment to writing into being." She posits memory as the factor that sustains that relationship—for both writers and characters. Additionally, Savory believes that if white women construct ex/isle differently from Black women (markedly affected by four hundred years of different history), this need not "marginalize anybody, rather complicate our understanding of what constitutes the sources of writing for Caribbean women."

Astrid H. Roemer, a Caribbean writer who has long lived in the metropolis, questions the effects exile can have on writing and reading. In her essay "Dangerous Liaison: Western Literary Values, Political Engagements, and My Own Esthetics," Roemer asserts: "the limits of my 'dangerous liaison' with Western literary values and my political engagement are measured through rethinking and reexperiencing the neighborhood," a process that allows her, as writer, to employ the trickster tradition. The resulting enterprise wrests from readers the comfortable notions and injections leading to a misreading of the text, themselves, and the world so that they will have no choice but to reread to find out where they went wrong. This she does to encourage readers "to remove cataracts" and to de-code the trickster. Readers and critics with a postcolonial predisposition appear to be the target of Roemer's enterprise. In terms of her own aesthetics, writing for her is taking responsibility: "making novels is entering the circle of the classical power plays: race-interests, gender-interests, class-interests, nation-interests. . . ."

Patricia Powell's essay "The Dynamics of Power and Desire and *The Pagoda*" is a practical example of the tenets called for by Paravisini-Gebert, Savory, and Roemer. Reflecting on her third novel, *The Pagoda*, Powell's essay identifies the features, intents, and concerns of the work. Powell employs the trickster tradition, questions Caribbean identity, and uses the letter as a frame for the voiceless in the novel. The result is an expansive history of the ethnic relations in the region itself. Her work grew out of a character's search for her lost identity. The character, part Black and part Chinese, led her to reflect on "images of Chinese that are portrayed in Caribbean literature and culture, the racial stereotypes [she] absorbed while growing up in Jamaica, and the complexities of otherness for people who are neither white nor black." What's more, the novel is organized around sexual longing as a manifestation of power and powerlessness. Powell proclaims that writing "sexuality so as to best illustrate the charged interactions that characters face is an unending struggle in [her] works."

In her essay "Voices of the Black Feminine Corpus in Contemporary Brazilian Literature," Leda Maria Martins calls for research and work to give visibility to Black women's writings, voices, and actions in the Brazilian cultural milieu as a means of eradicating the still prevalent stereotypes. According to Martins:

> The literary text is, then, the arena filled with diverse language modulations, which at the same time by means of reversal, disruption, confrontation, and self-celebration unveil and address the Black female body in the landscape of the literary idioms. By their intervention in the formulations of literary discourses, Black women writers enact the variety of textual archives and memories that dialogue within their texts, giving voice to their own desires and dilemmas.

Yet, Black women writers in Brazil are largely ignored by major publishers and do not reach a large number of readers. Black women writers aim to achieve a language of self-recognition and self-apprehension that mirrors their double condition, both as women and as Black women. In the works produced by contemporary Black women, Martin believes, "this feminine Blackness arises from some signifiers which are linked: voice, body, and desire."

In sum, these works articulate the varied experiences of exile and ex/isle within and without the psychological realm of the Caribbean region. Exile is reflected as a physical experience and is also connected with issues of language, insularity, and literary theory. The various voices of these women bring to the fore the problems of working within the frame of the politics of Western ideology and the physiological as well as spiritual representations of language, culture, and literary identity.

16. *Women Against the Grain: The Pitfalls of Theorizing Caribbean Women's Writing*

Lizabeth Paravisini-Gebert

If the Caribbean is indeed, as many have argued, the site of the first multinational, multi-cultural experiment, the crucible of diversity, the cradle of ethnic and cultural syncretism in the Americas, it should not surprise us, then, that as the West seeks to address its increasing eclecticism—the result of the third-worldlization it has undergone as waves of migrants from its former colonies descend upon its cities and towns—its scholars turn to the Caribbean, to its literature, culture, patterns of gender relations, for clues to an understanding of this newly found "hybridity." Aided and abetted by myriad theories developed for the purpose, they seek to determine what, if anything, the societies of the Caribbean—hybrid, mulatto, Creole, mestizo, take your pick—can teach the rest of the world about postcoloniality, transculturalism, postmodernity, transnationalism. In a climate of multicultural studies in which Black women—given their gender and race—have become the subject of almost feverish study, Caribbean women, by virtue of their race, gender, and postcolonial condition, have become the other's other, a valuable commodity, indeed. We—our writers particularly—can be scrutinized in all our pathologies and charming—when not exotic—aberrations, and set forth as examples of this, that, or the other post-something-or-other *condition*.

In the various interlocking theories of cultural and literary interpretation that comprise postcolonial scholarship, the condition of "postcoloniality" is taken as a given—one that may require articulation and elucidation (that being the happy task of the postcolonial scholar), but warrants no questioning as to its existence. They posit postcoloniality as the predicament of those fated to live in societies historically controlled from abroad, countries in which foreign interests mediated culture and politics. My main difficulty with their approaches is that in their elaborations, agency—however challenged, however deconstructed—rests with the colonizers and their traditions; they, more often than not, assign "an absolute power to the hegemonic discourse in constituting and disarticulating the native" (Perry). Seen from their vantage point, the colonized is perpetually condemned to reaction. Whether seen as assimilated by, revolting against, or elaborating a challenging discourse to colonial culture and mores, the postcolonial subject is perceived as always functioning in a configuration in which the colonizer's traditions, now apparently relegated to a "post" condition, retain their centrality throughout. The Caribbean subject—the male subject, that is—can cry his rage from the margins. The Caribbean woman—

or some carefully chosen examples of Caribbean womanhood—can bask in the warm glow of the very centrality of her marginality. She is of great interest to post-colonial scholarship because she is marginal. She can be brought in for analysis and then (hopefully) put back. In my moments of most profound distrust of totalizing theories I convince myself (unjustly, I am sure) that the theories are devised for the sole purpose of making sure we remain in our place, for some perverse amusement in watching us squirm.

I should briefly explain why I have moved from a vague uneasiness about being theorized from without to something akin to dread. A couple of years ago our best-known writer (by "our" I mean Puerto Rican), Rosario Ferré, announced an interest in claiming a Latino (as opposed to Caribbean or Latin American, or Puerto Rican) identity, which required that her next novel be written and published in English. She did, and the result, *The House on the Lagoon*, became a finalist for the National (i.e., American) Book Award. From my pro-independence nationalist (i.e., Puerto Rican) vantage point (which for my generation has meant a valoration of Spanish, or its Puerto Rican variant, as the unyielding rampart of cultural defense), the choice loomed like an unthinkable heresy.

I have calmed down considerably since then and am ready to discuss her decision as a most regrettable error of judgment, a seduction, a responding to the siren song of a multicultural, postcolonial book market which has opened a niche for a certain kind of female Caribbean writer whose work can be easily *consumed*, appropriated into a configuration where its serves the narrow purposes of theory, reassuring the reader that he or she understands the Caribbean without having to penetrate its multifarious realities. I was going to use Jamaica Kincaid's writings as another example of misappropriatable work, but Merle Hodge has analyzed, more eloquently and more insightfully than I could have done, the absence of a cultural dimension based on language in Kincaid's work that makes it so perilously accessible to essentializing theories of Caribbean womanhood. Suffice it to say that the Ferré incident brought to bear (at least to me) the perils of Caribbean women's writing being co-opted, seduced away from its glorious insularity (I will come back to this word) into postcolonial, postmodern, transnational space.

It is not my aim to argue that all conclusions based on postcolonial theories lack any validity: colonialism did indeed leave an indelible imprint on Caribbean nations, and anticolonial struggles have most clearly shaped the islands' political movements, particularly throughout the twentieth century. Caribbean societies, however, have managed to remain profoundly insular despite the colonial onslaught. By this I do not mean that they are unsophisticated, unworldly, or naive societies, but that they are driven as much, if not more, by internal, local concerns as they are by a persistent, continual, and continuous awareness of a colonial past. The peoples—the women—of the region have responded to their former colonization with myriad strategies for subverting the very history and identity imposed upon them by their metropolitan masters. It has long been a practice of Caribbean peoples to "carnivalize," at times to "cannibalize," the models imposed by officialdom.

The dethroning of colonial models extended to patterns of gender relations. Caribbean societies, precisely because of their prolonged colonial status, the far-reaching impact of the institution of slavery on gender roles and family relations, the correlation of race and class imposed by slavery, the gender imbalances created by the overwhelmingly male migration of the first half of the twentieth century, and myriad other factors, developed patterns of gender relations markedly different from those of the colonial metropolis. The standards familiar to the metropolis may have been closely imitated by the small enclaves of Europeanized white or light-skinned middle and upper-middle classes, but were frequently transformed by the masses of the people who wove new configurations out of the fabric of colonial mores. Official culture may have insisted on continuing to represent Eurocentric models as characteristic of Caribbean societies, making them, for example, the prerequisite for social mobility, but the reality was far more complex, more fluid, much more *sui generis*.

Among the Haitian peasantry, to offer a striking example, conventional marriage patterns hold little weight. Legal marriage, Wade Davis concludes in *Passage of Darkness*, has been "beyond the reach or desire" of the overwhelming majority of rural Haitians. *Plaçage*, a "socially if not legally sanctioned relationship that brings with it a recognized set of obligations for both man and woman," is a more common arrangement" (41, 43). Rural Haitian women, however, control the distribution of goods in the countryside and the marketplace—a role that guarantees them a strong voice and considerable power in the economic and social activities of the community, despite their apparent disadvantages in marital relations. Likewise, in "Slackness Hiding from Culture: Erotic Play in the Dancehall," one of the chapters of her remarkable book *Noises in the Blood*, Carolyn Cooper uses the metaphor of Slackness/Culture to investigate the "high/low," metropolitan/insular divide emblematic of Jamaican society as reproduced "in the hierarchical relations of gender and sexuality that pervade the dancehall" (11). Although the denigration of "slackness" that pervaded Jamaican colonial culture would appear to determine "the concomitant denigration of female sexuality" as manifested in the freedom of the dancehall, Cooper reads images of transgressive-woman-as-Slackness-personified as "an innocently transgressive celebration of freedom from sin and law" (ibid).

I underscore these factors, and offer these examples, simply to illustrate the limited applicability of theories of postcolonialism, postmodernism, even feminism, to a reality that may have been influenced by Euro-American cultural patterns, but which developed in fairly *local* ways in response to a collision between autochthonous and foreign cultures. These *local*—i.e., *insular* or Creole—responses to alien influences shaped the varieties of women's struggles to be found in the Caribbean, movements that often clash with each other as women of different classes and races strive to achieve sometimes contradictory goals. The insular factors affecting the development of the societies and cultures of the region—the indivisibility of gender relations from race and class, the intricate connections between sexual mores, skin pigmentation, and class mobility, the poverty and political repression that has left women's bodies exposed to abuse and exploitation—seem alien to the concerns of

Euro-American theoretical thought, which focuses on these factors as evidence of pathology.

This is nowhere clearer than in the frequent misreadings of the striking materiality of Caribbean women's depiction of the female body. Theorizations of Caribbean texts more often than not insist on interpreting bodies as symbolic constructs with cultural significance. The body thus exists as a form of discourse, "fictive or historical or speculative," but "never free of interpretation, never innocent" (Suleiman, 7). Female bodies and the perils to which they are subjected are often read as metaphors for some condition imposed upon us by pro-, virtual, or postcoloniality. The experience of many Caribbean women, historical experience as well as experience translated into literary texts, denies the body's existence as mere symbolic construct. During the media buildup leading to the most recent American intervention in Haiti, U.S. audiences heard, the majority for the first time, of the systematic use of rape by military forces as a means of political control. Haitian readers coming across the repeated, eventually murderous rape of Rose Normil in Marie Chauvet's *Colère* would reject feminist theorizing on the body's symbolism as superfluous, given the immediacy of the connection between women's rape and both historical and day-to-day reality in their country. Haiti's neighbors in the Dominican Republic, likewise, continue to be haunted by the story of the Mirabal sisters, the three courageous women murdered by Trujillo's henchmen because of their persistent efforts to oust the dictator. The account of their lives and deaths offered by Dominican-American writer Julia Alvarez in *In the Time of the Butterflies*, draws its strength from its close connection to history. One could indeed argue that the bodies of the Mirabal sisters are accessible to us through the symbolic discourse of texts such as Alvarez's. But only to a limited extent—for behind this discourse, however symbolic, stand the flesh-and-blood bodies of three vital young women, whose terror was real, whose bodies were torn apart, only to be used to inflict further torture—and through this torture a political lesson—on those to whom knowledge of their very real pain would bring immeasurable anguish and fear. In Dany Bébel-Gisler's testimonial text, *Léonora: L'histoire enfoui de la Guadeloupe*, as Ivette Romero has argued, Léonora brands her narrative with the many scars left on her body by her husband's abuse and the burden of work in the canefields, scars that attest to the palpability of her experiences, her very flesh bearing testimony to history.

The flesh-and-blood quality of women like Léonora, Rose Normil, and the Mirabal sisters serves as the vantage point from which Caribbean women writers and indeed most third-world women writers "read" and "write" the female body, from a materiality grounded in the specificities of history that set Caribbean writing apart from Euro-American theories of the body as text. This separateness, this unwillingness on the part of the Caribbean woman's textual body to yield easily to the demands of other women's theories, seems to me to be rooted in the complexities of intra-gender colonial relationships that postcolonial theory finds difficult to negotiate. Postcolonial theory is not so very comfortable with class (except insofar as the colonizer and colonized comprise different classes), or with race (ditto), or with gender issues (other than the vertical ones of male/female gender relationships). Caribbean women writers, on the other hand, have sought to reveal (horizontally, so to speak) the conflicting class and race realities of Caribbean women, conflicts in evidence from the early days of colonial society. C.L.R. James writes in *The Black Jacobins* of the underlying friction between women of different races and classes that characterized the colony of St. Dominique: "Passion," he writes, "was [the planters' daughters'] chief occupation, stimulated by over-feeding, idleness, and an undying jealousy of the black and Mulatto women who competed so successfully for the favours of their husbands and lovers" (30). The tensions to which James alludes, tensions stemming from profound class and race differences, have played perhaps a more central role in determining which women can write, which women we read, than other more decidedly colonial concerns, but that falls outside the purview of postcolonial theoreticians' interests.

Take the debate on women's rights in Puerto Rico as a case in point. The issue of women's rights began to be debated in the island in the early 1890s, when local newspapers began to focus on the subject of women's right to work, to own property, and to vote, and on women's role in the home and in society at large. The debate was led by two distinct and frequently opposed groups: working-class (i.e., Black and dark-skinned) women incorporated into the labor force after the American takeover, primarily in the tobacco and needlework industries, who sought union organization to fight economic exploitation; and middle-class (i.e., light-skinned) women, just entering the labor force as teachers, secretaries, bookkeepers, and clerks, who sought an end to their legal and social restrictions through their quest for the vote. The most glaring example of the split between the two feminist camps—one led by essayist and dramatist Luisa Capetillo, the other by novelist and journalist Ana Roqué—was the support given by the majority of middle-class suffragists to a project of law that would give the vote only to those women who could read and write. They received the vote in 1929. Most women had to wait until universal suffrage came into law in 1935. Poet Clara Lair, writing under the pseudonym of Hedda Gabler in the newspaper *Juan Bobo*, defended the middle-class position from the vantage point of her own self-perceived intellectual superiority thus: "I am going to declare that if the United States Congress decided to deprive of the vote Puerto Rican men who do not know how to read and write, it is an anomaly to request it for Puerto Rican women who, as a rule, don't know how to read and write either. . . . Most Free Congressman: it is a logical deduction that a woman who doesn't know how to write is a woman that has not wanted to read. And a woman who has not wanted to read is a woman who has not been able to think. This humble and amiable type of woman known as 'the Puerto Rican woman,' an atavistic servant, servant to a larger or lesser degree, servant to her master or to her father, or to her brother, or to her husband, but always a servant, is not the type of woman who thinks for herself, who acts for herself."[1] It is not the type of statement, addressed as it is against the political claims of another avowedly feminist group, that allows us to speak of women's solidarity in the region.

The tensions the Puerto Rican example illustrates touch upon the very vital issue of agency that postcolonial scholarship ascribes to colonial rather than intra-gender relationships. In this case, who has access to a congressman, whose agenda will be heard, who has power, and how will it be exercised? Which women, in short, can guide their own destiny? One resonant critique of Caribbean female writing, from the postcolonial theoretical viewpoint, is that of impatience with its characters' finding virtue and triumph in their ability to just come to terms with the limitations of their reality and endure. It goes against the theorists' grain. A central feature of Western theory as it relates to women is that of the emergence of a fully emancipated woman out of the mire of patriarchal culture. It is an image born of the myths of rugged individualism that have shaped the United States's image at home and abroad. Woman as maverick is the prevailing image in recent biographies of women like Eleanor Roosevelt, who emerges from the brilliant pages of Blanche Wiesen Cook's biography as symbol of American feminist womanhood in all its mythologizing power: crushed by her husband's affair with her own private secretary following her six pregnancies in the early chapters, Eleanor rises like a modern Phoenix to found a furniture factory, build her own house, engage in passionate friendships with women, run her own school for girls, learn to fly with Amelia Earhart, and become first lady on her own terms.[2] Dizzying stuff. But you can scan your memories in vain for similar images in the Caribbean and conclude that we lag behind the United States when it comes to heroic feminine material. To do so would be to judge heroism by standards that would never apply to the Caribbean region, where heroism, especially female heroism, as proven by glimpses into Beryl Gilroy's work and life, has been sought in the subsuming of individual aspirations and desires into the struggle for the betterment of the community, and where women have followed a tradition, in history as in literature, of grassroots activism and courageous resistance. More characteristic of the Caribbean historical process are the careers of women writers like Gilroy or Phyllis Allfrey, the latter credited with almost singlehandedly bringing democracy to Dominica through her efforts to found the Dominica Labor Party in 1955. In her attempt to wrest control of the Dominican political system from the hands of the landed and merchant elite, Allfrey had countless times crisscrossed the island on foot, traveling to near and remote villages and explaining in patois to gatherings of illiterate and semiliterate peasants the manifest advantages of allying themselves to a political party committed to furthering the workers' socioeconomic agenda. A young supporter remembers her campaign to found the Party as the island's "political awakening." While the upper class concentrated its fire on questioning Allfrey's political sincerity and accusing her of being a communist, he observed, the poor were happy, "drunk" with the feeling she had helped instill in them that "the day of the underprivileged was at hand" (Paravisini-Gebert).

Allfrey's career, tied as it was to the Caribbean's embryonic thrust toward political and cultural independence, also illustrates one significant aspect of women's progress toward fuller participation in all aspects of society: the impact of interregional and international migration on developing and spearheading women's efforts to become agents of their own fate. As a West Indian in London before the growth of a migrant community in the 1950s, Allfrey had mastered grassroots politics with the leftist branch of the Labor Party, working on campaigns led by birth-control proponents and feminists like Marie Stopes, Edith Summerskill, and Naomi Mitchison. Later she would make women's issues the focus of political activity in Dominica, pressing for the dissemination of birth control information, the availability of safe abortions, and the procuring of adequate medical care for women. Her activities were representative of a process of trans-island cross-pollinization that has nourished women's writing in the region.

Very often the process of migration, by forcing women into unfamiliar situations, experiences, and struggles, has resulted in a radicalization of political and social perspectives, leading women to assume roles not readily open to them in their home societies. Such is the case, for example, for Dominican women in the Washington Heights section of Manhattan, who have taken leadership roles in the domestic and community spheres, which would have been disallowed in the Dominican Republic. The organizational skills and leadership abilities nourished by these experiences have been invaluable both to their fledgling communities in the United States and to the home communities to which many of these women have eventually returned. Feminist leaders like Dominican poet and essayist Chiqui Vicioso, brought up and educated in the United States, have played central roles in grassroots ventures in the Dominican Republic as they have brought back with them often remarkable experiences in activism and the profound knowledge of their home societies to adapt those experiences to Caribbean needs and mores. Vicioso, returning to her home island as a UNESCO officer, organized peasant women into cultural cooperatives that fostered literary and artistic creativity as a means of empowering women to assume a greater level of control over their physical surroundings and economic activities. Likewise, Haitian women returned from abroad with organizational skills which furthered the struggle against the Duvalier's legacy of authoritarian military power. Recent interregional efforts to encourage communication and dialogue stemming from the trans-island communications fostered by migration have resulted in networks of communication that have proven invaluable in disseminating information and pinpointing successful strategies for women's community action and grassroots initiatives, countering the negative impact of free-zone development, securing information on health care and AIDS, developing ecological protection programs, limiting the alienating aspects of industrial work, and addressing such women-centered issues as abortion rights, child care, restrictions in access to education and jobs, battering, and child abuse.

In these interregional efforts we find women writers playing a leading role, as it has been in literature and the arts that these inter-island communications have developed with greater ease and cooperation (perhaps because they were seen as less threatening realms than political or economic collaborations). As in Allfrey's case, many Caribbean women writers have taken very active roles in feminist and political struggles: Marie Chauvet braved the Duvaliers in denouncing the Tonton Macoutes in *Amour, Colère et Folie* (1968) and *Les rapaces* (1986); Jacqueline Manicom, known primarily as the author of *Mon examen de blanc* (1972) and *La Graine* (1974), was cofounder of the feminist group Choisir and led a movement to make abortion legal in Guadeloupe (it is still rumored, such is the power of myth, that her fatal automobile accident in 1976 was the Silkwood-like result of these activities); Aída Cartagena Portalatin's founding of Brigadas Dominicanas to publish literary works banned by Trujillo placed her in constant danger. In their works, as in Ada Quayle's *The Mistress* (1957), Mayotte Capécia's *Je suis martiniquaise* (1948), the short stories of Olive Senior and Ana Lydia Vega, Paule Marshall's *The Chosen Place, the Timeless People* (1969), Michelle Cliff's *Abeng* (1984) and *No Telephone to Heaven* (1987), Elizabeth Nunez-Harrell's *When Rocks Dance* (1986), or Phyllis Allfrey's *The Orchid House* (1953), among many others, we find the salient elements of an emerging female and feminist creativity that seeks to examine the parameters of Caribbean writing from a vantage point that is truly Caribbean and appears to owe little to foreign concepts of women's power.

What I seek to suggest through these examples is that there has always been—throughout the history of women's orality and writing in the Caribbean—a fluid space in which women have defined the centrality of their bodies and voices through a deep connection to the specificities of our insularities. The voicelessness of the other's other that postcolonial theories assume to be our lot has been but the unwillingness or inability on the part of our colonizing others to listen to voices they have sought to delegitimize. The risk to Caribbean writing—women's writing in particular—is that of being lured away from our own creative spaces into the niche open to our writing by the various strands of postcolonial theories. They—in their interest in Condition, rather than Context, in their concern with isolated representation rather than contextualization within a national tradition—have the power of moving our writing, as in the extreme case of Rosario Ferré, away from its center into the floodlit centrality of a reimposed marginality. Like the trickster, Caribbean writing must negotiate the perilous terrain between a new readership open by the surge of postcolonial, multicultural scholarship and the lure of writing from that non-space. The best Caribbean writing has always come from a deep connection to the languages, cultures, religions, and traditions of our islands and their diasporas, from the very core of the various insularities of our myriad experiences. Postcolonial theories, like all mixed blessings, shall pass, but that insular space from which our writing can speak of the ethos of our peoples will remain. We leave it at our own peril.

17. Ex/Isle: Separation, Memory, and Desire in Caribbean Women's Writing

ELAINE SAVORY

> *I'm awfully jealous of this place (as you gather no doubt)*
> *I can't imagine anybody writing about it, daring to,*
> *without loving it—or living here twenty years, or being*
> *born here. And anyway I don't want strangers to love it*
> *except very few whom I'd choose—most sentimental.*
> *(But they are a bit patronizing you know.) However I've*
> *an idea that what with rain, cockroaches, and bad roads*
> *etc. Dominica will protect itself from vulgar loves.*
>
> —JEAN RHYS

> *Many-faceted and many-layered, this condition of exile is*
> *the legacy of colonialism and imperialism that first exiled*
> *Africans from their ethnicity and all its expressions—*
> *language, religion, education, music, patterns of family*
> *relations—into the pale and beyond, into the nether*
> *nether land of race.*
>
> —MARLENE NOURBESE PHILIP

This creative space which we call Caribbean women's writing is not and should not be predictable or easily definable. There is one essential feature we recognize: a strong attachment to the region, expressed often not just in content but in form, and we can adopt here Rhys's term *love*, in all of its complexity, to describe it. My own use of the term *desire* might suggest to those familiar with postmodern and post-colonial narratives that the intellectual line from Freud through Foucault and Lacan to Kristeva might be important here. But though that work has importantly informed contemporary discussion of subjectivity, bell hooks's frankly polemical construction of the concept of love as a potential political force in the African American community is more centrally important to the argument of this essay. hooks understands that subjectivity, the shape of feeling and identity, is culturally specific. In her essay, "Love as the Practice of Freedom" (from *Outlaw Culture: Resisting Representation*, 1994), she relates the idea of love to the history of African American culture through slavery and emancipation, through the history of racism and self-rejection. Caribbean women's writing, of whatever ethnic affiliation, is also part of that history in the sense that the construction of subjectivity, desire and love, is achieved in the shadow of consciousness of four hundred years of oppression and resistance. I argue here that the desire, which is the origin of writing, and manifests as a result of separation from the Caribbean—as a fractured, complex identification of love—is in effect the writer's condition of ex/isle.

Women writers who have fundamentally and formatively known the Caribbean region but for whatever reason do not live there now revisit it in their work. Those who were born overseas but shaped by Caribbean connection in their family lives write of that further incarnation of Caribbean identity, in the wider world. Those who were born in and have never left the region write of dramatic changes through the last years of the twentieth century. The point is, wherever you live in the world, if you live in a space which is connected to the Caribbean and you recognize Caribbean cultural sovereignty, you write within Caribbean space, where complexity, change, and political consciousness are crucially important. However we further define those, by linguistic markers or cultural parameters, our definitions are most productive (and most Caribbean) when they stimulate the possibility of further creative development, the possibility of new form.[1]

Of course we argue about placements because we are emotionally invested in our work and our work is our created territory, its contours our personal geography. Also because of still immensely durable neocolonial arrangements which lend support still to marginalization, suppression, and appropriation and which we struggle to oppose, subvert, and transform—a task which often means transforming ourselves to some degree. So our arguments about who we are and where we belong are vitally a part of the stimulation of writing. But it is the work—the survival of a range of inventive and accomplished writing—which marks Caribbean women's verbal artistry and the creative support of their critics and scholars, which is important. Our divisions, if set out oppositionally, or to privilege one identity over another, only weaken our communal capacity to share and then to go home to work alone in a fully creative way, whether we write fiction or criticism, poetry or theory, or all at once.

I distinguish between exile and what I call here ex/isle. Exile is the condition of separation from the country of birth. In my latter Caribbean-centered meaning, ex/isle, *isle* is not only the literal island but original cultural identity and connection, an identity which is based complexly in first self-definitions in terms of ethnicity, class, gender, nationality, generation. Ex/isle is the condition of separation from that identity, a separation in which, however, a new identity is reconstituted. Desire to make this new identity coherent with original subjectivity, never fulfilled but always pursued, works on fragments of memory: language itself becomes the agency for desire, and that is what brings the commitment to writing into being. This process can be just as evident in writers who have never left the region but who have complex relationships with their original cultural base, relationships which reflect a marked journey away from source. Indeed, perhaps all writing is about ex/isle in this sense:

even the most house-bound writer has inevitably to be away from origins, family, the world, in order to write.

So I do not interpret ex/isle as a negative experience. It is subjectivity separated from its origin, subjectivity which has the intention of remaining connected despite distance, but which is translocated and transformed by and into the desire to write. In the process of the writing, the original site of love, of subjectivity, the Caribbean itself, is reconstituted into other dimensions, images, identities. I defined love once, in a poem about women's writing, as "no fire, but a tremendous, quiet journeying on" ("love poem").[2] Edward Said has written of "traveling theory"; in relation to exile or migration it is helpful to adapt this and to speak of "traveling identity," a series of consecutive selves, linked together in the same life and resulting from the renewals of self in different environments. We can use major affiliations such as nationality or gender or race as temporary means to hold these selves together. But for a writer who migrates, who lives in ex/isle, language is itself a traveling space or series of spaces: a series of interconnected rooms or countries, reached only by passing through all of the others. Marlene Nourbese Philip has taken up Heidegger's definition of language as "the house of being" (69), a place where "life and death meet." Philip wants to "write from the center" but the center, in her case, has taken her far from home, even so far as to position herself as a Caucasianist, an expert on Europeans and their societies, by reason of cultural imperatives which have constructed whites and their cultures as a general norm. By moving so far from her own identity, she can the more definitively and excitingly explore it. In her prose poem "Looking for Livingstone," Philip creates a journey undertaken by a woman of African descent who discovers the complex identity of silence as well as the power of language. Livingstone is confounded by the self-confidence of this woman who finds him after journeying away from familiar territory through strange lands. To leave home is one way to come home: some people can understand their connection best without leaving; some need to go far away. The issue is not where the eye sits but what it sees.

Sometimes therefore it is only by means of moving outside the self that the center of the self can be seen, as in the Chinese yin-yang symbol, where the center of the white portion is black, and vice versa, and where the two colors are distinguished in equal space but divided by a curving, not a straight line. They therefore fit together as in a jigsaw puzzle, needing each other, interconnected. Perhaps we might rewrite Fanon in this context, for when he said, in Black Skin, White Masks, that "for the black man there is only one destiny. And it is white" (9), he might have said that for the white man (and woman) there is only one destiny, and it is black. Our black and white worlds are defined by difference but maintain that difference only by acute awareness of one another. When bell hooks speaks of going beyond resistance to transformation, she speaks of redefining identity in new creative terms, but that redefinition begins from acute awareness of the power relations which have defined human difference. The yin-yang symbol is the most positive metaphor for such a possibility: for difference articulated positively as identity, transition, and the possibility of balance rather than boundary, but nevertheless accepted as the starting point of creativity and a primary source of subjectivity.

Writers who have affiliations to more than one place must construct identity complexly. Paule Marshall is a major example of a writer who is equally affiliated to the Caribbean and to African America and whose contribution to Caribbean literary culture has been the more powerful for being mediated between two geographical locations: New York (not the same as the United States) and Barbados.[3] Marlene Nourbese Philip was born and grew up in the Caribbean[4] but now lives in Toronto, Canada. Jean Rhys was born and raised in Dominica,[5] though her father was from Britain; she went to Britain in her late teens and only returned once for a brief visit to the region. Pauline Melville[6] was born in Guyana and raised in England but has a strong connection to Guyana. Beryl Gilroy[7] left Guyana when she was a young woman to study in England in the fifties and has lived there ever since. Gilroy has written of the origins of her fiction in intense feelings provoked by living in England, feelings such as homesickness, depression, and rootlessness. The means to holding a sense of self healthily together in such circumstances lie in examining the past, working through memory and the desire for reconciliation of old and new versions of the self. We are constructed conventionally on the outside, but complexly on the inside: the two must speak to one another.

Though I have mentioned only five writers, in fact the number of Caribbean women writers who live outside the region is great—I could have chosen very many more important examples, such as Michelle Cliff, Dianne Brand, Olive Senior, Ramabai Espinet, Jan Shinebourne, and Joan Riley.

A character in a novel or a poem is only rarely a writer, but the journey which a character makes toward becoming coherent is like the journey through language from home to ex/isle to return. In the end, it is not where you locate the body but where you live in the mind which signifies.

I will take an example of this journey from texts of three of the writers I have mentioned. Anna Morgan in Rhys's *A Voyage in the Dark* lives in a time after the First World War when a physical reconnection with her Caribbean origins is very difficult, involving a long journey. The kinds of instant reconnections available to us through technological options like fast jet travel, the telephone, fax and modem and videotape are not possible for Anna. The journey which she takes is dangerous—indeed in Rhys's preferred version of the novel she dies at the end from a botched abortion. Desire for Anna does not lie in her sexual experiences, which are in various ways and degrees alienating or traumatic. It lies in her memories of her childhood home and identity, to which she journeys: it seems clear that it would be through a lover's willingness to connect with that childhood origin that Anna would discover sexual pleasure. This is particularly important since Anna is trying to construct her subjectivity after the physical rupture with childhood that migration has brought. Her English aunt sets out her cultural parameters by which Anna is for her suspect since she was brought up rather too close to the black Caribbean community. Anna spoke, as a child, "[e]xactly like a Nigger" (65), according to Aunt Hester.

There is, if you think about it, no sustained human relationship without memory. I learned this recently, when someone very close to me could not recognize me after an operation. It was a brief but terrifying moment: we can perhaps feel intense abstract desire for strangers sometimes, in the sense that all new lovers are strangers at the first moment of physical interaction, but once our humanity is involved, once we are revealed to another person, it is memory which stimulates the return of desire.

In Anna's case, an important moment in her affair with Walter Jeffries involves her memories of her West Indian childhood and her acceptance of too much alcohol. She is mildly rebuked by Walter for asking for whisky—she is nineteen—and she connects this to her family history; "It's in my blood" (51). This is a direct alliance with her "Uncle Bo," whom Aunt Hester thoroughly dislikes and condemns. Clearly Anna will not embrace the offer, by Aunt Hester, to make her a conventional English woman. She "goes upstairs" with Walter for sex anesthetized by alcohol. Her desire for her childhood is repudiated by him, much as it is in much less obvious but still crucial ways by Hester, and so he cannot become a pathway, as a mature affection might, toward her realization of her most coherent and happy self. Instead, he makes sure she knows he does not enjoy "hot places" (54). Anna's journey back to childhood becomes more and more private and divorced from her sexual life as the novel progresses and her sexual encounters become more about money and survival than any presence of feeling on either side. Rhys's original ending, while emotionally difficult for the reader, is logical: the divorce between desire and memory on the one hand and sexuality on the other leads directly to Anna's abandonment of self-esteem and the energy to go forward with her life. Anna's ex/isle is dramatically self-destructive because the culture in which she finds herself cannot make a place for her memories, for her self, and she lacks the inner resources to construct that place by herself except in retreating from reality. The inner self, or place of origin, and the outer self, or evident cultural attribution, are divorced dangerously from one another.

Paule Marshall's Avey Johnson used to know desire when as a young woman she and her husband maintained their connection to African cultural identities. He would make love to her then by talking to her about her desirability, making of her a Gullah beauty, a woman whose pride in herself flowered into sexual love for him as he went on talking—memory of ancestral past and racial pride made, through language, into desire, language as desire. But as Jay Johnson gave himself over to beating the system and making money, he drifted away from those origins. Avey was left a still proud but isolated wealthy woman, expressing her desires in expensive and elegant clothing, in pleasures bought by generous amounts of money and dictated by convention, like her annual Caribbean cruise. Her journey, in *Praisesong for the Widow* (127), is toward renewal of her desire for life through reconnection with African custom, in the form of rituals in Carriacou, in the Caribbean. Separation, in her case, has shut down too much of her memories and with it her desire for life. Through the ancient African dances performed in Carriacou—for dance is always in Paule Marshall's work a powerful metaphor for connection with life—Avey witnesses the falling away of years first from her guide Lebert Joseph and then from herself. She feels the heat of the dancers' bodies reaching her "in a strong, yeasty wave" (247).

Eventually, as she gives herself more and more to the dance, this stiff and apparently repressed older woman begins to find herself supple, "[a]ll of her moving suddenly with a vigor and passion she hadn't felt in years" (249). She does not need to stay on the island after this experience for it to be lasting and regenerative: she will return to the United States to live. She will be ex/isle but not exiled any longer from her innermost identity and spirit.

These examples move in opposite directions: Anna failing to reconnect with her origins and suffering a displacement in her desire for life as a result; Avey managing to return, owing to her financial ability to make a trip to the islands. Rhys's character is, like Rhys herself, a white Creole; Avey Johnson is, like Paule Marshall, of African descent. What if we were to find that white women construct ex/isle differently from black women, that the trajectory of relationship to memory, desire, and origins, their relations therefore to the wellspring of language from which their textuality is drawn, is markedly affected by four hundred years of different history? White women, after all, must face the history of their race as oppressor, of their gender as beneficiary of racial oppression, no matter where they are born and live; black women must face their race's history of marginalization and subordination. Both know that their gender identities are complexly involved with their racial histories. For black women, there is a proud ancestry of strong and surviving women, of resistance; for white women, there is a shameful history of female ancestors who lived by a double dependence on white men and black people. Rhys's character is brave enough to face her history, though she tries, problematically, to identify with a mulatto slave woman, Maillotte Boyd, as she endures the sexual act with Walter: in effect she tries to jettison her white identity and make herself into a black woman, the victim of white male lust. It is clearly too painful for her to see herself simply as white, especially because she is, as white Creole, constructed as inferior to British whites in England. But in her inability to understand her history clearly and to transcend it, Anna suffers terribly from lack of desire to protect herself from damage and to find the necessary energy for a happy life. By contrast, Avey Johnson throws off her evasion of her ancestral past and in the process liberates and reenergizes her spirit and even her body. Ex/isle is profoundly creative for both women, for even Anna can dream in complex images of her past. But for Avey Johnson the pathway is strengthening and positive, while for Anna it is draining and negative.

But both black and white history constructs all of us, whether we recognize it or not. Moreover, our personal identity is at a more subtle level less about the oppositional quantities of black and white than the continuum of complex identity which ranges through every shade of brown, gold, cream, and pink, informed by the affiliations we protect and cherish, as much by choice as by inheritance. These affiliations are cultural affiliations, they are Caribbean: African, Asian, European.

In Marlele Nourbese Philip's poem cycle in *She Tries Her Tongue, Her Silence Softly Breaks*, a woman searches for her mother, for her origins and cultural identity, "Where high and low meet I search / find can't, way down the islands' way" (28). The search is partly for place but mainly for recollection, memory, to retrieve intimate connection. "Sightings," the penultimate poem in the cycle, is a powerful evocation of desire, love, language, and landscape and is worth considering in full:

> Nose to ground—on all fours—I did once
> smell that smell,
> on a day of once—
> upon a time, tropic with blue
> when the new, newer and newest of leaves compete,
> in the season of suspicion she passed,
> then and ago trailed the wet and lost of smell,
> was it a trompe l'oeil—
> the voice of her sound, or didn't I once
> see her song, hear her image call
> me by name—my name—another sound, a song,
> the name of me we knew she named
> the sound of song sung long past time,
> as I cracked from her shell—
> the surf of surge
> the song of birth. (35)

Here, language, artistry, desire, the sexuality of birth itself, the imprinting which smell brings for humans, the vivid sight of tropical foliage and sky all combine: the journey is not to find a person but to find reentry into memory and desire as a way to continue both life and voice. The persona of the poem cycle struggles to maintain memory in the north: "To the north comes the sometime / blow of the North East trades— / skin hair heart beat / and I recognize the salt / sea" (29). The mother-daughter bond is metaphorically the connection between island and the creative condition of ex/isle, and that brings powerful words: "call and response in tongue and / word that buck up in strange" (31). There are seven "dream-skins": "sea-shell, sea-lace, feather-skin and rainbow flower, / afterbirth, foreskin and blood-cloth." (31) These terms become titles for sections of the long poem which follows, which is titled "Dream-skins" and is about a dream "in two languages" (32), the languages of the African and European worlds.

In the section "Feather-skin," the island/mother is suckled by the daughter and also suckles here, "thin like the / host / round and white / she swells enormous with / milk and child" (32). There is in this section "a choosing— / one breast / neither black nor white" (33). In "Foreskin," the mother is "wise black and fat" (33). In the last section, "Blood-cloths," the dream is now "in a different language," as if black and white have been metaphorically reconfigured, in the way that Caribbean culture is a creative reconfiguration of opposites into new identities, as elements combined in a crucible in the laboratory emerge as new compounds, with new futures.

Angela Ingram writes: "Geographical exile is often more a getting away from than a going to a place" (4). Much is made of this idea in some important recent studies of white women travelers who clearly left their own cultures because women were too confined there:[8] perhaps the same could be argued in the case of Jean Rhys, who left Dominica voluntarily and refused to return when asked by her family. But for women of African descent, ex/isle was, at least in earlier generations, often the result of involuntary migration, a leaving home on the part of parents in order to secure economic prospects for the family not available in the Caribbean, or in order to seek an education. Perhaps we might complicate both of these broad images by saying that ex/isle is often more a matter of changing inner space than outer location or identity. The inner self, as Beryl Gilroy has so often maintained, must be connected to the outer self, and that does not easily occur once the person moves out of childhood locales. Perhaps it is not so much that each and every black or white woman must follow a racial pathway to her literary voice but that there are cultural parameters which she must understand and to which she responds, consciously or not, along the way. Leaving home means opening up the possibility of complex decision, of complex realignments in terms of race, nationality, class, gender. Marlene Nourbese Philip's protagonist signifies her complex cultural identity by choosing the breast, which is neither black nor white.

I have made a distinction between exile and ex/isle, the first a matter of literal separation between birthplace and place of work or domicile, the second a creative if painful space in which a woman's writing becomes a means to construct images of progressively developing subjectivities. Celeste Schenk identifies "the politics of exclusion," or the ways in which women writers can be "exiled by genre" (225ff). Schenck calls for a "radical comparativism" of women's writing which can prevent us from marginalizing texts and writers through the imposition of culturally or politically determined criteria. What she has in mind is the way in which early women poets in Euro-America were shut out of the Modernist male poets' canons of experimentation, or if they chose experimental form, judged by other women as writing like men. In our development of canons and criteria of judgment for Caribbean women writers, I believe we can avoid both prescription and lack of precision: I think examining the journey from home through the alienation of a strange land to successive aesthetic resolutions of both together is helpful and leads us away from the unproductive oppositions of regional writers versus those overseas. More importantly, such a direction makes central the creative process itself: a process which, even when experienced at the writer's original home, requires a complex distancing from close connection as much as acknowledgment of it.

Works Cited

Angler, Carole. *Jean Rhys*. Boston: Little, Brown and Company, 1990.

Blunt, Alison and Gillian Rose, eds. *Writing Women and Space: Colonial and Postcolonial Geographies*. New York: The Guildford Press, 1994.

Broe, Mary Lynn and Angela Ingram, eds. *Women's Writing in Exile*. Chapel Hill: University of North Carolina Press, 1989.

Fanon, Frantz. *Black Skins, White Masks*. Trans. Charles Lam Markmann. London: Paladin, 1970.

Gilroy, Beryl. *Boy-Sandwich*. Oxford: Heinemann, 1989.

————. *Frangipani House*. London: Heinemann, 1986.

————. "I Write Because . . ." Ed. Selwyn Cudjoe *Caribbean Women Writers*. Wellesley, Mass.: Calaloux Publications, 1990. 195–201.

hooks, bell. *Outlaw Culture: Resisting Representations*. London: Routledge, 1994.

Lawrence, Karen R. *Penelope Voyages: Women and Travel in the British Literary Tradition*. Ithaca, NY: Cornell University Press, 1994.

Marshall, Paule. *Brown Girl, Brownstones*. Old Westbury, New York : The Feminist Press, 1981.

————. *The Chosen Place, The Timeless People*. New York: Random House, 1984.

————. *Daughters*. New York: Penguin Books, 1992.

————. *Praisesong for the Widow*. New York: G.P. Putnam's Sons, 1983.

Naipaul, V. S. *The Middle Passage*. Harmondsworth: Penguin 1969 .

Philip, Marlene Nourbese. *She Tries Her Tongue, Her Silence Softly Breaks*. Charlottetown: Ragweed Press, 1989.

————. *Frontiers: Essays and Writings on Racism and Culture*. Stratford, Ontario: The Mercury Press, 1992.

Rhys, Jean. *Voyage in the Dark*. New York: W.W. Norton, 1982.

Said, Edward W. *The World, the Text and the Critic*. Cambridge, Mass.: Harvard University Press, 1983.

Savory, Elaine. "Marlene Nourbese Philip." Eds. Bernth Lindfors and Reinhard Sander. *Dictionary of Literary Biography*. Washington D.C.: Gale Research Inc., 1996. 296–306

————. "Mathematical Limbs and Other Eventualities: Translocation of the Body in Pauline Melville's Shape-Shifter." Ed. Sue Thomas. *Decolonising Bodies: New Literatures Review*, vol. 30 (Winter 1995). 47–58.

Eds. Wyndham, Francis and Melly, Diana. *The Letters of Jean Rhys*. New York: Viking Penguin Inc., 1984.

18. *Dangerous Liaison: Western Literary Values, Political Engagements, and My Own Esthetics*

ASTRID H. ROEMER

> *Jesus.*
> *He says*
> *The man was born*
> *Long ago*
> *In the country of white man.*
> *He says*
> *When Jesus was born*
> *White man began*
> *To count years*
> *From one, then it became ten,*
> *Then one hundred*
> *Then one thousand*
> *And now it is*
> *One thousand*
> *Nine hundred*
> *And ninety six.*
> *My husband says*
> *Before the man was born*
> *white men counted years backwards*
> *Then it became*
> *One thousand*
> *Then one hundred*
> *Then ten,*
> *And when it became one*
> *Then Jesus was born.*
> *I cannot understand all this*
> *I do not understand it at all!*
> —OKOT P'BITEK

With the publication of *Song of Lawina*, Okot p'Bitek struck a chord that resonated in the hearts not just of East Africans, but indeed even African Americans like Alice Walker and African Caribbeans like me who intend to repeat: I cannot understand all this; I do not understand it at all!

Dear friends, I had to go that far even in paraphrasing one of the best critics, the

Goan Peter Nazareth, to make you understand that the notions of my reading are rooted in the history and future of a so-called Black living in the Diaspora. To me it is not a shame to confess that being influenced by the colonial and post-colonial power for more than a lifetime makes it a necessity, as Nazareth put it in his latest trickster book: "to roam the whole world looking for the pieces to make sense of my world, which was fragmented by colonialism and made to fit into the needs of the metropolitan center's rising capitalism, industrial and financial."[1]

Professor Nazareth found writers like Salkey, Ebejer, and Reed and bit by bit discovered the tricks so-called third-world writers are using to construct literary truth with their texts. Not to mislead or to hide and keep distance between art and artist or between novelist and audience, and not even to create a sort of special style to discuss any discourse: what Nazareth found was a "self-fulfilling tradition" of writing in the language of the colonial power but "out of the suppressing context."

And the "suppressing context" is what colonized writers share: "the experiences of having to struggle against the idea of powerlessness and of decisions always being made elsewhere." *In the Trickster Tradition* is one of the most important and brave essays about literary critics and close readings I have ever read, and because Nazareth's notions lightened up my own literariness, I would like to dedicate my reading to him and to all Caribbean tricksters.

"Dangerous Liason," the title of my reading, is directly related to my newest novel, *Dangerous Life*.[2] The main character is not, as people expected, female. For the first time I wanted to search for freedom and humanity through the eyes of a young African Caribbean boy. Onno, as I named him, is part of a so-called Creole family; his father is a minister and the family is surviving on the countryside of Suriname among Muslims, Hindus, and Buddhists after years and years of living in the midst of the natives in the rain forest of Suriname.

The liaison in this novel is between Christianity, the postcolonial administration ("the government"), and African resources. In terms of microanalysis some may say that *Dangerous Life* is the old tragedy of father, mother, and a son: the Oedipus drama. Even though all of these analyses are true in a way: my novel is just telling or exposing the struggle for dignity and a decent life for African Caribbean men and their families in a postcolonial context.

African Surinamese males called my book the most confronting thing they've ever passed through and women said that the novel is an archetype of the so-called Creole family. Even the white critics could not ignore the colonial ghost which all the characters in my book are fighting against in their own ways. For example: the minister articulates his fight by hating the institution of the church he works for, the mother hers by daily trying to keep the family together, and their son his by searching for serenity.

The metaphors which prompted me to subtitle my reading as "Western Literary Values, Political Engagements, and My Own Esthetics" are clearly projected in my characters: the minister is politically engaged in supporting the military regimes; the mother is trying to keep the family together with Western family norms such as "being an unhappy married woman is much better than being a happy single mother," and the son is looking for the esthetics of humanity. But the tragedy is that none of the characters could free themselves from the colonial dreams: truth, beauty, and justice. And right here the trickster strategy slips in, known as a vital metaphor in African Caribbean fables. The never articulated trick in African Caribbean lifestyles is this: by gathering power from the status of powerlessness, Anansi, the trickster, is constantly fooling the powerfuls by acting like them. So even his image is partly a lie: a sort of well-done ego as a mask to get a chair at the tables of the power plays; the Creoles or African Caribbeans are using their colonial images like a carnival costume to communicate with power. This could be identified as the non-articulated lifestyle of the African Caribbeans. Maybe the exhausting way colonized peoples celebrate their carnival is a symptom related to the trickster tradition. During some days we are allowed to play the trickster game completely unbidden!

Chinua Achebe's Ezeulu, the Chief Priest in the work *Arrow of God*, says to his son when deciding to send him to the Christian school at the point at which colonialism is consolidating itself in West Africa: "The world is like a Mask dancing, if you want to see it well, you do not stand in one place."[3] And we all know the lines Harry Belafonte sang so wonderfully, demanding: "Lord don't stop the carnival!"

In my country, Anansi has a wife he is very devoted to, and of course, as poors do, Anansi and his wife Akuba love to have a big family. Ma Akuba is very aware of the tricks her husband is playing, and she does believe that his way is the only decent one to survive and to dismantle the colonial power. She is the one supporting her husband by waiting at home, raising the kids, protecting the neighborhood, and being untouchable for the poisonous penetration of the colonial masters.

But—and this is the moral of the trick—as soon as Anansi is trying to betray his own family, he almost dies, gets mad, or gets lost in the wilderness, because Ma Akuba is no longer there waiting for him to come home. Ma Akuba, home, and neighborhood are metaphors for THE SELF of colonized peoples. The wife, the mother, the kids, the house, and the neighborhood ought to be FREE and UNTOUCHABLE because they function as clear mirrors, authentic images, healthy sources. In Anansi fables, the spiders don't even live together with other animals, and staying alive means "stick together."

What am I telling you with this strange prologue? Am I trying to catch you in a trickster web? How could an African Caribbean writer play games with the colonial powers without losing a grip on self-respect, dignity, and absolute locality to her/his own blood-rooted history-centered powerlessness? Why do some of us get drunk or get lost in "de guestroles," while we were only playing to dismantle the colonial power and gather "power-things" to share with the others waiting at home? Isn't it painful to watch too many of us being the colonizer while many others are still waiting in the neighborhood for better days without rude masters?

It was Toni Morrison who introduced the term "cataracts" in her reviews: cataracts is a disease of the eye, which can cause blindness, as we all know, but Morrison is taking the definition to the level of spiritual and intellectual blindness, that is taking away the transparency to see through the past, the future, and daily experiences. Isn't it strange that spiderwebs and cataracts do have the same structure?

On the analogy of Peter Nazareth's point that so-called third-world writers, as Caribbean writers, must deal with the context of the spider trickster Anansi and his wife Akuba to survive in the postcolonial context, which is only constructed to serve the needs of the Europeans, Toni Morrison is proudly begging the African American writers to remove the cataracts that dazzle their perception of reality. Conclusions: African Caribbean writers should be aware of the trickster tradition in their consciousness and use this anticolonial power strategy in their literary texts; African American writers should be attentive to the possibilities of cataracts and should mislead the disease with their usage of language and myth. With these two warnings in mind I'm taking you all to my own "dangerous liaison."

My first love was language (maybe the sound of "mamma"), and of course there was a point of no return for me when I discovered the magic of written words. In the magnum opus *Segu*,[4] by the distinguished Maryse Condé, there is that "point of no return" when one of the Bambara sons seems to be witched by the Koran—not because of its content but because of the magic of the written language. And that is where the tragedy started: a conflict between parole and script, between sound and silence; but more than that, Condé exposed the moment the Bambara son broke through his own tradition of language to let "the stranger" in. And by letting "the stranger (white, male, European, Christian) in," Africa lost her heritage, her land, and even her peoples. We are all devoted to the written texts; we are writers, novelists; our job is making books and selling the silence of the written speech. Even Socrates through Plato refused to let the script in, because he believed what the Bambara knew: script will change humanity in a frightful way.

It is now recognized that the earliest Hebrew scriptures were transmitted for hundreds of years before being committed to writing, and that even when the writing process began, about the time of King Solomon, the living tradition continued in prophecy and psalm until collections of these were made at the time of the Exile in Babylon, and books were directly written down. This period, from the initiation of the oral tradition to the point when it was written down, is very short compared with the Hindu scriptures, composed in a secret language, Sanskrit, and handed down with remarkably little deviation from generation to generation of Brahmin priests. The point when tradition becomes scripture is clearly a landmark in the history of a religion. The point of scripture is that the original revelation is preserved for all time, giving a norm by which conduct and teaching can be judged.[5]

Again I need a sort of historical context to say how much Western literary values are based upon the belief in "conducting and teaching" through the written text. Caribbean writers must accept that being a writer is being caught in one of the main colonial power programs of conducting, teaching, judging!

Being aware of this is being in contact with the trickster memory, or what in Jungian terms the collective unconsciousness of the Anansi archetype articulated as: I play the power game to gather "power-things" for the others "back home." So conducting, teaching, and judging should be interpreted as "carnival costumes" or as "cataracts" whether they come from us or from "agents of the colonial power." From this point I would like to introduce another qualification named "political engagement," a commitment rooted in our history as Africans in the Diaspora and in the history of the Renaissance of Western Europe.

It was in Germany that a single man named Imannuel Kant[6] gave his whole life to fight intellectually against the power of lyrics from the church, the state, metaphysics, and science. The Renaissance was the greatest period in Europe's history since the cultural dominance of ancient Rome: new riches spread among the bourgeoisie, science shook itself free from the shackles imposed by Christian dogma, the divine right of church and state began to be challenged. And the philosopher Kant, almost three centuries after the beginning of the Renaissance, had to state the matter again by the simple question: WHAT IS ENLIGHTENMENT?

Because in his time new dogmatisms began to replace the old ones. In religion, the rise of Protestantism led to Christian sectarianism on a massive scale, and in political life, the rise of individual towns and rulers led to wars which were as protracted as they were pointless.

In what Western philosophers are still calling the boldest move ever made by a philosopher, Kant developed a formal doctrine to measure "truth, beauty, and justice," and by breaking with traditional scripts and with the uncontrolled producing of written wisdom and knowledge, he gave room to construct a universal moral code by reason. In his essay *"Was Ist Aufklärung?,"* or "What Is Enlightenment?," he held an extreme methodological discourse to "free the mind from the power products of others," and with his intellectual and logical arguments he inspired people to start "thinking their own thinking" in search of the borders of reason. Although his method was quite "idealistic," he argued that reason is the means by which phenomena of experience are translated into understanding.

What Kant did was to remove cataracts from the eyes of his society, and he encouraged people to identify the interests of the "new masters." Did Kant realize that there were millions of people dragging others into slavery, and that the self-confidence Europeans had rediscovered led them to regard other parts of the world not as the home of equals, but as places to be "discovered," colonized, and plundered? Of course: in his famous essay he mentioned the cowards and the lazy minds, people too lazy and too cowardly to "start their own thinking" and use "reason" to dismantle their enemies. I mention that Kant, like so many other intellectuals in Europe, did not really know what was going on in the colonial program. And of course he made the mistake of his life when without verification, he believed the information of the slave masters: church and state, and science. However, Die Aufklärung in Germany and the Renaissance in France gave their experiences to art and science; and literature standing in between had to generate values from both science and art.

Looking at Western literary values from that point of view means accepting that these values are all developed in an intellectual, artistic, and philosophical context where Africans were nothing more than slaves and humanity was defined from a white male bourgeois perspective called "humanity" or "Christianity," or "science."

Again I use a historical close-up to clarify the position of African Caribbean and African American writers. In our trying to get the attention of publishers, editors, critics, and the rest of the world: our readers, we must play the sublime trickster games by using Western values in behalf of our own interests.

It is an irony drama that the books we loved and the books that made us love books were not made to "conduct, teach, judge" Blacks. So the literary values which slipped into our esthetics, minds, and body are mostly against our own esthetic nature. And these values are still dominant.

In a conversation with her, Bill Moyers attacked Toni Morrison by saying: "The best-selling novels on the eve of the Civil War were sappy stories written by women about courageous orphans. Your people never show up in the novels of that time. How do you explain that?" And Morrison answered with a bullet: "They do show up. They are everywhere. They are in the writers' preoccupation with blackness. They are in all the dark symbols."[7]

But this tragedy of slumbering in the darkness of the colonial powers is not that extreme: African Caribbeans have their *Anansi* stories, their spiritual myths, their songs, their music and rituals. And those are sources to "come home" or to "feel in the neighborhood" when playing the masters-ego is driving one tired and crazy. Without the "untouchable measures of home" not only does a writer get lost in the interests which are against her people, but also the characters and their lives won't be able to mislead and remove cataracts. In an interview Morrison mentioned that every art is political. Morrison's approach is in conflict with the European standard that a writer should not be a storyteller, a message-bringer, or a teacher but an enchantress, a witch, because "Literature is Magic."

But, dear friends, who is mastering the definition of magic? And why couldn't African Caribbeans start their own tradition of literature not by trial and error but by grounded intellectual discourse? As Morrison once said: "Critics have vested interests in the survival of art as economics, have vested interest in making art into whatever fad that happens to be needed at the time. So it's very easy to dislike. But Black people must be the only people who set out our criteria in criticism. White people can't do it for us. That's our responsibility."[8] With this notion it is time to complete the love triangle by letting my own esthetics in.

Last year at Wellesley College I tried to explain how I prepare myself to write. What I wanted to state is that writing to me is taking responsibility: making novels is entering the circle of the classic power plays: race-interests, gender-interests, class-interests, nation-interests, and so forth. It is the enduring and penetrating power of fixed words which are holding the whole world in a sort of grip and the end is not there yet. Information of all kinds is fighting for attention.

Again, the continent of our ancestors and African Caribbeans generally is mostly out of this game. The old stereotypes about us aren't really knocked out, or new ones are waiting to drive me and the peoples I feel at home with aside. Instead of reading good books and looking for serenity in poetry, the youth is up to listen and to watch.

And even though I'm almost fifty I must confess that the best poetry I'm letting in is by listening to the lyrics of songs. As if the Bambara's point of no return has turned upside down: the spirituality of life has not been shaped for script. Language is sound and not silence; life is image and not word. But why do I love *Sula* by Morrison, *The Color Purple*, by Walker, and *Segu*, by Condé, in the way that I love listening to Sarah Vaughan, Harry Belafonte, Bob Marley, and so many others?

The arguments given to estimate my answer are triggering the pain of the dangerous liaison: once I've entered the power circle of the written word with my trickster consciousness I will not return without gathering all valuable things for myself and my neighborhood. But which are the valuable things now, and do I still have a neighborhood at the end of this century?

The peoples back home in Suriname hate their writers overseas: because they do not want our novels and fame, they want us! They want us in the neighborhood to hear if the sound of our laugh is authentic and if the smile on our face is not a sign of the fixed masters' ego. And I think that they are right: who am I after so many years of trickster games in Europe without the senses of the untouchables? The difference between African Caribbean writers and African American writers is that the latter don't have to live in exile. I mention Angela Davis, who took the risk during the Soledad Case to be killed rather than to run to another country; and so did the Greek Socrates.

Because how could one wear the trickster mask when there is no one to identify the unmasked; and how could one play the trickster game when there is no one around to play the game with? What is the truth, beauty, and justice of life when the carnival is going on and on?

What I'm saying is that when one is lost in a liaison there is no safety, no tie, no home; there is just the game and the excitement it brings. And there will be a point where there is no difference between lies and truths, love and hate, pain and pleasure, enemy and lover. And such a dilemma is taking one back to the state of mind where the master-slave relationship was a drug of neurotic contradictions. Transforming this to the position of African Caribbean writers is not too difficult. But I don't like generalizations and I promised to say something about my own esthetics.

The notion of Kant is a real light bringer: in African tradition there is not something like a Renaissance; people should believe the tradition, and even dreams and other "strange experiences" should be taken to "a special person" to translate in the traditional ways. Discussing the tradition was a sin: a symptom of the evil.

Africans in the Diaspora had to discuss their reality and were pushed into a state of mind which forced them to do their own thinking and use reason to call their reality into question. So we African Caribbeans do have a tradition of "the intellectual work called thinking," and I add Kant's notion of rethinking traditional knowledge to this, plus his basic argument that knowledge should be brought to the society to be "purified": there is no truth without the falsification and verification of the society. Because that's how morality (ethics) starts.

Transforming it into writing: there is no novel without a neighborhood, no writer without a home, no sentence without the writer's logic. No book without a moral code. But if there *is* no novel without a neighborhood! If there is no writer without a home, no sentence without a writer's logic, not a single story without a moral code, then literature must be engaged. Literature can't exist without exploring the interests of one's neighborhood, one's home, one's logical concept, and one's moral codes. And I guess that Morrison's notion that literature is political is comparable to my point of view that there is no novel, no story, no poem without interests.

Another notion is based upon an old statement of mine that the colonial language should be reconstructed by colonized writers before using it: language is a power medium and I must unpower it for my own longings.[9] It is a necessity that the neighborhood "understands" the language and that the outside world just "overstands" the text because it is not made "in their size," and the text is not dealing with their interests. It takes a well-done trickster mentality to produce certain kinds of scriptures without taking risks to be killed or molested by enemies but rather remain charming enough to be published—"sell-able."

My last point is typical because it is rooted in Africa, where griots are telling stories over and over again, sometimes without marked changes. Traditions are kept alive by storytellers who, by some mysterious faculty beyond the grasp of literate people, are able to remember great epics and lists without effort; they are handed down because they hold meaning for the culture concerned. Broadly speaking, oral traditions fulfill two social functions. First, they may be a means of teaching the values and beliefs which are integral to the culture; second, they may serve to validate the particular social and political arrangements which currently prevail—the distribution of land, the claims of one powerful lineage to the chiefship, or the pattern of relations with a neighboring people. Most of the standard oral stories we have made in the Caribbean are exploring the brutality of the colonial power and sometimes the genius to dismantle or handle it. I like to use standard-oral-stories as metaphors in a new context.

In *Dangerous Life*, my latest novel, I've used the standard that new religion is poisoning a tradition: a nation, a tribe, a family, even an individual. And through the use of this standard in a modern Creole family in the Caribbean new dimensions are showing up: for example, that sun, son, and father are archetypical metaphors for conducting, teaching, and judging. Plus that the difference between religion and spirituality or revelation is a struggle between man and woman, body and spirit, scripture and speech, silence and sound, death and life. And where, for God's sake, will the African Caribbean as a man and as a writer be when his woman is calling him back home?

In the tradition of the trickster no power play is dangerous as long as I'm in touch with the trickster consciousness. Even a liaison with the Renaissance with the German Immanuel Kant and his "reasonable morality," will not transform me into "an agent of the postcolonial power." Do you remember Dorcas in Toni Morrison's *Jazz* and how she died? It wasn't even bizarre, the way the neighborhood protected her lover, the man who killed her. I quote from *Jazz*:[10]

"How did you get rid of her?"
"Killed her. Then I killed the me that killed her."
"Who's left?"
"Me." (209)

Morrison used the trickster strategy; Anansi did the decent job and Akuba was waiting at home and the whole neighborhood protected Anansi when the masters came to get him.

In an interview with Robert Stepto in 1976, Morrison mentioned the neighborhood:

> My tendency is to focus on neighborhood and communities. And the black community was always there, only we called it "neighborhood." And there was this life-giving, very, very strong sustenance that people got from the neighborhood. One lives really in the neighborhood. And all the legal responsibilities that agencies now have, were the responsibilities of the neighborhood. So that people were taken care of, or locked up or whatever. If they were sick, other people took care of them; if they needed something to eat, other people took care of them; if they were old, other people took care of them; if they were mad, other people provided a small space for them, or related to their madness or tried to find out the limits of their madness.[11]

Talking about limits: the limits of my "dangerous liaison" with Western literary values and my political engagements are measured through rethinking and reexperiencing the neighborhood, and this intellectual and emotional journey has taken me right there where I'm feeling safe enough to handle the responsibilities taken as a third world or African Caribbean writer in the trickster tradition. And that means "using myself in different ways in my fiction and to go as far as possible to let the readers misread the text, themselves, and the world so that they have no choice but to reread to find out where they went wrong."[12] And at this point of return (to reread the text and rethink the mix-reading) the reader will be moved into the state of mind to remove cataracts and to decode the trickster!

So I don't care. I do not care at all what colonized critics or readers with cataracts are saying while hearing or reading my texts, mistreating the lines of the native woman in *Song of Lawina:*

> I cannot understand all this
> I do not understand it at all.

19. *The Dynamics of Power and Desire in* The Pagoda

Patricia Powell

*T*he Pagoda grew out of a character's search for a lost identity. I was writing a short story about a woman trying to find out the Asian origins of her Jamaican father, who is part Black, part Chinese. I drew a blank, for at some point in the story I realized that I knew nothing at all about the Chinese in Jamaica. The extent of my knowledge was that many owned restaurants and supermarkets, and bakeries and groceries, and that many were quite well-off and therefore, as one article suggested, a tremendous economic threat since they supposedly constituted Jamaica's true middle class; some still spoke foreign languages which as children my friends and I mimicked in the most disparaging way. I remember a family of Yaps who were our neighbors; the daughters attended my high school, and would sometimes offer a ride in their Benz. Mr. Yap ran a bakery, as did Mr. Chen, another neighbor, who was married to an East Indian. But though their children played with us we knew somehow that there were unspoken barriers—that there were things we couldn't talk about, things we couldn't share. All Chinese were Mr. or Miss Chin regardless of name, and we called them so behind their backs and sometimes to their faces; some were Chinee, the Chinaman, names we whispered.

But somehow my character's search for her father's Asian identity was not unlike my own search for what Jamaica is: an island bereft of its original inhabitants and composed of a transplanted citizenry, some of whom are Chinese people who have contributed greatly to Jamaica but whose efforts are often minimized in the pages of history and literature. The story enabled me to reflect on the images of Chinese that are portrayed in Caribbean literature and culture, the racial stereotypes I absorbed while growing up in Jamaica and the complexities of "otherness" for people who are neither white nor black, and those racial and social and political spaces they occupy in the minds of the dominant racial groups, their experiences of exile and displacement, their experiences of home, there on the island.

As my own knowledge of Chinese history grew, a knowledge garnered from the dusty archives at the University of the West Indies at Mona where I went on a faculty development grant from UMass, and from scraps of conversations with Chinese and other Jamaicans, from unpublished dissertations and published articles, from the films of Richard Fung, and from the works of V. S. Naipaul about the East Indians in Trinidad and in Africa, the short story swelled to proportions so enormous I decided it would be a novel about immigration—a story about a Chinese woman living in Jamaica during the nineteenth century. I wanted to explore the conditions in China that impelled her to leave home: internal strife that exploded into violent clan fights and secret societies, wars and a hunger so severe it drove people to sign immigration contracts, to kill children and sell wives, to imprison and sell their own people. I also wanted to explore the treatment afforded contract laborers on the Jamaican plantations, where they were often overworked and underpaid and mutilated and subjected to starvation; where the terms of their contracts were never realized; where many were killed while trying to escape and others simply killed themselves in order to escape. I wanted to know my character's experiences in a new country with a new language, new cultural codes, and her experiences as a single woman, a woman without a husband or father.

Immediately the technical problems began. I wanted a woman protagonist, but records showed that Chinese laws prohibited women from emigrating until the third wave of Chinese immigration to Jamaica, much later than the time period I had allotted for my characters. Even if she were able to survive the daily beatings inflicted on laborers while they waited in baracoons for foreign ships to come, how would she be able to slip by Chinese authorities and survive in one piece in a boatload of drunken sailors and immigrant Chinese men during that other middle passage from China to the Caribbean, where immigrants died from sadness or starvation or suffocation or infectious diseases on board ships where they were beaten to death if suspected of revolt; where so many vessels sunk or were gutted by fires and the charred, bloated Chinese bodies were swallowed by the jagged jaws of circling sharks; where only one third of them ever survived a passage, the rest left behind, their bones scattered, sunken in beds in the middle of ocean? These were just some of the problems that had to be ironed out once the novel began.

Set in the nineteenth century, *The Pagoda* follows the experiences of Lowe, a Chinese woman passing as a male shopkeeper at a time when Jamaican society is fraught with the racial, political, and economic tensions left over from emancipation and the newly instituted contract labor system that brought in workers from all over the British empire. Written in a third person narration throughout, the novel refers to Lowe in the masculine at all times, though, little by little, over the course of the work, the reader comes to realize that Lowe is not male but female, though s/he has been married to Miss Sylvie for thirty years and they have raised a daughter together. It is a novel about immigration and racial politics, about identity and sexuality, and about violence and power and powerlessness and desire.

Much of the work centers on Lowe's experiences at the shop and with the Black villagers, and on her relationships with Cecil, the white shipmaster who owns the vessel on which she is a stowaway; with Miss Sylvie, the arranged wife, and with Lowe's daughter, who is the result of a union of violation with Cecil. These charged interactions that cross boundaries of race, class, sex, and gender have allowed me to investigate the dynamics of power and desire between characters. When Cecil finds Lowe hiding in the hull of the ship, a fight ensues. Cecil is victorious and he brings Lowe to his cabin, where Lowe remains his mistress for the remainder of the journey. The relationship that develops in the cabin between Lowe and Cecil is an intriguing one that raises important questions about desire, for Cecil's desire for Lowe has everything to do with her cross-dressed status, a fantastical construction that has little to do with who she really is. I was curious about the ways in which memory and image and standards of beauty dictate desire, and how Cecil sees or cannot see her.

As they prepare for arrival, Cecil shortens Lowe's hair and sews trousers and shirts for her so she will pass even more effectively, but marks her at the same time. Lowe is now different from the other Chinese onboard the ship because Cecil has made her more of a Europeanized masculine figure. She no longer wears the padded jackets and half trousers of the other Chinese; she no longer carries the queue of hair. He teaches her to read and write English so she will have skills with which to survive on the island. Once they are on the island, he gives her capital to start a business, and he provides the initial costume for her masquerade. There is the wife he will acquire so there will be a "real" mother for the child he makes with her on the boat. There is the house he provides for them to live in, and along with several acres of land. I wanted to explore Cecil's fantasies regarding power and family and social class and race and desire.

It is important that Lowe is not simply a victim. When she fights Cecil on the ship, he is left partially blind, so he too is marked; is partially deprived of sight. In addition, Lowe never lets up on her dislike of him, she never comes to love him, never sees him as a savior; there is no ecstasy in their sex, she is never a willing participant, there is no gratitude, only constant antagonism. By the novel's end, however, she does come to acknowledge that maybe Cecil is in need of a family too, that he too is a stranger there on the island, and in need of the very kind of mothering he offers her.

Another set of power dynamics is examined once they arrive on the island. She is not in Kingston's downtown, which studies show was the main location of Chinese grocers. She is in the countryside. I was interested in exploring the social interactions between the Chinese shopkeeper and the Black people who inhabit the village. I was curious about the ways in which she may have "appeared" to the villagers. Did they see her only as a prosperous shopkeeper making money off them, or did they see her as a "man" mothering a mixed-race child? Or as a Chinese foreigner whose presence indicates that their own efforts at freedom are being sabotaged, a Chinese "man" clearly aligning him/herself with Cecil who is white and later with Sylvie who appears white and who employs a dark-skinned housekeeper? I wanted to unearth the complexities of Lowe living there among them, listening to their frozen dreams, looking at their broken lives, their attempts at wholeness after emancipation, but never getting close enough to them to reveal herself, let her guard down, talk about her isolation, her fears, her homesickness, her struggles at passing. A boundary is maintained that separates her from them, an actual shop counter that heightens the differences and imbalances.

Lowe must have appeared to the villagers as indeed a powerful figure and at the same time as completely vulnerable, which would have fed their rage against her in complicated ways. The villagers would want to destroy her because she not only has transcended class boundaries but several race and gender categories as well. They want to return her to her place, for how could she have appeared so abruptly into their lives and so quickly formed relationships that are imbued with the society's obsession with class hierarchies and domination based on color. There is also the suggestion that some of them may know that she is a woman passing, and this further fuels their anxiety.

Cecil dies in the blaze set by villagers that razes the shop, and his death and the destroyed shop are symbolic for a number of reasons. Without the shop which consumes her existence, which creates her identity, which masks her vulnerabilities and true self, Lowe is nothing. She must now renegotiate her position of power there in the village and create a new sense of self and identity. The villagers who set the fire are well aware that Cecil is the mastermind behind all that Lowe is, and to them, Cecil is representative of the holders of unfathomable power and they are always reminded of their powerlessness and positions of disenfranchisement.

It is only through Cecil's death that Lowe can begin to live and objectively look at the relationship with Miss Sylvie, look at concerns around sexuality and desire, and begin to repair self. Without Cecil, she can now begin to face her/his own complicated feelings for Cecil, who is a complex figure himself, for all the reasons outlined earlier, due to his role as protector and violator. Through Cecil's death and the loss of the shop, Lowe can begin to sort through her own sexual life, her sexual feelings that have been thwarted somewhat by Cecil's violations, but also by the arranged wife, Miss Sylvie's desires, Lowe's own fears, and her own sense of body—a body that transgresses space, a body with a foot in both a masculine and a feminine world, privy to both spheres and swelling with the complications of each. Hers is a body that cannot be one thing or another, but at all times must be wearing costumes and masks, a myriad of selves hiding the true form. It is a body full of psychic and physical wounds, a body tingling with memories, a body on which desires and fantasies are negotiated, a foreign body trying to create a wholesome self.

In this novel, as in all my novels, sex has little to do with love or with committed relations or with idyllic unions but everything to do with characters' bottomless longings, their insatiable cravings and fears, their feelings of helplessness, and power and powerlessness, their desires spurred on by fantasies and dreams, their struggles with race and racism and the intersections of class and hybridity, of colorism and colonialism. How to write sexuality so as to best illustrate the charged interactions that characters face is an unending struggle in my works. I attempted it in *A Small Gathering of Bones* by chopping up Dale's anonymous sexual encounter in the park with an attention to detail that highlights his constant fear, a terror gnawing in the back of the subconscious. So that at the same time that the scene arouses the reader, and I overload the page with sensory details to do just that, the arousal is interrupted by the character's constant reminder of the hostile world around him and his own fragile, vulnerable position. So there are the street sounds of people passing and of laughter, but there is the fear of beating or incarceration if found; there is the fear of death. Though the anonymity and the illicitness of the situation bring their own charge, there is always the reminder that this encounter is not a shared idyllic experience, but rather an individual and pleasurable one.

Much of this information Lowe tries to cram into the letter to her estranged daughter that opens the novel, to which she returns over and over again in the work, and which she never completes or sends, but through which she tries to explain the circumstances of her life in China that caused her to leave and the fashion in which she did, and the conditions onboard the ship and Cecil's role in the smuggling of Chinese bodies to the Caribbean. And of course there are Lowe's own complicated feelings for her, for she is not simply the constant reminder of a rape, of a violated union with Cecil, but she has gone ahead to cross boundaries even Lowe hasn't the courage to do. She leaves the convent school that would have provided her with an education to survive there in the island outside of retail and elopes with a black man markedly older than she is, a man as old as Lowe, a man who harbors resentments against Chinese businesses, a man who in Lowe's eyes is the exact replica of Cecil in looks and in gestures, a man who confesses to Lowe that he himself is haunted by his wife's obsession with Cecil. The letter is an important thread that winds throughout the book, for it is a letter that enables Lowe a voice to express desires, it is a letter about China, a letter in which Lowe tries to define a place for her/himself, a letter that allows a voice, a letter that allows her/him to record her/his history, and that of people scattered throughout the Diaspora, a letter that is unmasked, unfettered, and without costumes.

There are similar intimate though frustrating confrontations in *The Pagoda*, due in part to Lowe's first sexual encounter being one of involuntary bondage on the ship with Cecil. She is forever marked by this experience, and the memories crop up again and again during intimate moments. One such scene is where Lowe is seduced by a customer, who eventually kisses him/her one day when they are in the shop. (Though Lowe's gender is known to the reader, it is not clear whether or not the customer knows.) Lowe's fear of being found out, of being seen, whether by the woman's husband or by the villagers, her fear of the complications that are bound to arise in terms of race and class and sexuality should her true identity be realized, is so great, it creates an emotional and physical split. I portray this separation in the text by flooding the page with sensory details, and by completely subverting the emotional response.

Another example occurs when Lowe has her first sexual encounter with Miss Sylvie. Though it occurs in a closed space, it is not a safe one, as the power dynamics between Lowe and Sylvie and the circumstances under which they meet are lopsided. Lowe no longer has a space entirely her own since she has lost the shop, and she feels completely at her mercy. Though they are the only two in the room, neither Lowe nor Miss Sylvie sees the other. She begins her velvet words of seduction by telling him of her dreams haunted by an Oriental man who was to be her lover. Therefore her desires for Lowe precede Lowe and are informed by her fantasy of dreams, not by who or what Lowe truly is. While she undresses Lowe, Lowe's thoughts are only of flight, and the world Lowe conjures in her head are of escape, the safety of her shop, the comfort of the men who share their broken dreams and laugh deep throttling laughs;

the fear that splits up her body is not unlike earlier experiences of bondage, where she had to escape inside the self. This time the page is filled with images that interrupt the sexual experience, images that are both concrete and illusory.

Because of the novel's particular historicity, and because it is a work so imbued with the issue of power among characters, I struggled with the authority implicit in writing a novel about the Chinese in Jamaica. Several strategies allowed me to work through some of the dilemmas implicit in undertaking such a work and also to raise questions about the ways in which history is written. One included the use of an unreliable third person narrator, Lowe, the Chinese woman passing as a male shopkeeper. Not only is she passing for someone she is not, but the factual nature of her statement is never clear since she is now older and plagued with forgetfulness and her stories are often a conglomeration of fantastical creations; the very boundaries of fact and fiction are not always clear, even to her. In addition, the narrative structure of the text will often break to include photographs, labor contracts, and certificates, fractures meant to rupture the seemingly seamless narrative, to further conflate the lines between fact and fiction, and to mirror the renegotiations of identity that characters undergo during immigration.

The novel also features the letter that Lowe tries to write to her estranged daughter. The letter, which serves as the only concrete document about Lowe's Chinese history, is never completed or sent to the daughter, though the reader is privy to its contents. I wanted to convey the idea of a Chinese history in Jamaica still writing itself, still making itself, still largely undocumented.

Another theme that runs through the work is the building of the Pagoda, the Chinese cultural center, which is the one dream Lowe holds on to after her shop is razed to the ground by arsonist villagers. The building of the center is a metaphor for the rebuilding of Lowe's own life, for creating a space that houses the history and culture of her people, for creating an identity politic on the island; it is a way for Lowe to incorporate her loss of China into her life. Like the letter to the daughter, however, the Pagoda will not be completed by the novel's end. I wanted to create this open-ended feel to the novel as another way of reflecting on the absence of a conclusive Chinese history and alerting readers to the fact that the story is simply part of an ongoing dialogue about the documentation of Chinese history and culture in the Caribbean. There are still so many stories to be told about the Chinese in Jamaica, there is still so much unfinished history to be unearthed, and I wanted to leave room for other storytellers, other versions of history. There are still so many other Pagodas to be built.

20. *Voices of the Black Feminine Corpus in Contemporary Brazilian Literature*

LEDA MARIA MARTINS

In the last decade the debate about women's role and figurations within the context of Brazilian literature and society has been very fruitful. A variety of essays not only give focus to women's social conditions in our society but also critically unveils the masculine gaze from which the representation of feminine characters had risen in Brazilian literature and social imagination. The debate has also focused women's literary production, though the research about Black women writers is still at its beginning.

In one of her books, Ruth Silviano Brandão argues that in the arena of Brazilian literature, woman, particularly the white woman, has been portrayed as an idealized figure, as a model either of virtue or of madness, inhabiting the scene of masculine fantasy. In these texts, which have a long tradition in Brazilian literature, the masculine imagination voices the female characters with men's desires:

> The female character, constructed and produced by the masculine register, does not coincide with the woman. It isn't her faithful replica, as many times the naive reader may believe. She is instead the product of an alien dream and as such she circulates in this privileged space that fiction makes possible.[1]

As Brandão goes on to argue, it is as a "mirage of the feminine" created by language that the female body becomes an object of men's desires, the text "being the place where these objects of desire are embodied by the materiality of the signifiers."[2] In the locus of the text the female character is the "passenger of an alien voice," "built as a phallic body, as the complement that heals the [men's] void."[3] As Rosemary Curb also points out:

> The woman may be perceived by self and others as virgin mother, femme fatale or mother Earth. She may be seen as politically powerless and emotionally passive, or imbued with mythic powers; but the image is never self-defined.[5]

Encovered by this narcissistic gaze, these female figurations, in the literary scene and the social imagination, engender woman's annihilation and delusion. As such, they inhabit what Josefina Ludner names "fictions of exclusion," fictions that tend to conceal the difference.[5]

This frozen frame is broken particularly in women's contemporary writings, where female characters face new agendas and shape different roles, giving visibility to their own experiences as human beings. The women's texts remodel the representation of womanhood with new significations and appearances, deeply interfering in the whole process of literary construction and language annunciation.

But even when the women's writings bring to focus new agendas concerning the feminine condition, the lights barely touch the modes of representation of Black women, either in literature or in the social context.[6]

In the Brazilian literary tradition, the Black female character, with rare exceptions, has been figured as three main images: the Black mammy, the prototype of the generous Black mother, always smiling, always singing, always taking care of and feeding the white children; the Black maid, the white's housekeeper, that usually has no face or has some facial features considered "ugly," and finally the "lascivious" *mulata*.

It's interesting to observe that during the Romantic period, in the nineteenth century, when a project to create a national Brazilian literature (and culture) was in progress, the native Indian woman was regarded as the ideal image of Brazilian ancestry, the legendary and celebrated mother of the Brazilian "race": a sign of the New World, a figure that embodied qualities of motherhood, beauty, and silent renunciation, as is designed in Alencar's character Iracema, whose name is an anagram of *America*.

While the native Indian female character was portrayed as "a figure through whom the writer could celebrate the good qualities of the land, the purity of the people, and the values of an admirable culture," the *mulata* was used to fulfill and justify the sexual desires and adventures of the white men.[7] Her figure is thus always confined within a pattern that inexorably points to sensuality, lasciviousness, malice, mundanity, immorality, vice, selfishness, complicity, and pleasure. From the seventeenth century in Gregório De Matos's poetry, to Brazilian contemporary fiction, theater, TV series, and so on, this overeroticized body of the Black woman has played the main role, and is best exemplified by Gabriela, the "clove and cinnamon" character of Jorge Amado's novel *Gabriela*.

To trace the various tracks Black women writers have been following in order to break away from these violent images of ourselves isn't an easy task. We still need much research and work to give visibility to Black women's writings, voices, and actions in the Brazilian cultural milieu. Even an author like Carolina de Jesus, whose writings have been translated into several languages all over the world, does not receive enough attention in our academic institutions. Most of the production of contemporary Black women writers is not welcomed by the major publishers and does not reach a large number of readers. Nevertheless, their poems and fiction continue to be produced and to circulate in anthologies and smaller editions. Some of these writings have also begun to be studied at the universities, particularly by the new generations of Black women scholars and readers.

To bring into focus Black women's writings and conditions is a disturbing issue in Brazilian cultural debates. Usually even the Black male writer, when writing about the attitudes toward the African descendants and toward Blackness in Brazilian literary and cultural contexts, approaches Black women's selfhood as an extension of his own identity, or regards it as a minor issue. Talking about her own experience at *Quilombhoje* group, Miriam Alves affirms:

> When we attempted to talk about groups of writers, we ended up joking. I analyzed the jokes in this way: a white man, when he's not taking me seriously, jokes about the most serious thing I have—myself; the black brother, when he's not taking me seriously as a woman writer, jokes about something even more serious—my being.[8]

In the same interview, given to *Callaloo*, Miriam Alves reaffirms the use of the literary language as a tool to negotiate relationships and to dramatize the Black woman's voice in the sexist and racist Brazilian society. Writing is viewed, then, as a device to engender self-liberation:

> Literature is my instrument. If I am able to communicate by filling the pages with commas, and the reader understands that I am talking about the place that Brazil is, about the misery in which the Black population finds itself, if I manage to speak with commas, I'm going to fill the page with commas.[9]

In most of the literary pieces I refer to in this paper, the Black woman writer aims to achieve a language of self-recognition and self-apprehension that mirrors her double condition, both as a woman and as a Black woman. Being Black and being a woman becomes, then, a thematic from which the literary craft derives.

In the poetry produced by contemporary Black women, this feminine Blackness arises from some signifiers which are linked: voice, body, and desire. The literary text is, then, the arena filled with diverse language modulations, which at the same time by means of reversal, disruption, confrontation, and self-celebration unveil and dress the Black female body in the landscapes of the literary idioms. By their intervention in the formulations of literary discourses, Black women writers enact the variety of textual archives and memories that dialogue within their texts, giving voice to their own desires and dilemmas. In their craft and language rituals they put into motion different tunes that seed their writings with new translations of female figurations:

> A drop of milk
> runs down between my breasts.
> A stain of blood
> adorns me between my legs.
> Half a word choked off

brakes my mouth.
Vague desires insinuate hopes.[10]

In this poem by Conceição Evaristo, the woman defines herself as someone floating "in red rivers," whose words "rape the eardrums of the world." In this short piece, the building of womanhood is formulated and stressed by the repetition of the pronoun I, repeated at the beginning in eight of the twenty-one verses. The movement of this I, as a subject, transforms the image of woman from a "female matrix" into a matrix power that paints the feminine figure in a new dimension:

> I—woman
> Shelter of the seed continued motion
> of the world.[11]

The metaphor of this voyage through the territories of language is repeated in many poems, where the female body is located in special narrative images. Literature is viewed as a continent also occupied by feminine tongues, whose phrases and frames are signatures of selfhood, metaphors of woman as lady of her own voice. In her poem "Endless Continent," Esmeralda Ribeiro begins with a special metaphor:

> At the bend of the river
> the
> image
> of poetry without
> limits
> goes along

And she ends the poem with the same territorial imagery, revisiting the place and voice of the woman in a cartography which was once men's domain:

> On the bed
> the body
> anoints itself with
> verse and prose. [12]

This metaphor of woman's dislocation and revisiting, which condenses women's internal and external struggles, also points to the new meaning of the Nation itself, addressed not as an exclusive male territory, but as a conceptual landscape and notion, also redesigned and refigured by women. To write the woman is then to rewrite the Nation, and both tasks are accomplished by braiding the signs in the tapestry of language. Thus to write the woman:

> It is to trace the lines

of the map of a nation.
It is to write on your head
a black song.[13]

To redefine feminine territories and self is also to rename the subject or the
woman as subject. In this sense womanhood is not taken by the poems as a sign of
completeness, but as a sign of nonlinear movement, a kind of curvature inscribed in
the modes of enunciation. The pronoun I, that renames and voices the subject, is best
defined as a vicarious term, a signifier that represents woman as a voyager, a migrant,
always in search of her words, her language; someone who is able, through continuous relocation, to free herself and to give birth to new idioms and voodoo languages.
In her poem "Voodoo," Miriam Alves writes:

> There's a road
> sliding up the hill
> hidden
> where a curve works overtime.
>
> This road penetrates the wilderness
> it runs back out
> where the curve waves
> to hidden sadnesses
> I buried there the voodoo of uncertainties
> stuck with pins
> of sorrows
> in order to free my womb.[14]

To free the womb from alien desires is also to use the word as a knife, reshaping
the female libido with images of joy and demystification. In another poem, Miriam
Alves articulates:

> It is I
> in bed who embrace
> consume you with the ardor of sex.[15]

And in "Pieces," Roseli Nascimento plays with language to break old expectations toward female sexuality:

> sheltered
> united
> mapping
> libido
> orchestrating

cries
nakednessexogenous
nakednessexogenous[16]

This intervention operated on language but also by language brings us to focus another important issue in contemporary women's writings: their forms of speech and the role memory plays. In her book *Black Women, Writing and Identity*, Carole B. Davies calls our attention to how some acts of speech are rearticulated in women's writings. As she puts it: "Play between the articulation of language, silence, and other modes of expression weaves its way through women's writing."[17] She also highlights "the multiple ways of voicing that reside in Black women's textualities," affirming that a "significant amount of creative work by Black women writers" offers us "ways of reading a range of signifying practices which give voice to material and historical specificities of Black female experiences."[18]

Very briefly I will approach some of these modes of voicing in two narratives, first by viewing the articulation of memory as a rhetorical sign that signals the character's elaboration of a Black feminine tongue, and second by naming as acts of speech the voice that derives from the tension and friction between two boundaries: the feminine interior narration, built by diverse recollections, and the external gaze and language that also figure her.

Black women remember. Many times a Black woman remembers in silence. Memory is her intimate house, a site where she also locates herself, where she mirrors herself and the world. Some narratives dramatize the gaps in between this internal voice, created both by memory and the recollection of experience, and by an external, public gaze that comes from the "others" represented not only by white people but also by Black men. This tension that rises from the struggle between the voices of intimacy and the public view is enacted by acts of silence or indirect acts of speech. In Conceição Evaristo's short story "Maria," a Black maid is going back home after a hard day's work. She is tired, her children are at home, hungry and sick. Suddenly a man, her former husband, sits at her side and whispers words in her ear. During all the narration, Maria doesn't say a single word. She remembers. She thinks. Deep in her mind, other voices and narrations struggle—her private memories, her stories of love and abandonment, her desires and fears, her history and identity. Her action is mainly an act of sewing her most personal reminiscences.

"This time he whispered a little more loudly," says the narrator, and "she still guessed what he was saying, without hearing him directly: a hug, a kiss, love for the child."[19] Suddenly the man and his partners rob the other passengers, take their money and leave the bus. "It was then that she remembered the anger of the others." Maria is then caught by the voices and gazes toward her that come from everywhere: "Calm down people! If she was with them, she would have gotten off too," "That whore, that shameless black woman was with the thieves." "Lynch her, lynch her, lynch her!" "Just look at her, still black and bold."[20]

"Bleeding from the mouth, the nose and the ears," Maria is seriously injured by the passengers and we hear (from the narrator or from herself?) that "Maria wanted so much to tell her son that his father had sent a hug, a kiss and love."[21] How do we, readers, hear Maria's voice in this narrative? Only through her memory, dramatized by silence. We hear and see her on the very edge of language, where she dwells. It is in the frontiers and borders of conflicting discourses that her silent voice is articulated.

In Esmeralda Ribeiro's short story "Guarde Segredo," the act of narration is an act of historical reconstruction. Here the author portrays memory as written references that are quoted by reversing the models, by inscribing some traces over the text of the literary tradition, thus operating a change. In this story, the narrator, a young Black woman, writes a letter to a friend, confessing that she has killed her white lover, Cassi Jones. Amazingly, Cassi Jones is also a character of the novel *Clara dos Anjos*, written in the beginning of twentieth century by the Black writer Lima Barreto. In his novel, Clara, a young *mulata*, is seduced by Cassi Jones and is abandoned after she becomes pregnant. The novel ends in a chorus of lamentation, where the narrator criticizes the education of Black women, which does not enable them to face their desire for whiteness. In Esmeralda Ribiero's narrative, Lima Barreto himself becomes a character, either as a photograph or as a ghost inside the house. After the female narrator murders Cassi Jones, Lima Barreto becomes visible and says: "Bravo! This was the other end I wanted to that scoundrel Cassi Jones." Her grandmother adds then: "It had to be this way, my darling. We can't accept destiny with resignation."[22]

In this narrative, memory is an instrument of action and change. The literary sources are voiced in the text only to be dislocated, revisited, rewritten differently and not to be accepted with resignation. Nevertheless, at the end of "Guarde Segredo," Clara confesses that it was good to tell someone her story by writing it, but asks her friend to keep the secret. Here again silence becomes a sign of self-preservation, which reminds me of what Carole B. Davies names as the "left overs" in Black women's tongues, something that is there as "excess," as "supplement"; and, I would add, even as silence. She affirms:

> It is this tension in between articulation and aphasia, between the limitations of spoken language and the possibility of expression, between space for certain forms of talk, and lack of space for Black women's speech, the location between the public and the private, that some Black women writers address.[23]

In Conceição Evaristo's story, Maria's silent act of recollection displays her voice as an oppressed speech pushing toward the act of telling, toward the act of liberation. The woman narrator in Esmeralda Ribiero's short story, by the act of writing, already speaks and rearticulates memory as a device to transform the literary discourse and to relocate Black women's roles and figurations. In both narratives, to be silent or to keep silent signals the actions of self-preservation and camouflage; it also signals the formulation of acts of speech engendered on the edge of sound and silence, enunciation and announcing, the hidden and the unveiled, past and future. This rhetorical acts also points to the Black women writers present time.

The pronoun "I" migrates along all these texts, speaking aloud or by murmurs. Both modes of rhetorical articulation present to us new tunes on female figurations but also reveal the very conditions of the writers, as women and as Black.

I myself do not value a piece of work based on the author's color or gender. Nevertheless, we should never forget the roles gender and "race" play in the formulation of the canons, in the inclusion or exclusion of the texts chosen to be read and honored. The writings I've mentioned here are just a small part of the current production of Black Brazilian women writers, at whose side, modestly, I include myself. These voices challenge the literary criticism daily, disrupting and enriching the literary idioms. And as Toni Morrison once said: "All of us, readers and writers, are bereft if ashen criticism remains too polite or too fearful to notice a disrupting darkness before its eyes."[24]

I will conclude by adding to this chorus of tongues my own poetic words:

> The hollowness of the word
> enacts the duration of memory
> imaginary texture
> of a strange and familiar desire.

> History is nothing
> but Tabulation.
> Memory is always
> an invasion of the void.

> And the suburbs of the night
> are webbed in the interspace of alleys
> in the relics and ruins of the future
> in the figures of oblivion
> flaring shadows
> under the luminaries.[25]

Notes

Introduction

1. Selwyn R. Cudjoe, ed., *Caribbean Women Writers: Essays from the First International Conference* (Wellesley, Massachusetts: Calaloux Publications, 1990), 5.

2. Cudjoe, 6.

3. M.J. Fenwich, "Female Calibans: Contemporary Women Poets of the Caribbean," *The Zora Neale Hurston Forum* 4, no. 1 (fall 1989), 1.

4. Thomas Pringle, preface to *Six Women's Slave Narratives*, ed. William L. Andrews (New York: Oxford University Press, 1988), iii.

5. William L. Andrews, ed. *Six Women's Slave Narratives* (New York: Oxford University Press, 1988), xxxii.

6. Paula Burnett, ed., *The Penguin Book of Caribbean Verse in English* (London: Penguin Books, 1986), xvii.

7. Maryse Condé, *I, Tituba, Black Witch of Salem* (New York: Ballantine Books, 1992), 203.

8. Ibid., 209–210.

Part One: Language, Orality, and Voice

1. *De Language Reflect Dem Ethos: Some Issues with Nation Language,* by Opal Palmer Adisa

1. June Jordan, *Civil Wars* (Boston: Beacon Press, 1981), 72.

2. Frederic G. Cassidy, *Jamaica Talk: Three Hundred Years of the English Language in Jamaica* (London: Macmillan, 1982), 405.

3. Mervyn Alleyne, *Roots of Jamaican Culture* (Cambridge: Cambridge University Press, 1966), 120.

4. Alleyne, 132.

5. Geneva Smitherman, *Talkin and Testifyin'* (Boston: Houghton Mifflin Company, 1977), 171.

6. Jordan, 66.

7. Sally Lodge, "Interview with Paule Marshall," *Publishers Weekly* (January 20, 1984): 90.

8. Amon Saba Saakana, *The Colonial Legacy in Caribbean Literature*, vol. 1 (Trenton, New Jersey: Africa World Press, 1987), 26.

9. Ibid., 133.

10. Ibid.

11. Ibid., 49.

12. VèVè A. Clark. "Developing Diaspora Literacy and Marasa Consciousness," in *Comparative American Identities: Race, Sex and Nationality in the Modern Text*, ed. Hortense J. Spillers (New York: Routledge, 1991), 45.

13. Frantz Fanon, *Black Skin, White Masks* (New York: Grove Press, 1967), 17–18.

14. Ibid., 18.

15. Joan Cambridge, *Clarise Cumberbatch Want to Go Home* (New York: Ticknor & Fields, 1987), 201.

16. Ngũgĩ wa Thiong'o, *Homecoming* (Westport, Connecticut: Lawrence Hill, 1972), 16.

17. Sylvia Wynter, "Afterword: "Beyond Miranda's Meanings: Un/silencing the 'Demonic Ground' of Caliban's 'Woman,'" in *Out of the Kumbla*, eds., Carole Boyce Davies and Elaine Fido (Trenton, New Jersey: Africa World Press, 1990), 360.

18. Paule Marshall, "Brazil," in *Soul Clap Hands and Sing* (Washington, D.C.: Howard University Press, 1988), 170.

19. Ibid., 175.

20. George Lamming, "A Monster, a Child, a Slave," in *The Pleasures of Exile* (London: Allison & Busby, 1984), 110.

21. Chinua Achebe, *Hopes and Impediments* (New York: Doubleday, 1989), 133.

22. Louise Bennett, "Dutty Tough (The Ground Is Hard)," in *Creation Fire: A CAFRA Anthology of Caribbean Women's Poetry*, ed. Ramabai Espinet (Toronto: Sister Vision, 1990), 201.

23. Marlene Nourbese Philip, "Discourse on the Logic of Language," in *She Tries Her Tongue, Her Silence Softly Breaks* (Charlottetown, Canada: Ragweed Press, 1989), 56.

24. Audre Lorde, *Sister Outsider* (Freedom, California: Crossing Press, 1984), 56.

25. Opal Palmer Adisa, "She Scrape She Knee: The Theme of My Work," in *Caribbean Women Writers: Essays from the First International Conference* ed. Selwyn Cudjoe (Wellesley, Massachusetts: Calaloux Publications, 1990), 147–148.

26. Lorde, 41.

27. Ibid., 42.

28. Ibid., 43.

2. *Language and Identity: The Use of Different Codes in Jamaican Poetry,* by Velma Pollard

1. Gerald Moore, "The Language of West Indian Poetry," in *Critics on Caribbean Literature*, ed. Edward Baugh (New York: St. Martin's Press, 1978), 130.

2. Jean D'Costa, "The West Indian Novelist and Language: A Search for a Literary Medium," in *Studies in Caribbean Language*, ed. Edward Baugh (New York: St. Martin's Press, 1978), 252.

3. Ibid.

4. Velma Pollard, "Mother Tongue: Voices in the Writing of Olive Senior and Lorna Goodison," in *Motherlands: Black Woman's Writing from Africa, the Caribbean, and South Asia*, ed. Susheila Nasta (New Brunswick, New Jersey: Rutgers University Press, 1992), 240.

5. Moore, 131.

6. Pamela Mordecai, "Wooing with Words: Some Comments on the Poetry of Lorna Goodison," *Jamaica Journal* 45 (1981): 34.

7. J. E. Chamberlin, *Come Back to Me My Language: Poetry and the West Indies* (Toronto: McClell and Steward, 1993), 211.

8. Mordecai, 37.

9. Edward Baugh ed. *Studies in Caribbean Language* (New York: St. Martin's Press, 1978), 20.

10. Lorna Goodison's poem "Ocho Rios" is analyzed in detail in Mordecai's essay.

11. R. B. LePage and Andree Tabouret-Keller, *Acts of Identity: Creole Based Approaches to Lan-*

guage and Ethnicity (Cambridge: Cambridge University Press, 1985), 247.

3. *Orality and Writing: A Revisitation,* by Merle Collins

1. Walter Ong, *Orality and Literacy: The Technologizing of the Word* (London: Routledge, 1988), 11–15.

2. Gordon Rohlehr, *Calypso and Society in Pre-Independence Trinidad* (Port-of-Spain., unp. 1994), 166.

3. Ruth Finnegan, *Oral Literature in Africa* (Oxford: Oxford University Press, 1970), 2.

4. Ngũgĩ wa Thiong'o, *Decolonizing the Mind: The Politics of Language in African Literature* (London: James Currey, 1986), 12.

5. Finnegan, 92, 166.

6. Merle Collins, interview with Kofi Anyidoho, Accra, Ghana, October 1995.

7. Merle Collins, interview with Kofi Awoonor, Accra, Ghana, October 1995.

8. Merle Collins, interview with Agovi, Accra, Ghana, October 1995.

9. Anyidoho interview.

10. Merle Collins, interview with Carlton Gabriel, St. George's, Grenada, 1995.

11. Merle Collins, radio interview with Maureen Warner-Lewis, University of the West Indies, Kingston, Jamaica, taped by BBC Studios.

12. Agovi interview.

13. Shara McCallum, "Descubriendo una fotografía de mi madre," unpublished poem.

4. *Caribbean Writers and Caribbean Language: A Study of Jamaica Kincaid's* Annie John, by Merle Hodge

1. Jamaica Kincaid, *Annie John* (New York: Farrar, Straus and Giroux, 1983), 102; *Lucy* (London: Jonathan Cape, 1991), 90. Subsequent references to *Annie John* and *Lucy* are cited by page numbers within the text.

2. Jamaica Kincaid, *A Small Place* (London: Jonathan Cape, 1991), 25. All subsequent references will be indicated within the text.

5. *Francophone Caribbean Women Writers and the Diasporic Quest for Identity: Marie Chauvet's* Amour *and Maryse Condé's* Hérémakhonon, by Régine Altagrâce Latortue

1. Maryse Condé, *Hérémakhonon* (Paris: UGE, 1976). I will also refer to the English edition, trans. Richard Philcox (Washington, D.C.: Three Continents Press, 1982). All references will be indicated within the text.

2. Marie Chauvet, *Amour, Colère et Folie* (Paris: Gallimard, 1968). References to this work are cited by page numbers within the text. The English translations are mine.

3. Nella Larsen, *Quicksand* (New York: Knopf, 1928).

4. Richard Wright, *Native Son* (New York: Harper & Brothers, 1940).

5. Ralph Ellison, *Invisible Man* (New York: Random House, 1952).

6. VèVè Clark, "Developing Diaspora Literacy and *Marasa* Consciousness," in *Comparative American Identities: Race, Sex and Nationality in the Modern Text,* ed. Hortense, Spillers (New York & London: Routledge, 1991), 47.

7. Maryse Condé, *La Parole des femmes: essai sur des romancières des Antilles de langue française* (Paris: L'Harmattan, 1979), 82.

8. Régine Latortue, "In Search of Women's Voice: The Woman Novelist in Haiti," in *Wild Women in the Whirlwind: Afra-American Culture and the Contemporary Literary Renaissance*, eds. Joanne Braxton and Andrée McLaughlin (New Brunswick, New Jersey, Rutgers University Press, 1990), 193.

9. Françoise Lyonnet, *Autobiographical Voices: Race, Gender, Self-Portraiture* (Ithaca & London: Cornell University Press, 1989), 179.

10. "Interview with Yanick Lahens," in *Callaloo: A Journal of African American and African Arts and Letters*, 15, no. 2 (1992): 442.

11. Clark, 315–16.

6. Unheard Voice: Suzanne Césaire and the Construct of a Caribbean Identity, by Maryse Condé

1. Gordon Lewis, "Slavery, Imperialism and Freedom." (New York Monthly Review Press, 1978).

2. Franklin Knight, *The Modern Caribbean* (Chapel Hill: University of North Carolina Press, 1989).

3. Derek Walcott, *The Antilles: Fragments of Epic Memory* (New York: Farrar, Straus & Giroux, 1992).

4. André Breton, preface to *Cahier d'un Retour au Pays Natal* (Paris: Presence Africaine,) 1971.

5. George N'Gal, *Aimé Césaire: un homme à la recherche d'une patrie* (Dakar: Nouvelles Editions Africaines, 1975).

6. Daniel Maximin, *L'Isolé Soeil* (Paris: Seuil, 1981).

7. Suzanne Césaire and Aimé-Menil Rene Césaire, eds. "Tropiques 1941–1945" (Paris: Jean-Michel Place, 1978).

8. Aimé Césaire.

9. Suzanne Césaire.

10. Ibid.

11. Ibid.

12. Ibid.

13. Ibid.

14. Jean Bernabé, Patrick Chamoiseau, and Raphael Confiant. *Eloge de la Créolité* (Paris: Gallimard, 1989).

15. Sara Suleri, "Skin Deep: Feminism and the Postcolonial Condition in Colonial Discourse," in *Colonial Discourse and Post-Colonial Theory: A Reader*, ed. Patrick Williams and Laura Christian (New York: Columbia University Press).

Part Two: Politics and Economics of Caribbean Life

Overview

1. Wilfred Cartey, *Whispers from the Caribbean: I Going Away, I Going Home* (Los Angeles: Center for Afro-American Studies, 1991), xiii.

8. *The Politics of Literature: Dominican Women and the Suffrage Movement Case Study: DeliaWeber,* by Daisy Cocco De Filippis

1. Angela Hernández, *Emergencia del silencio: La mujer Dominicana en la educación formal* (Santo Domingo: Publicaciones de la Universidad Autónoma de Santo Domingo, vol. 538, 1986), 92.

2. Livia Veloz, *Historia del feminismo en la República Dominicana* (Santo Domingo: Secretaría del Estado de Educación Bellas Artes y Cultos, 1977), 7.

3. Ibid., 18.

4. Hernández, 107.

5. Veloz, 17.

6. Hernández, 108–114.

7. Ibid., 114–120.

8. Delia Weber, *Pensamiento inédito* (Santo Domingo: Casa Weber, 1987), 41.

9. Weber, *Pesamiento*, 41, 45.

10. Ibid., 36.

11. Ibid.

12. Ibid., 38–39.

13. Rodolfo Coiscou Weber, introduction to *La India, renacimiento en Bengala/Personalidad de Rebindranath Tagore* by Delia Weber (Santo Domingo: Casa Weber, 1985), unp.

14. Delia Weber, *Los viajeros* (Santo Domingo: Imprenta La Opinión, 1944; 2nd ed., (Casa Weber, 1991), 21.

15. Norma Celeste Reyes, García Rodríguez, and José Enrique, "*Para una descripcíon temática del cuento dominicano,*" *Eme-Eme III*, 16 (1975), 72.

16. Delia Weber, "*Doran,*" in *Dora y otros cuentos* (Santo Domingo: Imprenta de la Librería Dominicana, 1952), 8.

17. Gabriela Mora, "Crítica feminista: apuntes sobre deficiones y problemas." 5-7.

9. *Children in Haitian Popular Migration as Seen by Maryse Condé and Edwidge Danticat,* by Marie-José N'Zengo-Tayo

1. Dawn Marshall, *The Haitian Problem: Illegal Migration to the Bahamas* (Mona, Jamaica: Institute of Social and Economic Research, the University of the West Indies, 1979): xiii.

2. Jean-Claude Charles, *De si jokes petites places* (Paris: Stock, 1982), unp.

3. Jean-Claude Icart, *Négriers d'eux-même: Essai sur les boat people haïtiens en Floride* (Montréal: CIDIHCA, 1978): 29.

4. The push-pull factor is a classic notion used in social science but abandoned today: see Glick Schiller, Basch, and Blanc-Szanton, 1992.

5. Maryse Condé, *Haiti Chérie* (Paris: Collection "Je Bouquine" Bayard Poche, 1991), 37.

6. Ibid.

7. Condé, 43-44.

8. Ibid.

9. Ibid., 48.

10. Edwidge Danticat, *Breath, Eyes, Memory* (New York: Soho Press, 1994): 8.

11. Ibid., 42.

12. Ibid., 44.
13. Ibid. ,49.
14. Ibid., 51.
15. Ibid., 61.
16. Ibid., 69.
17. Ibid., 67.
18. Ibid., 72.
19. Ibid., 80.
20. Ibid.
21. Ibid., 201.

Part Three: Beryl A. Gilroy: World Griot

Overview

1. Beryl A. Gilroy, "I Write Because," in *Caribbean Women Writers: Essays from the First International Conference*, ed. Selwyn R. Cudjoe (Wellesley, Massachusetts: Calaloux Publications, 1990). 200.
2. Beryl A. Gilroy, *Sunlight on Sweet Water* (Leeds, Yorkshire, England: Peepal Tree Press, 1994): 22.
3. Beryl A. Gilroy, "The Oral Culture—Effects and Expression," *Wasafiri*, 63.
4. Ibid., 65.
5. Richard Daveson, "The Life of the Political Past," *Times Literary Supplement*, 1187.
6. Beryl A. Gilroy, "Site and Style—Two Works," 1.
7. Beryl A. Gilroy, "Caribbean Women Writers," 201.
8. Beryl A. Gilroy, *In Praise of Love and Children*, (Peepal Tree Press, 1996). 77–78.
9. Beryl A. Gilroy, quoted in *Something about the Author*, 84.
10. Beryl A. Gilroy, "Caribbean Women Writers," Citations in this paragraph are from pages 197 and 198.

13. Frangipani House: *Beryl Gilroy's Praise Song for Grandmothers*, by Australia Tarver

1. Beryl A. Gilroy, "Writing, Ancestry, Childhood and Self," in *Moving beyond Boundaries: International Dimensions of Black Women's Writing*, eds. Carole Boyce Davies and Molara Ogundipe-Leslie (New York: New York University Press, 1995), 53–60.
2. For the praise poem to Mnkabyi, see Judith Gleason, *Leaf and Bone, African Praise-Poems* (New York: Viking Press, 1980), 14–15.
3. Isidore Okpewho, *The Epic in Africa: Toward a Poetics of the Oral Performance* (New York: Columbia University Press, 1979), 237.
4. Beryl A. Gilroy, *Frangipani House* (Portsmouth, New Hampshire: Heinemann, 1986), 1. Subsequent citations are from this edition and appear in the text in parenthesis. "Writing and Ancestry."
5. Gilroy, "Writing, Ancestry," 55.
6. Ibid., 53.

7. Lucy Wilson, "Aging and Ageism in *Praisesong for the Widow* and *Frangipani House*," *Journal of Caribbean Studies* 7 (winter 1989): 189–199.

8. Alice Walker, *The Temple of My Familiar* (New York: Harcourt Brace Jovanovich, 1989), 48; my emphasis.

9. Gilroy, "Writing, Ancestry," 53.

10. Ibid., 60.

14. *Anguish and the Absurd: "Key moments," Recreated Lives, and the Emergence of New Figures of Black Womanhood in the Narrative works of Beryl Gilroy,* by Joan Anim-Addo

1. Beryl A. Gilroy, *Frangipani House* (London, 1986), Heinemann and *Boy Sandwich* (London, 1989), Heinemann. All references to these publications will be indicated in the text.

2. Beryl A. Gilroy, "Autobiography as Social Interaction for Change," unp. (1991), 1.

3. *Chrystal Rose, What a Bitch* (London: Fourth Estate: 1996) drew unusual media attention for a Black British woman's debut publication and heralded the arrival of the "Black woman as Bitch" stereotype on the Black British literary scene.

4. For a lucid discussion of authorship and intention, see Martin Montgomery et al., "Ways of Reading (London: Routledge, 1992).

5. See, for example, S. Cohan and L. Shires, *Telling Stories* (New York and London: Routledge, 1988), 30, for discussion on textual analysis emphasizing a plurality of meanings.

6. R. Barthes. *Image, Music, Text* (Glasgow: Fontana, 1977), 157–159.

7. See, for example, Joan Anim-Addo and Susanna Steele, "Availability, Accessibility and Acceptability," in *Framing the Word: Gender and Genre in Caribbean Women's Writing*, ed. Joan Anim-Addo (Whiting and Birch, 1996), 96–102.

8. Beryl A. Gilroy, "Writing, Ancestry, Childhood and Self," in Carole Boyce Davies and Molara Ogundipe-Leslie, *Moving Beyond Boundaries, International Dimensions of Black Women's Writing*, vol.1 (Pluto Press: London), 53.

9. Gay Wilentz, *Binding Cultures* (Bloomington: Indiana University Press, 1992), xii.

10. Beryl A. Gilroy, "On Creativity, Autarchy, and Memory," unpublished paper delivered at the Second International Conference of Caribbean Women Writers, Goldsmith College, London, 1996.

11. See Gilroy, "On Creativity."

12. *Tyrone, the Man,* a forthcoming publication, was originally constructed as the second half of a single Beryl A. Gilroy work, the first half of which is currently in print as *Boy Sandwich.*

13. Beryl A. Gilroy, *In Praise of Love and Children* (Leeds, Yorkshire, England: Peepal Tree Press, 1996). References will be indicated in the text.

14. See, for example, the discussion in Walter Odajnk, *Marxism, and Existentialism* (New York: Anchor Books, 1965).

15. Beryl A. Gilroy, "*Frangipani House:* Exterior Experiences," unpublished paper.

16. Odanjk, 14.

17. Mikhail Bahktin, *The Dialogic Imagination* (Austin: University of Texas Press: 1981), 23.

18. Ibid.

19. Ibid.

20. Gilroy, "Exterior Experiences."

21. Bahktin, ibid.

22. Ibid.

23. Gilroy, "Writing, Ancestry, Childhood," ibid.

24. See H. Bhaba, Cited in Abena P. A. Busia, "Performance, Transcription and the Language of the Self: Interrogating Identity as a Post Colonial Poet," in *Theorizing Black Feminisms*, ed. S. James & A. P. Busia (London and New York: Routledge, 1993), 204.

25. Ibid., 204.

26. Gilroy, *Boy Sandwich*.

27. Information given at the 1996 International Conference of Caribbean Women Writers and Scholars, Florida International University, Miami, Florida.

28. Gilroy, unpublished manuscript.

29. See, for example, editorial in *Mango Season*, no.2 (Spring 1995), 3.

30. See, for example, *Mango Season*, (London) vol.7 (December 1996), 5.

31. This is not to suggest by any means that there is a single writing project which is the same for all women writers.

32. Bhaba cited in Busia, ibid.

33. Gilroy, "*Frangipani House*," in *Framing the Word: Gender and Genre in Caribbean Women's Writing*, ed. Anim-Addo (London: Whiting & Birch, 1996), 197.

34. Gilroy, "On Creativity," 197.

Part Four: Expressions: Literary Theory and Exile

16. *Women Against the Grain: The Pitfalls of Theorizing Caribbean Women's Writing*, by Lizabeth Paravisini-Gebert

1. Clara Lair, "*Que no voten las Puertorriqueñas*," *Juan Bobo* (17 June 1916): 15.

2. Blanche Wiesen Cook, *Eleanor Roosevelt*, vol, *1884–1933* (New York: Viking Penguin, 1992).

17. *Ex/Isle: Separation, Memory and Desire in Caribbean Women's Writing*, by Elaine Savory

1. Though I would not expect V. S. Naipaul to agree now with the notorious remark he first made in *The Middle Passage* (1969) some thirty years ago that "nothing was created in the West Indies," it is still important to locate and footnote such an idea. The West Indies has both significantly invented and adapted in everything from music (e.g., steel pan) to intellectual thought to cuisine. But perhaps the most important contribution the Caribbean has made to the world is the Caribbean person, someone born into an enormously complex culture and whose vision is both historical and acutely, creatively contemporary.

2. "love poem" appeared in *Pathways* (Mona, Jamaica) 8 (July 1987):25–26.

3. Marshall's extraordinary achievement in fiction is only just becoming recognized: for a long time she received proper attention within neither American nor Caribbean literature. Her novels, such as *Brown Girl, Brownstones* (1959), *The Chosen Place, the Timeless People (1969)*, and *Daughters* (1991), chronicle succeeding generations of interactions between African Americans and the Caribbean.

4. Philip, a novelist, essayist, and poet, grew up in Tobago. For lengthy discussion of her work from a cultural and literary perspective, see Elaine Savory, *Marlene Nourbese Philip* (1996).

5. For biographical details and a substantial bibliography, see Carole Angier's biography.

6. For a substantial bibliography, see Carole Angier's biography, *Jean Rhys* (1990).

7. See Beryl Gilroy's essay "I Write Because" (1990). Her novels, poems, and essays have contributed importantly to the development of Caribbean women's writing in Britain, just as her work as a cross-cultural psychologist broke new ground in educational theory. Her novel, *Boy-Sandwich* (1989) is a sequel, set in London, to her earlier novel, *Frangipani House* (1986), which is set in Guyana.

8. See, for example, Karen Lawrence Penelope, "Voyages: Women and Travel in the British Literary Tradition" eds. Alison Blunt and Gillian Rose *Writing, Women, and Space*, (1994).

18. *Dangerous Liaison: Western Literary Values, Political Engagements and My Own Esthetics*, by Astrid H. Roemer

1. Peter Nazareth. *In the Trickster Tradition: The Novels of Andrew Salkey, Francis Ebejer and Ishmael Reed* (London, Bogle L'Overture Press, 1994).

2. Astrid Roemer, *Gewad Leven* (Dangerous Life) (Amsterdam: A. Arbeiders Pers, 1996)

3. Chinua Achebe, *Arrow of God* (New York, Anchor Doubleday, 1964), 46.

4. Maryse Condé. *Segú* (Amsterdam, De Knipscher: 1984).

5. See Kenneth McLeish, *Guide to Key Ideas in Human Thought*. New York: Facts on File, 1993.

6. Immanuel Kant. *Bantwortung der Frage: Was Ist Aukflang?*. intro. and trans. B. Delfgaaw (Kok Agora: Kampen, 1988).

7. Danille Taylor-Guthrie, ed. In *Conversations with Toni Morrison* (Jackson: University Press of Mississippi, 1994).

8. Ibid., 11.

9. Astrid H. Roemer, "In Search of My Own Voice," speech delivered at Wellesley College, 1995.

10. Toni Morrison, *Jazz* (New York: Random House, 1992)

11. Danielle Taylor-Guthrie, ibid.

12. "In Search of My Voice," ibid.

20. *Voices of the Black Feminine Corpus in Contemporary Brazilian Literature*, by Leda Maria Martins

1. Ruth Silviano Brandão. "*Passageiras da voz alheia: A escritia feminina*," in eds. *A escrita Feminina*, ed. S. R.S. Brandão and L. Castello Branco (Rio de Janeiro: Casa Maria Editorial, 1989), 17. The English translation of Brandão quotations in this paper is my responsibility.

2. Ibid., 17–18.

3. Ruth Silviano Brandão. *Literara e psicanalise* (Belo Horizonte: NAPq/UFMG, 1993), 20.

4. Rosemary Curb, "Re/cognition, Re/presentation, Re/creation in Woman-Conscious Drama," in *Theatre Journal* 37, no.3 (October 1985): 303.

5. Ludner, Josefina, "Ficciones se exclusion," in org. Heloisa Buarque de Hollanda, *Y nosotros Latinoamericanas?: Estudos sobre genero e raca* (Sao Paulo: Fundacão Memorial da American Latina, 1992), 25.

6. During Slavery, the Black woman was viewed as a womb for reproduction, as a member of

the work force, or, more frequently, as a sexual object to fulfill white men and women's desires. See Sonia Maria Giacomini, *Muhler e escraca, uma introdicao historica ao estudo da mulher negra no Brasil* (Petropolis, Brazil: Vozes, 1988).

7. Teofilo de Queiroz, Jr. *Preconceito de cor e a mulata na literatura Brasileira* (São Paulo: Atica, 1975), 31.

8. Miriam Alves, interview in *Callaloo*, "African Brazilian Literature: A Special Issue," vol. 18, no.4 (Baltimore: Johns Hopkins University Press, 1995), 803.

9. Ibid.

10. Conceicão Evaristo. "I Woman," in *Finally Us: Contemporary Black Brazilian Women Writers*, ed. Miriam Alves, trans. Carolyn R. Durhan (Colorado Springs, Colorado: Three Continents Press, 1994), 71.

11. Ibid.

12. Esmerelda Ribeiro, "Endless Continent," in *Finally Us*, 83.

13. Chant Celinha, in *Finally Us*, 55.

14. Miriam Alves, "Voodoo," in *Finally Us*, 181.

15. Miriam Alves, "Pieces of a Woman," in *Callaloo*, "*African Brazilian Literature: A Special Issues*," 801.

16. Roseli Nascimento, "Pieces," in *Finally Us*, 192.

17. Carol Boyce Davies. *Black Women, Writing and Identity: Migrations of the Subject* (London and New York: Routledge, 1994), 163.

18. Ibid., 164.

19. Conceicão Evaristo, "Maria," in *Callaloo*, "*African Brazilian Literature: a Special Issue*," ed. Charles H. Howell, Phyliss Peres, Leda Maria Martins, and Carolyn Richardson Durham, 772.

20. Ibid.

21. Ibid.

22. Esmerelda Ribiero, "Guarde Segredo," in *Cadernos Negros*, no. 14, contos. (São Paulo: Quilombhoje, 1991), 29. The English translation of Ribeiro quotations in this paper is my responsibility.

23. Davies, *Black Women*, 153.

24. Toni Morrison, *Playing in the Dark: Whiteness and the Literary Imagination* (Cambridge, Massachusetts: Harvard University Press, 1992), 91.

25. Leda Maria Martins, "Soltice," in: *Callaloo*, "*African Brazilian Literature: A Special Issue*," 871.

Bibliography

Achebe, Chinua. *Hopes and Impediments*. New York: Doubleday, 1989.

Alexander, Ziggi, and Audrey Dewjee, eds. *The Wonderful Adventures of Mrs. Seacole in Many Lands*. Bristol, England: Falling Press, 1984.

Alleyne, Mervyn. *Roots of Jamaican Culture*. London: Pluto Press, 1988.

Alvarez, Julia. *In the Time of the Butterflies*. Chapel Hill, North Carolina: Algonqin Books, 1994.

Andrews, William L., ed. *Six Women's Slave Narratives*. New York: Oxford University Press, 1988.

Angier, Carole. *Jean Rhys*. Boston: Little, Brown, 1990.

Bailey, Beryl Loftman. *Jamaican Creole Syntax*. Cambridge: Cambridge University Press, 1966.

Barron, W.R. J. *English and Medieval Romance*. London and New York: Longman, 1987.

Baugh, Edward, ed. *Critics on Caribbean Literature*. London: Allen & Unwin, 1978.

Belgrave, Valerie. *Sun Valley Romance*. London: Heinemann, 1993.

Blunt, Alison, and Gillian Rose, eds. *Writing Women and Space: Colonial and Postcolonial Geographies*. New York: Guilford Press, 1994.

Boyce-Davies, Carole, and Elaine Savory Fido, eds. *Out of the Kumbla*. Trenton, New Jersey: Africa World Press, 1990.

Broe, Mary Lynn, and Angela Ingram, eds. *Women's Writing in Exile*. Chapel Hill: University of North Carolina Press, 1989.

Brontë, Charlotte. *Jane Eyre*. New York: W. W. Norton, 1987.

Brontë, Emily. *Wuthering Heights*. London: Everyman's Library, 1987.

Burnett, Paula, ed. *The Penguin Book of Caribbean Verse in English*. London: Penguin Books, 1986.

Cambridge, Joan. *Clarise Cumberbatch Want to Go Home*. New York: Ticknor & Fields, 1987.

Cartey, Wilfred G. *Whispers from the Caribbean: I Going Away, I Going Home*. Los Angeles: University of California, 1991.

Cassidy, Frederick G. *Jamaica Talk: Three Hundred Years of the English Language in Jamaica*. London: Macmillan, 1982.

Charles, Annette. *Love in Hiding*. London: Heinemann, 1993.

Colleton, Lucille. *Merchant of Dreams*. London: Heinemann, 1993.

Condé, Maryse. *Segu*. Amsterdam: De Knipscher, 1984.

Cook, Blanche Wiesen. *Eleanor Roosevelt: Vol. 1, 1884–1933*. New York: Viking Penguin, 1992.

Coombs, Orde, ed. *Is Massa Day Dead?* Garden City, New York: Anchor Books, 1974.

Cooper, Carolyn. *Noises in the Blood: Orality, Gender and the "Vulgar" Body of Jamaican Popular Culture*. London: Macmillan, 1993.

Cudjoe, Selwyn R., ed. *Caribbean Women Writers: Essays from the First International Conference*. Wellesley, Massachusetts: Calaloux Publications, 1990.

D'Allan, Deidre. *Fantasy of Love*. London: Heinemann, 1993.

Dalphinis, Morgan. *Caribbean and African Languages*. London: Karia Press, 1985.

Davis, Wade. *Passage of Darkness: The Ethnobiology of the Haitian Zombie.* Chapel Hill: North Carolina: University of North Carolina Press, 1988.

Den Ouden, Bernard D. *Language and Creativity.* Lisse, Netherlands: Peter De Ridder Press, 1975.

Devonish Hubert. *Language and Liberation: Creole Language Politics in the Caribbean.* London: Karia Press, 1986.

Ebejer, Francis, and Ishmael Reed, eds. *The Trickster Tradition: The Novels of Andrew Salkey.* London: Bogle L'Overture Press, 1994.

Espinet, Ramabai, ed. *Creation Fire: A CAFRA Anthology of Caribbean Women's Poetry.* Toronto: Sister Vision, 1990.

Fanon, Frantz. *Black Skin, White Masks.* New York: Grove Press, 1967.

Fenwich, M. J. "Female Calibans: Contemporary Women Poets of the Caribbean." *The Zora Neale Hurston Forum* 4, no. 1 (fall 1989): 1–8.

Fowler, Roger, ed. *A Dictionary of Modern Critical Terms.* London: Routledge, 1991.

Garis, Leslie. "Through West Indian Eyes." *New York Times Magazine,* 7 October 1990, 42.

Gates, Henry Louis, Jr., ed. *The Classic Slave Narratives.* New York: Mentor Books, 1987.

Gilbert, Sandra M., and Susan Gubar. *The Madwoman in the Attic: The Woman Writer and the Nineteenth-Century Literary Imagination.* New Haven: Yale University Press, 1979.

Gilroy, Beryl. *Boy-Sandwich.* Oxford: Henemann, 1989.

_____. *Frangipani House.* London: Heinemann, 1986.

hooks, bell. *Outlaw Culture: Resisting Representations.* London: Routledge, 1994.

James, C. L. R. *The Black Jacobins: Toussaint L'Ouverture and the San Domingo Revolution.* New York: Vintage Books, 1963.

Jensen, Margaret Ann. *Love's Sweet Return: The Harlequin Story.* Bowling Green, Ohio: Bowling Green State University Popular Press, 1984.

Jolly, Dorothy. *Heartache and Roses.* London: Heinemann, 1993.

Jordan, June. *Civil Wars.* Boston: Beacon Press, 1981.

Kincaid, Jamaica. *Annie John.* New York: Farrar, Straus & Giroux, 1988.

_____. *Lucy.* London: Jonathan Cape, 1991.

_____. *A Small Place.* New York: Farrar ,Straus & Giroux, 1988.

Lair, Clara. *"Que no voten las puertorriquenas."* *Juan Bobo,* 17 June 1916, 15.

Lamming, George. *The Emmigrants.* London: Michael Joseph, 1954.

Lawrence, Karen R. *Penelope Voyages: Women and Travel in the British Literary Tradition.* Ithaca, New York: Cornell University Press, 1994.

Le Page, R.B. *The National Language Questions.* London: Oxford University Press, 1964.

Lodge, Sally. "Interview with Paule Marshall." *Publishers Weekly,* 20 January 1984, 90–91.

Lorde, Audre. *Sister Outsider.* Freedom, California: Crossing Press, 1984.

Lovelace, Earl. *The Dragon Can't Dance.* Essex, England: Longman, 1979.

Marshall, Paule. *Brown Girl, Brownstones.* Old Westbury, New York: Feminist Press, 1959.

_____. *The Chosen Place, the Timeless People.* New York: Random House, 1984.

_____. *Daughters.* New York: Penguin Books, 1992.

_____. *Praisesong for the Widow.* New York: G. P. Putnam's Sons, 1983.

_____. *Soul Clap Hands and Sing.* Washington, D.C.: Howard University Press, 1988.

Nachbar, Jack, and Kevin Lause, eds. *Popular Culture: An Introductory Text.* Bowling Green, Ohio: Bowling Green State University Popular Press, 1992.

Naipaul, V. S. *The Middle Passage.* Harmondsworth: Penguin, 1969.

Ngũgĩ wa Thiong'o. *Homecoming.* Westport; Connecticut: Lawrence Hill, 1972.

_____. *She Tries Her Tongue, Her Silence Softly Breaks.* Charlottetown, Canada: Ragweed Press, 1989.

Paravisini-Gebert, Lizabeth. *Phyllis Shand Allfrey: A Caribbean Life.* New Brunswick, New Jersey: Rutgers University Press, 1996.

Perry, Benitta. "Problems in Current Theories of Colonial Discourse." *Oxford Literary Review* 9, nos. 1–2 (1987).

Philip, Marlene Nourbese, ed. *Essays and Writings on Racism and Culture.* Stratford, Ontario: Mercury Press, 1992.

Ramchand, Kenneth. *The West Indian Novel and Its Background.* London: Heinemann, 1983.

Rhys, Jean. *The Letters of Jean Rhys.* Edited by Grancis Wyndham and Diana Melly. New York: Viking Penguin, 1984.

_____. *Voyage in the Dark.* New York: W. W. Norton, 1982.

Roemer, Astrid H. *Gewaagd Leven.* Amsterdam, Roman Arbeiders Pers, 1996.

Saakana, Amon Saba. *The Colonial Legacy in Caribbean Literature,* VOL. 1,. Trenton, New Jersey: Africa World Press, 1987.

Said, Edward W. *The World, the Text and the Critic.* Cambridge, Massachusetts: Harvard University Press, 1983.

Selvon, Samuel. *A Brighter Sun.* London: Allan Wingate, 1952.

Smitherman, Geneva. *Talkin' and Testifyin'.* Boston: Houghton Mifflin, 1977.

Spillers, Hortense J., ed. *Comparative American Identities: Race, Sex and Nationality in the Modern Text.* New York: Routledge, 1991.

Suleiman, Susan Rubin, ed. *The Female Body in Western Culture: Contemporary Perspectives.* Cambridge, Massachusetts: Harvard University Press, 1986.

Thomas, Sue, ed. *Decolonising Bodies: New Literatures Review,* 30 (winter 1995).

Walker, Alice. *Living by the Word.* New York: Harvest/HBJ, 1988.

Wright, Louis B., and Virginia A. La Mar, eds. *The Tempest: Shakespeare.* New York: Washington Square Press, 1961.

Contributors

OPAL PALMER ADISA, born in Jamaica, is a literary critic, writer, and storyteller. Her published works include *Tamarind and Mango Women* (1992) which won the PEN Oakland/Josephine Miles Award; *Traveling Women* (1989); *Bake-Face and Other Guava Stories* (1986); and *Pina, the Many-Eyed Fruit* (1985). She has made audio and video recordings of her poetry and has published extensively on oral literature and the literature of the Black Diaspora. She currently teaches in and chairs the Ethnic Studies/Cultural Diversity Program at California College of Arts and Crafts.

JOAN ANIM-ADDO, born in Grenada and educated in the Caribbean and London, is a writer, editor, and lecturer. She divides her time between teaching in higher education and writing. She teaches at the Caribbean Studies Centre, Goldsmiths College, University of London. She is Chair of the Caribbean Women Writers Alliance (CWWA) and cofounder of the London-based literary publication *Mango Season*, which maintains a central focus on Caribbean women's writing. A research historian as well as a creative writer and critic, Joan Anim-Addo includes among her recent publications *Longest Journey: A Black History of Lewisham* (1995), *Framing the Word: Gender and Genre in Caribbean Women's Writing* (1996), and *Sugar, Spices and Human Cargo* (1996). Her poems and short stories are widely anthologized. She is currently engaged in writing a biography of Beryl Gilroy.

MARION BETHEL was born in the Bahamas, where she currently lives and works. Her works have appeared in *Junction, Lignum Vitae, At Random, The Massachusetts Review*, and *The Caribbean Writer*. She was awarded the Casa de Las Americas prize for her book of poetry *Guanahani, My Love* (1994) and in 1991, a James Michener Fellowship.

MERLE COLLINS, born in Grenada, is currently Professor of English and Comparative Literature at the University of Maryland. Her publications include *The Colour of Forgetting* (1995), *Rotten Pomerack* (1992), *Rain Darling* (1990), *Angel* (1987), and *Watchers and Seekers: Creative Writing by Black Women in Britain*, edited with Rhonda Cobham (1987).

MARYSE CONDÉ, born in Guadeloupe, has lectured widely in Africa, Europe, the Caribbean, and the United States, where she is currently a tenured Professor of Francophone Literature at Columbia University. A noted critic and essayist, Condé has also published ten novels, many of which have been translated into English. A recipient of Guggenheim and Rockefeller Fellowships, she was the first woman to receive the Puterbaugh Award. Her most recent work is *Les Migrations du Coeur*.

DAISY COCCO DE FILIPPIS, born in the Dominican Republic, is Professor of Spanish and Chair of the Department of Foreign Languages at York College in New York City. She has edited eight books, including *Sin Otro Profeta que su Canto* (1988) and *Combatidas, Combativas y Combatientes* (1992), which are anthologies of creative writing by Dominican women. Her most recent work is *Stories of Washington Heights and Other Corners of the World*, a bilingual anthology of short stories by Dominicans in the United States.

BERYL A. GILROY, born in Guyana (then British Guiana), is the author of seven fictional works, a volume of poetry, several children's books, and an autobiographical account of her experiences as the first Black female teacher in London, *Black Teacher* (1976). In 1996, Peepal Tree Press published three new titles by Gilroy: *In Praise of Love and Children, Inkle and Yarico*, and *Gather the Faces*. Additionally, Gilroy is a clinical psychologist who counsels women under stress and children with behavioral problems.

MERLE HODGE, born in Trinidad, completed her primary and secondary education in Trinidad, then studied French language and literature at the University of London. Her postgraduate work is in the area of Francophone Caribbean and African literatures. She has published two novels, *For the Life of Laetitia* (1993) and *Crick Crack, Monkey* (1970), as well as numerous short stories. Currently she is a Lecturer in the Department of Language and Linguistics at the University of the West Indies in Trinidad.

RÉGINE ALTAGRÂCE LATORTUE, born in Port-au-Prince, Haiti, is a Professor of Comparative Literature and Chairperson of the Africana Studies Department at Brooklyn College of the City University of New York. She earned her Ph.D. at Yale University, and has been a Rockefeller Humanist-in-Residence and a Ford Foundation Post-Doctoral Fellow. Her publications include a coauthored bilingual edition of Louisianan poetry, *Les Cenelles: A Collection of Poems by Creole Writers of the Early Nineteenth Century*, a coedited monograph on Haitian women immigrants, *La Femme Haitienne en Diaspora*, and several articles on Francophone literature and comparative studies of women writers of the African Diaspora. She is currently working on a text about women and the novel in Haiti.

LEDA MARIA MARTINS was born in Rio de Janeiro, Brazil. A professor, theatre director, and poet, she wrote *Afrografias de Memoria* (1996), *A Cena em Sombras* (1995), *O, Modern Oteatro de Corpo-Santo* (1991), and *Cantigas de Amares* (1983). She received a Fulbright Scholarship to Berkeley in 1989, an M.A. in Luso-Brazilian literature from Indiana University in 1981, and a Ph.D. in comparative literature at the Universidade Federal de Minas Gerais, Brazil, in 1991. She is also the Subcoodinator of the Graduate Program in Literature at Universidade Federal de Minas Gerais, Brazil.

ADELE S. NEWSON, born in the United States, is an Associate Professor in the Department of English at Florida International University. Her research and teaching areas include African, African American, and Caribbean women writers. In addition to the 1987 publication *Zora Neale Hurston: A Reference Guide*, she has to her credit numerous articles, reviews, and essays, including contributions to *The Oxford Companion to Women's Writing in the United States* (1995).

MARIE-JOSÉ N'ZENGO-TAYO, born in Haiti, is a lecturer in the Department of French at the University of the West Indies, Mona, Jamaica. Her fields of study include comparative literature of the French-speaking Caribbean. She is currently working on Haitian popular migration and its literary representation. Her publications include "Maitre ou Mentor: L'ombre de Glissant dans *Texaco* de Patrick Chamoiseau" (1995), "Women, Literature and Politics: Haitian Popular Migration as Viewed by Marie-Therese Coliman and the Haitian Female Writer" (1995), and "Discourse, Madness and the Neurotic Heroine in French Caribbean Women Novelists" (1993).

LIZABETH PARAVISINI-GEBERT, a Professor in the Department of Hispanic Studies at Vassar College, is the editor of *Green Cane and Juicy Flotsam* (with C.C. Estevez, 1993), *Pleasure in the Word: Erotic Writings by Latin American Women* (with M. Olmos, 1993), and *Remaking a Lost Harmony: Contemporary Fiction from the Hispanic Caribbean* (with M. Olmos, 1995). She has published extensively on Caribbean and Hispanic feminism and has translated works by Ferré, Yañez, Vega, Poujol-Oriol, and Contreras. She has received research grants from the Schomburg Center and the National Endowment for the Humanities.

VELMA POLLARD, born in Jamaica, is a Senior Lecturer in Language Education and Dean of the Faculty of Education at the University of the West Indies, Mona, Jamaica. Her major research interests are Creole languages of the Anglophone Caribbean, the language of Caribbean literature, and Caribbean women's writing. She is also involved in creative writing and has published poems and short stories in regional and international journals. *Crown Point and Other Poems* (1988) and *Shame Trees Don't Grow Here* (1992) are both available through Peepal Tree Press. A volume of short fiction, *Considering Women*, was published by the Women's Press in 1989. Her novella *Karl* (1992) won the Casa de Las Americas literary award and has been published by Casa as a bilingual (English and Spanish) text. Her novel *Homestretch* was published by Longman in 1994.

PATRICIA POWELL was born in Jamaica. She is the author of *Me Dying Trial* (1993) and *A Small Gathering of Bones* (1994). Her forthcoming novel, *The Pagoda*, is about the Chinese in nineteenth century Jamaica. Powell is an Assistant Professor of Creative Writing at the University of Massachusetts, Boston.

ASTRID H. ROEMER was born in Paramaribo, Suriname, and emigrated to The Netherlands to study Dutch literature. She has earned a B.A. in teaching, a B.A. in familly therapy, and an M.A. in the humanities. She has written short stories, novels, poetry, plays, columns, and essays. A well-known creative writing teacher, she is also editor, and family therapist. She is currently working on a trilogy which will be published by Arbeiderspers in Amsterdam.

ELAINE SAVORY lives between New York City and Barbados. She coedited the first feminist collection of essays on Caribbean literature, *Out of the Kumbla: Women and Caribbean Literature* (1990), with Carole Boyce Davies. Her first volume of poems, *Flame Tree Time* (1993), was published by Sandberry Press, Kingston, Jamaica. She has written short stories as well as numerous articles and chapters in books on Caribbean, African, and Indian women writers. She has also directed, acted, written, and produced for theater and television. She has taught at the University of the West Indies, the University of Ghana at Legon, and New York University. A Visiting Scholar at Brown University she has guest lectured in the United Kingdom, the United States, India, and the Caribbean. She teaches at the New School for Social Research in New York City and is completing a study of Jean Rhys for Cambridge University Press, her second volume of poetry, *gingerbread house,* and a volume of creative nonfiction, *Bringing It All Back Home.*

SYBIL SEAFORTH was born in Trinidad, where she lives and works. She has written plays and short stories and is currently working on a fictional piece about Caribbean women in long-term relationships. She is the author of *Skiff Bay* (1997) and *Growing Up with Miss Milly* (1988). A member of the Caribbean Association for Feminist Research and Action, she was the coordinator of CAFRA's Women's Creative Expression Project from 1989 to 1994. A recent Fellow at the Virginia Center for the Creative Arts, Seaforth is a graduate of the University College of Swansea, Wales.

LINDA STRONG-LEEK, born in the United States, received her Ph.D. from Michigan State University in African and African American literature and history. She is an Assistant Professor of English at Florida International University, where her major areas of teaching and research include the literature of Black women in the Diaspora, African and African American literature, and American literature. Her most recent publications include chapters in the upcoming releases from Africa World Press, *Flora Nwapa: Emerging Perspectives* edited by Marie Umeh, and *Ama Ata Aidoo: Emerging Perspectives,* edited by Gay Wilentz and Adu U. Azodo, respectively. She is currently working on a manuscript which focuses on the issue of female circumcision in the novels of Ngũgĩ wa Thiong'o, Flora Nwapa, and Alice Walker, and on an historical work on the continued legacy of slavery and miscegenation in the American South.

Australia Tarver is an Associate Professor of English at Texas Christian University. She teaches modern American fiction, African American literature, and the literature of Africa and the African Diaspora. She has contributed to *The Dictionary of Literary Biography* and *The Oxford Companion to African American Literature*. She is currently working on a book on Black Southern novelists.

Lourdes Vázquez was born in Puerto Rico. Her published books include *The Broken Heart* (1996), *El Amor Urgente* (1995), *La Rosa Mecanica: Short Stories* (1991), *Marina Arzola: The Poet's Biography* (1990), and *Las Hembras: Poetry* (1986). She writes essays for *FEM*, a feminist journal in Mexico, and articles for newspapers in Puerto Rico. She earned a B.A. from the University of Puerto Rico, an M.L.S. from the University of Puerto Rico, and an M.A. from New York University.

Sherezada (Chiqui) Vicioso is a poet with four volumes to her credit, *Wish-ky Sour* (1995), *Internamiento* (1993), *Un Extrano Ulular Traia El Viento* (1983), and *Viaje Desde El Agua* (1981). She has written three books of essays and has worked as a journalist for the past ten years. She is also a sociologist, an educator, and a feminist critic. She earned her B.A. from Brooklyn College and her M.A. from Columbia University, and is enrolled in the Graduate Studies Program at Fundação Getuli Vargas, Rio de Janeiro.

Caribbean Women Writers and Scholars: A Select Bibliography

Opal-Palmer Adisa

Adisa, Opal Palmer. *It Begins with Tears.* London: Heinemann, 1997.

_____. *Tamarind and Mango Women.* Toronto: Sister Vision, 1992.

_____. *Bake-Face and Other Guava Stories.* Berkeley: Kelsey Street Press, 1986.

_____. "Duppy Get Her." In *Caribbean New Wave: Contemporary Short Stories,* edited by Stewart Brown, London: Heinemann, 1990.

_____. "Three Jamaican Women Writers at Home and the Diaspora." *Dissertation Abstracts International* 54:8, 1994.

_____. "Journey into Speech—A Writer between Two Worlds: An Interview with Michelle Cliff." *African American Review,* 28:2 (summer 1994): 273–281.

_____. "She Scrape She Knee: The Theme of My Work." *ARIEL: A Review of International English Literature* (Calgary) 24:1, (1993).

About Opal Palmer Adisa

Flockemmann, Miki. "Language and Self in Opal Palmer Adisa's Bake Face and Other Guava Stories." *ARIEL: A Review of International English Literature* (Calgary) 24:1 (January 1993) 59–73.

Miriam Alves

Alves, Miriam, ed. Trans. Carolyn R. Durhan. *Enfim—nos: Escritoras Negras Brasileiras contemporaneas (Finally—Us: Contemporary Black Brazilian Women Writers).* (Colorado Springs, Colorado: Three Continents Press, 1994.

Marion Bethel

Bethel, Marion. *Guanahani, My Love.* Havana : Casa de las Americas, 1994.

_____. "Of Pirates and Junkanoo." *River City* (University of Memphis), 16, no. 2, (summer 1996).

_____. "Bougainvillea Ring Play" In *Womanspeak,* Vol. 3. Nassau, Bahamas: Woman Speak Press, 1996.

_____. "Bringing Myself into Fiction, The Primary Years," *In Moving beyond Boundaries.* Vol. 1., *International Dimensions of Black Women's Writing,* edited by Carole Boyce Davies and Molara Ogundipe-Leslie. London: Pluto Press, 1995.

_____. "Taino Rebirth," *The Massachusetts Review.* (autumn/winter 1994). (Mount Holyoke and Smith Colleges and the University of Massachusetts).

_____. "Womancycle," and "April in Nassau" In *Womanspeak.* Vol. 2. Nassau, Bahamas: Woman Speak Press, 1994.

_____. "In the Shallow Seas," "Miss Jane's Hands," "This Tamarind Season," and "Blood Moon" In *At Random*. Vol. 5. Humanities Division of the College of the Bahamas, 1994.

Merle Collins

Collins, Merle. *Angel*. Seattle: Seal Press, 1988.
_____. "Themes and Trends in Caribbean Writing Today." In *From My Gypsy to Sci-Fi: Genre and Women's Writing in the Postmodern World.*, edited by Helen Carr. London: Pandora, 1989.

About Collins, Merle

DoHarris, Brenda. "*Angel*: A Novel by Merle Collins." *The Zora Neale Hurston Forum* 4:1 (fall 1989) 25–28.
Lima, Maria Helena. "Revolutionary Developments: Michelle Cliff's *No Telephone to Heaven* and Merle Collins's *Angel*." *ARIEL: A Review of International English Literature* (Calgary): 24:1 (January 1993): 35–56.
Wilson, Betty. "An Interview with Merle Collins." *Callaloo: A Journal of African American and African Arts and Letters* 16:1 (winter 1993): 94–107.
Woodcock, Bruce. "Long Memoried Women: Caribbean Women Poets." In *Black Women's Writing*, edited by Gina Wisker. New York: St. Martin's Press, 1993.

Maryse Condé

Condé, Maryse. *Crossing the Mangrove*. New York: Anchor Books, 1995.
_____. *Hérémakhonon: a Novel*. Washington, D.C.: Three Continents Press, 1992.
_____. *I, Tituba, Black Witch of Salem*. Charlottesville: University Press of Virginia, 1992.
_____. *Tree of Life*. New York: Ballantine Books, 1992.
_____. *The Children of Segu*. New York: Viking Penguin, 1989.
_____. *A Season in Rihata*. Portsmouth, New Hampshire: Heinemann, 1988.
_____. *Segu*. New York: Viking Penguin,
_____. "Language and Power: Words as Miraculous Weapons." *College Language Association Journal* 39: 1 (September 1995): 18–25.
_____. "Order, Disorder, Freedom, and the West Indian Writer." *Yale French Studies* 83 (1993): 121–135.

About Maryse Condé

Andrade, Susan Z. "The Nigger of the Narcissist: History, Sexuality and Intertextuality in Maryse Condé's *Hérémakhonon*." *Callaloo: A Journal of African American and African Arts and Letters*. 16:1 (winter 1993) 213–226.
Adjarian, Maude Madeleine. "Looking for Home: Postcolonial Women's Writing and the Displaced Female Self." *Dissertation Abstracts International* 56: 1 (July 1995).
Berrian, Brenda F. "Masculine Roles and Triangular Relationships in Maryse Condé's *Une Saison a Rihata*." *Bridges: An African Journal of English Studies Revue, Africaine d'Etudes Anglaises* (Dakar, Senegal) 3 (1991): 5-20.
_____. "Maryse Condé and Rita Dove." *Callaloo: A Journal of African American and*

African Arts and Letters 14:2 (spring 1991): 347–438.

Bruner, Charlotte, and David Bruner. "Return of a Native Daughter: An Interview with Paule Marshall and Maryse Condé." *SAGE: A Scholarly Journal on Black Women* 3:2 (fall 1986): 52–53.

_____. "Buchi Emecheta and Maryse Condé: Contemporary Writing from Africa and the Caribbean." *World Literature Today: A Literary Quarterly of the University of Oklahoma* 59:1 (winter 1985): 9–13.

Clark, VéVé A., and Cecile Daheny (translators). "*'Je me suis reconciliée avec mon ile' : Une Interview de Maryse Condé*" ("'I Have Made Peace with My Island': An Interview with Maryse Condé." *Callaloo: A Journal of African American and African Arts and Letters* 12:1 (winter 1989):85–133.

Chamoiseau, Patrick, and Kathleen M. Balutansky. "Reflections on Maryse Condé's Traversée de la mangrove." *Callaloo: A Journal of African American and African Arts and Letters.* 14:2 (spring 1991): 395–398.

Dukats, Mara-Laimdot. "Antillean Challenges to Universalism: Narrativizing the Diverse: A Study of Selected Works by Patrick Chamoiseau, Maryse Condé, Edouard Glissant, and Daniel Maximin." *Dissertation Abstracts International* 54:11 (May 1993).

Flannigan, Arthur "Reading below the Belt: Sex and Sexuality in Francoise Ega and Maryse Condé." *The French Review: Journal of the American Association of Teachers of French.* Champaign, Illinois, 62:2 (December 1988): 300–312.

Hardy, Sarah-Boykin. "A Poetics of Immediacy: The Short Story and Oral Narrative." *Dissertation Abstracts International* Vol. 54:5 (November 1993).

Herndon, Crystal Gerise. "Gendered Fictions of Self and Community: Autobiography and Autoethnography in Caribbean Women's Writing." *Dissertation Abstracts International* 54:8 (February 1994).

Hewitt, Uah D. "Inventing Antillean Narrative: Maryse Condé and Literary Tradition." *Studies in Twentieth Century Literature* 17:1 (winter 1993): 79–96.

Mekkawi, Mohamed. *Maryse Condé: Novelist, Playwright, Critic, Teacher: An Introductory Biobibliogaphy.* Washington, D.C.: Howard University Press, 1991.

Mudimbe-Boyi, Elisabeth. "Giving a Voice to Tituba: The Death of the Author?" *World Literature Today: A Literary Quarterly of the University of Oklahoma* 67:4 (fall 1993): 751–756.

Proulx, Patrice June. "Speaking from the Margins: Exiles, Madwomen and Witches in Marie Cardianl, Maryse Condé, and Miriam Warner-Viera." *Dissertation Abstracts International* 52:8 (Febuary 1992).

Smith, Arlette M. "Maryse Condé's *Hérémakhonon*: A Triangular Structure of Alienation." In *International Women's Writing: New Landscapes of Identity,* edited by Brown, Anne E. and Marjanee E. Goose. Westport, Connecticut: Greenwood Press, 1995. 63-69

_____. "The Semiotics of Exile in Maryse Condé's Fictional Works." *Callaloo: A Journal of African American and African Arts and Letters.* 14:2 (spring 1991):381–388.

Snitgen, Jeanne. "History, Identity and the Constitution of the Female Subject: Maryse Condé's Tituba." *Matatu: Journal for African Culture and Society* (Amsterdam) 3:6 (1989): 55–73.

Soestwohner, Bettina Anna. "Narrative Margins in Maryse Condé's Novels *Hérémakhonon* and *La vie scelerate*: Between the Myth of History and the Memories of the Mothers." *Disser-*

tation Abstracts International 54:8 (February 1994).

Taleb-Khyar, Mohamed B. "An Interview with Maryse Condé and Rita Dove." *Callaloo: A Journal of African American and African Arts and Letters.* 14:2 (spring 1991): 347–366.

Williams, John "Beyond Languages and Color." *Discourse: Journal for Theoretical Studies in Media and Culture* 11:2 (spring-summer 1989): 109–113.

Daisy Cocco De Filippis

De Filippis, Daisy. "Out of Their Men Built: Dominican Women Writers in the Twentieth Century." In *In Their Sisters' Hands: Caribbean Women Writers,* edited by Merle Collins. Oxford: Heinemann Press, forthcoming.

_____. ed. *Dominican Literature at the End of the Century: The Rapport Between and Diaspora and Its Homeland.* Proceedings of the June 1994 Conference. New York: CUNY Dominican Studies Institute, 1996.

_____. ed. *Asian Culture: Tradition and Diaspora.* Proceedings of the November 1993 Conference. New York: York College, Executive Report 1, vol. 3, 1995.

_____. co-editor with F. Gutierrez. *Stories from Washington Heights and Other Corners of the World: A Bilingual Selection of Short Stories Written by Dominicans in the U.S.* New York: CUNY Latin American Writers Institute, 1994.

_____. ed. *The Women of Hispanola, Moving Towards Tomorrow.* Selected Proceedings of the May 5, 1993, Conference. New York: York College, Executive Report, vol 1, 1993.

_____. ed., *Combatidas es y combatientes, entologia de cuentos escritos por Dominicanas.* Santo Domingo: Talker, Publicacion del Instituto del Libro, Libreria Trinitaria, Camara Dominicana de Libro, 1992.

_____. editor and co-translator. *From Desolation to Compromise: The Poetry of Aida Cateagena Portalatin.* Santo Domingo: Ediciones Montesinos no. 10, 1988.

_____. co-editor and translator with E. J. Robinett. *Poems of Exile and Other Concerns: A Bilingual Selection of Poetry Written by Dominicans in the United States.* New York: Ediciones Alcance, 1988.

_____. *Estudios semioticos de poesia dominicana.* Santo Domingo: Bilblioteca Taller no. 178, 1984.

_____. "Behind the Hedge of Towering Hibiscus, Not Far from the Anacahuita Tree: Julia Alvarez' Journey Home," In *Proceedings of the Third Annual Caribbean Women Writers Conference,* edited by Selwyn Cudjoe. Wellesley, Massachusetts: Calaloux Publications, 1995.

_____. "Dominican Writers at the Crossroads: Reflections on a Conversation in Progress" *CELAC* (SUNY Albany) 2:3, (fall 1996).

_____. "Aida Cartegena Portalatin: A Literary Life" In *Moving beyond Boundaries.* Vol. 2, *Critical Responses,* edited by Carole Boyce Davies and Molara Ogundipe-Leslie. London: Pluto Press, 1995.

_____. "Singing to the Beat of Their Own Drums: Dominican Women Writers in the 1980's." In *Gender, Culture and the Arts,* edited by Ronald Dotterer and Susan Bowers affiliate of Associated University Presses, Cranbury, New Jersey: Susquehanna University Press, 1993.

Ramabai Espinet

Espinet, Ramabai. "The Invisible Woman in West Indian Fiction." *World Literature Written in English* (Singapore) 29:2 (autumn 1989) 116–126.

_____. ed. *Creation Fire: A CAFRA Anthology of Caribbean Women's Poetry.* Toronto: Sister Vision; Tunapuna, Trinidad and Tobago: CAFRA. 1990.

_____. *Nuclear Seasons: Poems.* Toronto: Sister Vision, 1991.

Merle Hodge

Hodge, Merle. *For the Life of Laetitia.* New York: Farrar, Straus, & Giroux, 1993.

_____. "Challenges of the Struggle for Sovereignty: Changing the World versus Writing Stories." In *Caribbean Women Writers: Essays from the First International Conference,* edited by Selwyn Cudjoe, Wellesley, Massachusetts: Calaloux, 1990.

_____. "Critical Perspectives on Leon Gontran Damas." In *Beyond Negritude: The Love Poems,* edited by Keith Q. Warner. Washington, D.C.: Three Continents Press, 1988.

_____. *Is Freedom We Making.* St. George's, Grenada: Government Information Service, 1981.

_____. *Crick, Crack, Monkey.* London: Heinemann, 1981.

About Merle Hodge

Abruna, Laura Niesen de. "Twentieth Century Women Writers from the English Speaking Caribbean." In *Caribbean Women Writers: Essays from the First International Conference,* edited by Selwyn Cudjoe. Wellesley, Massachusetts: Calaloux, 1990.

Balutansy, Kathleen M. "We Are All Activists: An Interview with Merle Hodge." *Callaloo: A Journal of African American and African Arts and Letters.* 12:4 (fall 1989): 651–662.

_____. "Revisioning Our Kumblas: Transforming Feminist and Nationalist Agendas in Three Caribbean Women's Texts." *Callaloo: A Journal of African American and African Arts and Letters* 16:1 (winter 1993): 44–64.

Gikandi, Simon. "Narration in the Post-Colonial Moment: Merle Hodge's *Crick Crack Monkey.*" *ARIEL: A Review of International English Literature* (Calgary) 20:4 (1989): 18–30.

Kemp, Yakini. "Woman and Womanchild: Bonding and Selfhood in Three West Indian Novels." *SAGE: A Scholarly Journal on Black Women* 2:1 (spring 1985): 24–27.

Stevenson, Peggy-Lee-Denise. "Conflicts of Culture, Class and Gender in Selected Caribbean-American and Caribbean Women's Literature." *Dissertation Abstracts International,* 50: 10 (April 1990).

Thomas, Ena V. "*Crick Crack Monkey:* A Picaresque Perspective." In *Caribbean Women Writers: Essays from the First International Conference,* edited by Selywn Cudjoe, Wellesley, Massachusetts: Calaloux, 1990.

Régine Altagrace Latortue

Latortue. Regine Altagrace. "The Woman in the Haitian Novel." *Dissertation Abstracts International* 44:1 (July 1983).

_____. ed. *Le Cenelles: A Collection of Poems by Creole Writers of the Early Nineteenth Century.* Boston: G. K. Hall, 1979.

Leda Maria Martins

Martins, Leda Maria. *Afrografias da memoria; O reinado do Rosario no Jatoba*. Belo Horizonte, Brazil: Mazza Edicoes, forthcoming.

_____. *A Cena em Sombras*. São Paolo: Editora Perspective, 1995.

_____. *O Moderno Teatro de Qorpo-Santo*. Belo Horizonte, Brazil: Editora UFMG:1991.

_____. *Cantigas de Amores*. Belo Horizonte, Brazil: Edicao de Autor, 1993.

_____. *Gestures of Memory: Transplanting Black African Networks*. In *Brazil and the Discovery of America*, edited by B. McQuirk and Sr. Oliverira Sr.,England: Mellen Press, 1995.

_____. "*Rito e Celebracão.*" In *Anais do l Encountro de Professores de Literaturas Africanas de Lingua Portuguesa, 1991*. Niterói, Brazil: Universidade Federal Fluminense, 1995, 383–394.

_____. "A Ritual Choreography." In *Callaloo, A Journal of African American and African Arts and Letters*. 18: 14 (November 1995) 83–70.

_____. "*Cultura Negra e Identidades.*" In *Africas Gerais*. Belo Horizonte, Brazil: Secretaria Municipal de Cultura, no. 2 (1995) 2–4.

_____. "*Na Encruzilhada dos Discursos Oitocentistas.*" In *Cadernos Pedagogicos e Culturais*. Niterói, Brazil: Centro Educacional de Niterói (1994) 15–19.

_____. "*Coreografia de Imagens e Tons: O Navio Negreiro de Castro Alves e Slaveship de Amiri Baraka.*" In *Com Textos* Revista do Departamento de Letras, Mariana, 1993.

Lizabeth Paravisini-Gebert

Paravisini-Gebert, Lizabeth. *Jamaica Kincaid: A Critical Companion*. Westport, Connecticut: Greenwood. forthcoming.

_____. and Margarite Fernandez Olmos, eds. *Sacred Possessions: Vodon, Santeria, Obeah and the Caribbean*. New Brunswick, New Jersey: Rutgers University Press, forthcoming.

_____. trans. and intro. *How to Gather the Shadows of the Flowers and Other Stories by Angela Hernandez*. Fredonia, New York: White Pine Press, forthcoming.

_____. *Shand, Phillis Allfrey: A Caribbean Life*. New Brunswick, New Jersey: Rutgers University Press, 1996.

_____, and Margarite Fernandez Olmos, eds. *Remaking a Lost Harmony: Contemporary Fiction from the Hispanic Caribbean*. Fredonia, New York: White Pine Press, 1995.

_____, and Carmen C. Esteves, eds. *Green Cane and Juicy Flotsom: Short Stories by Caribbean Women*. New Brunswick, New Jersey: Rutgers University Press, 1994.

_____, comp. and annot. and Olga Torres-Seda, comp. and annot. *Caribbean Women Novelists: An Annotated Critical Bibliography*. Westport, Connecticut: Greenwood Press, 1993.

_____, and Margarite Fernande Olmos eds. *Pleasure in the Word: Erotic Writings by Latin American Women*. Fredonia, New York: White Pine Press, 1993.

_____, and Margarite Fernandez Olmos eds. *El placer de papbra: literature erotica femenina de America Latina*. Mexico: Planeta, 1991.

_____, ed. and intro. *Luz y sombra de Ana Roque*. Rio Piedras, Puerto Rico: Editorial de la Universidad de Puerto Rico/Instituto de Cultura. Puertorriquena, 1991; rpt. 1994.

_____, "Forging a Theory of the Latino Novel: The Role of Politics and Ideology." In *New Voices in Latin American Literature/Nuevas voces en la literature Latino America*. Jackson

Heights, New York: OLLANRAY, 1993.

_____, "The White Witch of Rosehall and the Legitimacy of Female Power in the Caribbean Plantation." *Journal of West Indian Literature* (Kingston, Jamaica) 4:2 (November 1990).

Velma Pollard

Pollard, Velma. *Karl and Other Stories.* Harlow, Essex, England: Longman, 1994

_____. *Homestretch.* Harlow, Essex, England: Longman, 1994.

_____. *From Jamaican Creole to Standard English: A Handbook for Teachers.* New York: Caribbean Research Center, Medgar Evers College (CUNY), 1993.

_____. *Anansesem: A Collection of Caribbean Folk Talkes, Legends, and Poems for Juniors.* Longman: (Kingston, Jamaica): 1985.

_____, and Jean D'Costa, *Over Our Way: Caribbean Short Stories.* intro. and notes. Harlow Essex, England: Longman, 1980.

_____. *Nine West Indian Poets: An Anthology for the CXC English Examination.* Glasgow: Collins, 1980.

_____. "The Speech of the Rastafarians of Jamaica, in the Eastern Caribbean: The Case of St. Lucia." *International Journal of the Sociology of Language* (Berlin) 85 (1990) 81–90.

_____. "Caribbean Languages: Lesser-Known Varieties." *International Journal of the Sociology of Language,* (Berlin) 85 (1990).

_____. "The Particle *en* in Jamaican Creole: A Discourse Related Account." *English World Wide: A Journal of Varieties of English* (Amsterdam), 10:1 (1989):55–68.

_____. "Olive Senior: Journalist, Researcher, Poet, Fiction Writer." *Callaloo: A Journal of African American and African Arts and Letters* 11:3, (summer 1988).

_____. "An Introduction to the Poetry and Fiction of Olive Senior." *Callaloo: A Journal of African American and African Arts and Letters* 11:3 (summer 1988): 540–545.

_____. "Innovation in Jamaican Creole: The Speech of Rastafari." In *Focus on the Caribbean,* edited by Manfred Gorlach and John A. Holm. Amsterdam: Benjamins. Vol. 9, 1986.

_____. "Cultural Connections in Paule Marshall's Praise Song for the Widow." *World Literature Written in English* (Singapore) 25:2 (autumn 1985): 285–298.

_____. "The Social History of Dread Talk." edited by Lawrence D. Carrington, Dennis Craig, and Ramon Todd. In *Studies in Caribbean Language,* St. Augustine, Trinidad: Society for Caribbean Language, 1983. Vol. 11.

Marie-Jose N'Zengo-Tayo

Tayo-N'Zengo, Marie-Jose. "Women, Literature and Politics: The Haitian Popular Migration as viewed by Marie-Therese Colima and the Haitian Female Novelsits." In *Moving Beyond Boundaries,* edited by Carole Boyce Davies and Molara Ogundipe-Leslie. Vol. 2 *Critical Responses.* London: Pluto Press, 1995.

_____. "Maître ou mentor? L'ombre de Glissant dans *Texaco* de Patrick Chamoiseau." ("Master or Mentor: Glissant's ghost in Chamoiseau's *Texaco*"). In *The Reordering of Culture: Latin* American, the Caribbean and Canada, edited by Alvina Ruprecht and Cecilia

Taiana. Ottawa: Carelton University Press, 1995.

_____. "Litterature et Diglossie: Creer une langue métisse ou la "Chamoisification" de français dans *Texaco* de Patrick Chamoisseau." *TTR: Traduction, Terminologie, Redaction* (University of Concordia, Montréal) 9 no. 1 (Summer 1996): 155–176.

_____. "Re-imagining history: The Caribbean Vision of the Haitian Revolution and of the Early Independence Days." *Espace Caraibe*. No. 3 (Guadeloupe, West Indies: GEREC) 1995.

_____. "Discourse, Madness and the Neurotic Heroine in French Women Novelists." *The Journal of West Indian Literature* 6 no. 1 (July 1993): 29–44.

Patricia Powell

Powell, Patricia. *A Small Gathering of Bones*. Oxford: Heinemann Educational, 1994.

_____. *Me Dying Trial*. Oxford; Portsmouth, New Hampshire: Heinemann, 1993.

_____. "An Investigation of Selected Syntactical and Morphological Structures in the Conversation of Secondary Students After Two Years' Study of French." *Dissertation Abstracts International*, 34:2.

Astrid H. Roemer

Roemer, Astrid H. *"Levenslang gedicht: roman."* Haarlem: De Knipscher, 1987.

_____. *"Ijn terug Suriname."* Haarlem: De Knipscher, 1974. 2nd ed. The Hague: Pressag, 1975.

_____. *Nergens, ergens*. Haarlem: De Knipscher, 1983.

_____. *Schoon en schofterig*. Haarlem: De Knipscher, 1985.

_____. *"De Orde van de dag: Novelle"*. Schoorl: Conserve, 1988.

_____. *"Het Spoor van de jakhals: Novelle."* Schoorl: Conserve, 1988.

_____. *"Waaron zou je huilen mijn lieve mijn lieve: Novelle."* Zoetermeer: Z & Co., 1977. rpt. Haarlem: Knipscheer, 1976, Schoorl: Conserve, 1987.

About Astrid H. Roemer

Phaf, Ineke. "Interview with Astrid Roemer." In *Unheard Words: Women and Literature in Africa, the Arab World, Asia, the Caribbean, and Latin America*. edited by Mineke Schipper. London: Allison & Busby, 1985.

Elaine Savory

Savory, Elaine, and Carole Boyce Davies, eds. "African Women Writers: Toward a Literary History." In *A History of Twentieth-Century African Literatures*, vol. 9, edited by Owomoyela Oyekan. Lincoln: University of Nebraska Press, 1993.

_____. "Freeing Up: Politics, Gender, and Theatrical Form in the Anglophone Caribbean." In *Gender in Performance: The Presentation of Difference in the Performing Arts*, edited by Lawrence Senelick. Hanover, New Hampshire: Tufts University Press, 1992.

_____. "The Politics of Colour and the Politics of Writing in the Fiction of Jean Rhys." *Jean Rhys Review* 4:2 (1991):3–12.

_____. "A Question of Realities: Zuzu Sofola's 'The Sweet Trap.'" *ARIEL: A Review of In-*

ternational English Literature (Calgary) 18:4 (October 1987) 53–66.

_____. "Island & Overseas: Visions." *Journal of West Indian Literature* (Kingston, Jamaica) 1:2 (June 1987): 58–64.

_____. "Naming Caribbean Women Writers." *Callaloo: A Journal of African American and African* Arts and Letters 13:3, 539–550.

_____. "Finding a Truer Form: Rawle Gibbon's Carnival Play I, Lawah." *Theatre Research International (Eynsham, Oxford, England) 15:3 (autumn 1990): 249–259.*

_____. *"Okigbo's Labyrinths and the Context of Igbo Attitudes to the Female Principle."* In Ngambika: Studies of Women in African Literature. Trenton, New Jersey: Africa World, 1986.

_____. "Value Judgements on Art and the Question of Macho Attitudes: The Case of Derek Walcott." *The Journal of Commonwealth Literature* (London) 21:1 (1986): 109–119.

Sybil Seaforth
Seaforth, Sybil. *A Boundary for Vimal.* Addison Wesley, England: Longman, 1996.

_____. *Growing Up with Miss Milly.* Wellesley, Massachussetts: Calaloux Publications, 1988.

_____. "Only a Housewife." *You Caribbean Women's Magazine* 4, no. 13. (Trinidad) 1982.

_____. "A Season to Remember." *The Trinidad Guardian.* 16 March 1980.

_____. "Bright Rosy's First Christmas." *The Trinidad Express Newspaper.* 2 December 25.

Lourdes Vázquez
Vázquez, Lourdes. *The Broken Heart.* New York: La Candelaria, 1996.

_____. *El amour urgente.* New York: La Candelaria, 1995.

_____. *Configuraciones: An art piece.* San Juan: 1992.

_____. *La rosa mecanica.* Puerto Rico: Editorial Huracan, 1991.

_____. *Aterrada de cuernos y cuervos: Marina Arzola, el testimonio, a biography.* San Juan: El Gallo Rojo, 1990.

_____. *La rosa mecanica.* Colombia: Museo Omar Rayo, 1988.

Works about Vázquez, Lourdes
Duchesne, William. *"Un album para Marina Arzola."* El Mundo, (September 1990).

Grau, Maria Mercedes. "Recuentan vida de Marina Arzola." *Dialogo* (April, 1991).

Martinez, Elena M. *Interview: "Coversacion con Lourdes Vázquez."* Revista FEM 16, 112 (June 1992).

Rodriguez, Capo J. "Con hembras y lagartijas." *El Mundo* (May 1987).

Rodriguez Martino, Graciela. "Aterrada de cuernos y cuervos." *Claridad* (August 1990).

Trelles, Carmen Dolores. Review: *La rosa mecanica. El Nuevo Dia* (February 1992).

_____. "Aterrada de cuernos y cuervos: Marina Arzola, el testimonio." *El Nuevo Dia* (August 1990).

_____. "Para leer en femenino." *El Nuevo Dia* (September 1990).

Sherezada (Chiqui) Vicioso

Vicioso, Sherezada. *Wish-ky Sour.* 1995.

————. *Internamiento.* 1993.

————. *Algo que decir: ensayos sobre literatura femenina, 1981–1991.* Santo Domingo, Dominican Republic: Editora Buho, 1991.

————. *Un extrano ulular traia el viento.* Santo Domingo, Dominican Republic: Alfa y Omega, 1985.

————. *Viaje desde el agua.* Santo Domingo, Dominican Republic: Fundacion del Libro Casa de Teatro, 1981.